FIVE ELEVENTH CENTURY
HUNGARIAN KINGS: THEIR POLICIES
AND THEIR RELATIONS WITH ROME

Z. J. KOSZTOLNYIK

EAST EUROPEAN MONOGRAPHS, BOULDER
DISTRIBUTED BY COLUMBIA UNIVERSITY PRESS
NEW YORK

1981

Z. J. Kosztolnyik is Professor of History
at Texas A & M University

To Penelope, for being what she is

TABLE OF CONTENTS

LIST OF ABBREVIATIONS

ASS	Acta sanctorum Bollandiana
ITK	Irodalomtörténeti Közlemények
Mansi, *Concilia*	J.D. Mansi (ed) Sacrorum conciliorum collectio
Marczali, *Enchiridion*	H. Marczali *et al* (ed), Enchiridion fontium historiae Hungarorum
Migne, *PG*	J.P. Migne (ed), Patrologiae cursus completus, series latina
Migne, *PL*	J.P. Migne (ed), Patrologiae cursus completus, series graeca
MGHLL	Monumenta Germaniae historica, Legum collectio
MGHSS	Monumenta Germaniae historica, Scriptores
RHM	St. L. Endlicher (ed), Rerum Hungaricarum monumenta Arpadiana
SIE	J. Card. Serédi (ed), Szent István Emlékkönyv
SSH	E. Szentpétery (ed), Scriptores rerum Hungaricarum
Szentpétery, *Regesta*	E. Szentpétery (ed), Regesta regum stirpis Arpadianae critico-diplomatica
Závodszky	L. Závodszky (ed), A szent István, szent László és Kálmán korabeli tárvények és zsinati határozatok forrásai

PREFACE

The purpose of this work is to determine the policies of five eleventh century Hungarian kings, especially the policy of King Stephen I of Hungary, the founder king of the Christian Hungarian realm in 1000, with special attention to the role of Bishop Gerard of Csanád. This policy may be characterized as a political and cultural undertaking because Christianization of the realm in those days meant a thorough reorganization of the then at least 150 year-old Hungarian social–political structure according to western lines of political thought and stressing cultural adherence to the European body politic.

The work is based upon contemporary evidence: the *vitae* of King Stephen and of Bishop Gerard; the legal statutes enacted by Stephen and his council, and Stephen's political testament, his *Admonitiones* to his successors on the throne; the mid-fourteenth century *Chronicon pictum*, whose appropriate paragraphs are based upon the reports of contemporary eleventh century writers and chroniclers, such as, for instance, Bishop Nicholas of Veszprém, the chancellor of King Andrew I; the reports of the *Chronicon* duly cross-referenced by the *Gesta Hungarorum* of the Hungarian Anonymus of the late twelfth century; the letters of popes Gregory VII and Urban II addressed to the Hungarian court, and the documents issued, the laws enacted by Ladislas I of Hungary. The bishop of Csanád was also a writer whose incomplete major opus, *Deliberatio supra hymnum trium puerorum*, a theological treatise on the Book of Daniel, 3:57ff., is so filled with allusions to the contemporary Hungarian scene in the early 1040s, that it may be considered the major historical source of the period. To cite but a few examples: Gerard made mention of investiture and simony in Hungary,—in the early 1040s. He deplored the unworthy behavior of the new and undereducated Hungarian clergy; he disagreed with the forced religious policy of the royal court, a policy that proved to be of lasting value only under the iron rule of King Stephen. Upon his death, the policy backfired miserably. The bishop so wrote, and the annals support his assertions. Gerard was critical of the behavior of the Hungarian nobles of the time, and maintained that although old age was a requirement, education was also needed for the royal council to assess correctly the political situation of the new Hungarian realm in its relations with the rest of continental Europe.

King Stephen strove for and successfully maintained a good foreign policy. Stephen's successors faced challenges of a different nature: they had to struggle with the expansionist politics of the German emperors, while, in the 1070s, the Hungarian court had become an unwilling participant in the power struggle between Rome and the Franconian dynasty in the Germanies. The country was rent asunder by civil war, and only the determined attitude of King Ladislas could restore law and tranquility. Through his legislative acts,—based, in fact, upon fulfilling the laws of King Stephen,—Ladislas reorganized the administration of the realm, introduced common law (which he enforced through his itinerant justices and county judges), and was able, with the approval and the cooperation of the Holy See, to confirm membership for his people within the framework of the late eleventh century European community.

To the best of my knowledge, this treatment of Hungarian history is entirely new and original. I also feel that, due to the unfamiliarity of the reader with this era and area of European history, a thorough documentation of this work is a must. It is my hope and desire that this book makes a contribution to a better understanding of this particular phase of the political and intellectual-religious history of eleventh century Europe.

For help in preparing this manuscript, I owe thanks to my wife for her encouragement and patience.

Texas A & M University   Z.J. Kosztolnyik

INTRODUCTION

MAGYAR BEGINNINGS IN THE REPORTS OF HUNGARIAN AND BYZANTINE CHRONICLERS

Ergo sicut dicit Sacra Scriptura et sancti doctores, Hungari descenderunt a Magor, filio Iaphet, . . . a quo Magari sunt nominati.

Chronicon pictum, c.4

The predecessors of the Magyars descended from the Finno-Ugrian family of the Ural branch of the Ural-Altaic peoples. The younger Ural branch developed into Samoyed and Finno-Ugrian. Finno-Ugrian branched off into (1) *Finn,* with its Lapp, Finn-Estonian, Tsermiss and Mordvin families; (2) *Permish,* with Zyrian and Votyak; and (3) *Ugrian,* with its Magyar, Vogul and Ostyak groups. The Altaic branch comprised Turks, Mongols and Manshu-Tungus, and their descendants.[1]

The Proto-Magyas came down into the region of the *Palus Meotis* (Sea of Azov) from Siberia in the fifth century A.D. According to the author-compiler of the *Chronicon pictum,* a fourteenth century Hungarian chronicle in Latin,[2] these were the descendants of the biblical Japhet,[3] and his grandsons (through *Magog*), *Magor* and *Hunor* are the eponyms of the Magyars and Huns;[4] Magor and Hunor, in fact, led the Magyars on a raid against the territory of their neighbor (in the region of the sea of Azov), Prince Bereka, and kidnapped Bereka's wives and his grandsons. Two of the captured women were daughters of Dule of the Alans, a Scythian prince, and Magor and Hunor took them to wife.[5] The *Chronicon pictum* relates the following about the raid: "in deserto loco sine maribus in tabernaculis permanentes uxores ac filios filiorum Bereka, cum festum tube colerent et coreas ducerent ad sonitum simphonie, casu repererunt."[6] This is to say: [the Magyars] came upon the wives and the grandsons of Bereka by chance, abiding in the wilderness, without [mature] males, in tents, while they were keeping the festival of the trumpet and were dancing to the accompaniment of the tambourine. The language of the *Chronicon pictum* here suggest the Jewish feast of Tabernacles.[7] It suggests that, since they were celebrating in Jewish fashion a Jewish feast, the women captured by Magor and his party were of the Jewish faith. The description of the chronicler may be an allusion to Leviticus, 23:43: "quod in tabernaculis habitare fecerim filios Israel,"[8] and to Peter Comestor who speaks of a *festum tubarum vel clangores.*[9] Assuming that the chronicler recorded the legendary element of an actual historical event, it may be that, according to this fourteenth century account, the ancestors of the Magyars married Jewish women, or women of the Jewish religion.

Simon de Keza, the second of the three medieval Hungarian chroniclers under consideration here, in his *Gesta Hungarorum,* composed in the late thirteenth century,[10] asserts that *Menroth* was the forefather of the Magyars,[11] and that it was Menroth's two sons, *Hunor* and *Magor* respectively, who, while hunting "inter paludes Meotidas," had come upon "in tabernaculis permanents uxores ac pueros filiorum Belar;" among them, according to Keza, were the daughters of Prince Dule of the Alans, whom Hunor and Magor took to wife.[12] Keza says nothing about the feast.

Anonymus *P. dictus magister,*[13] chronicler of the late twelfth-early thirteenth centuries,[14] although proud of his learning and of being well informed,[15] recorded nothing in his *Gesta Hungarorum* about the raid or the wives of Bereka. Anonymus did say, however, that the inhabited by the *Dentumoger*), was *Magog,*[16] the son of Japhet, and that Magog's people were called the *Moger.*[17] From the family of Magog, says Anonymus, descended Almos, "a quo reges et duces Hungarie originem duxerunt."[18] In other words, Anonymus confirms the exalted position Magog held in early Hungarian historical tradition by making him the eponym of the *Moger*—terms like Moger, Magor, Magari having a familiar ring in the spelling of *Magyar,* i.e., Hungarian.

Because Anonymus, Keza, and the compiler of the *Chronicon pictum* made use of the work, now lost, of an early national chronicler of the eleventh-twelfth centuries,[19] who in turn obtained some of his information from the *Exordia Scythica;*[20] and because the compiler of the

Chronicon pictum, be he a Benedictine monk or a Franciscan friar,[21] relied for information upon the *Chronographia* by Sigebert of Gembloux;[22] the *Chronicon pictum,* by recording the capture by Magor and his party of the women of Bereka and Dule, may have preserved for posterity information that, for centuries, remained hidden in a nearly forgotten historical tradition. Perhaps the compiler of the *Chronicon pictum* described the feast in an attempt to authenticate the information he received from the *magister ystoriarum* Peter Comestor[23] who in his desscription of the seven Jewish feasts of the year had mentioned a *festum tubarum.*[24]

By the ninth century A.D., the Magyars (now a partly Israelitish people) are settled south and west of the region of their raid, *Atelcosu* (Bessarabia),[25] where in an interesting inversion *they* are preyed upon by the Petchenegs, and *their* (i.e., the Magyars') women are stolen.[26] The Magyars then migrate to Hungary.[27]

Byzantine chroniclers, as, for instance, Leo VI the Wise,[28] Constantine VII Porphyrogenitus,[29] and Theophanes Continuatus,[30] describe the (Proto-) Magyars as *Turkoi, Unnoi,* and *Ungroi* (Ungroi derives from *Onogur* [=ten Ugors],[31] while *Ungry* in ecclesiastical Slavic, and *Vengry* in Russian derives from *Ungroi.*) An early tenth century source refers to the Magyars as "depopulantibus Agarenis," the descendants of Agar, wife of the patriarch Abraham.[32] And Remigius of Auxerre, of about the same time, in his writ addressed to Bishop Dado of Verdun expresses doubt concerning the Scythian ancestry of the Magyars.[33] But Ioannes Malalas, a Byzantine chronicler of the sixth century,[34] may, in describing the activities of King Muageris, have been the first, in the opinion of the learned Gyula Moravcsik, to use the term *Magyar.*[35]

In the critical Bonn edition of the Malalas text, Grod, a king of the Huns who ruled Bosporus,[36] paid a visit to Constantinople, where he was graciously received by the emperor. Overhelmed with gifts, he was sent home as advocate of the interests of the emperor and as guardian of Bosporus,[37] the city that served as the point of commercial exchange between the Romans and the Huns.[38] In recording the incident, Malalas states that the "above mentioned" king, Grod, became a Christian and remained in Bosporus.[39] And having accomplished his assignment, Grod gained, as a reward for faithful service to the emperor, admission to the Byzantine Church and entry into a spiritual relationship with Emperor Justinian who had become his godfather.

Grod suppressed the cult of pagan idols among his people, angering the pagan priests.[40] They revolted, killed Grod, and elected Mougel, Grod's brother, king.[41] Because Mougel feared the revenge of the Byzantine court, he and his supporters occupied Bosporus, massacred the Byzantine garrison there, and fled before the arrival of the imperial forces. The Byzantine court had no other alternative but to repopulate the devastated city.[42]

On the grounds that the name of the ruler may be held identical with the name of, and language spoken by, the people over whom he exercised authority,[43] it may be that Malalas is describing here a confrontation between Grod—and Mougel—speaking factions of the ruling element among the Huns in the Crimea. Though he failed ultimately, Grod sought contact with the Byzantine court to confirm the political ascendancy of his Grod-people in the Hunish society of the Crimea. He must have been concerned about the fundamentalist opposition of the pagan priests and of his brother Mougel, lest it endanger the relationship he was trying to build with the Byzantine administration.

There may, however, have been another dimension to the Grod/Mougel political situation of the Huns in the Crimea. Though Mougel's determination to stand aloof from Byzantine politics and his decision to flee the peninsula, the sphere of Byzantine political-religious and cultural influence, make unlikely any detailed Byzantine historical record proving the existence of the Magyars in the sixth century, it may be argued that the Grod/Mougel groups were politically divided thus: Grod and his faction wished to effect political compromise and to live within the framework and under the protection of a world-state, while Mougel and his faction wanted to break away from, to avoid contact with, the civilized world. The Spartan Mougel, leader of the Huns in the Crimea, made a fateful decision which delayed the early incorporation of his people into the political structure of a cultured world-state.[44]

It is the variations of the name Mougel: Mouger, Mougar, and Magyar, that underline the name of Professor Moravcsik's King Muageris.[45]

The legislation and correspondence of Justinian provide, in fact, evidence for the reasoning of Grod and for the reliability of the Malalas report. Justinian's legislation emphasized that other peoples should join the administration of the empire in order to expand the religio-political and territorial influence of the court.[46] "Nihil est enim quod lumine

clariore praefulgeat, quam recta fides in principe; nihil est quod ita ne-
queat occasui subiacere, quam vera religio" (There is nothing that shines
with a brighter light than orthodoxy in a [foreign, allied] prince; there
is nothing less subject to eclipse than the true religion.)[47] The Emperor
recognized the primacy of Rome,[48] and yet he conducted an independent
policy. "Quomodo ergo . . . dignas Deo gratias agere valeamus, quod
per me, ultimum servum suum, . . . dignatus est et tantarum provinciarum
populos a iugo servitudinis eripere" (How might we render worthy enough
thanks, therefore, unto God, because through me, the remotest of his servants, he has deigned [by engineering their conversion] to rescue from the
yoke of slavery [to the devil] the peoples of even so great provinces?)[49]
The Huns led by Grod/Mougel may have been small in numbers, but
they occupied an important geographical location in the Crimea.[50]

The correspondence of the Emperor proves that from early on the
court had conducted an energetic missionary policy among the "bar-
barians" and had drawn them into the court's sphere of influence.[51]
As a result, Bosporus and Phanagoria in the Crimea had become ecclesiastical centers in the fourth century. The court identified the success
of this missionary policy with the growth of its political influence; therefore, the Huns were brought within the orbit of Byzantine policy. These
Huns were identified with the Utigors, Kutigors, and Onongurs by Balint
Hóman, whose views were accepted by Gyula Moravcsik who said that
the Onogurs lived in the Kuban river region and that the Hun-Onogurs
played a role in the formation of the Magyars as a people.[52] (The argu-
ments of both Hóman and Morvcsik, however, were recently questioned
by Elemér Moór.)[53] Because the Ugors, Utigors, and Onogurs settled
near Armenian territory and because the Armenians were Christians, the
ancestors of the Magyars must have gained some acquaintance with
Christianity.[54]

A smaller portion of the Magyars' ancestors was converted by Bishop
Quardusat, alias Theokletos of Armenia, whose missionary activities were
recorded in Pseudo-Zachary's lost *Historia ecclesiastica,* around 569.[55]
The Syriac translation of Pseudo-Zachary, prepared about 669, subsumes
all of the converted peoples under one designation: "Huns," as if to
convey the notion that the Byzantine Church and court had no interest
in the conversion of individual peoples.[56]

The (Onogur-) Huns made their appearance in the Causasus and Kuban regions during the fifth century and formed the ruling element of the Bulgarian realm that was destroyed by the Khazars in the mid-seventh century.[57] Patriarch Nicephorus frequently refers to the Huns as Bulgarians, and so does an entry in the *Acta Sanctorum.*[58] Cosmas Indicopleustes, describing the Christian -Bulgarians, says that the territory named "Hunnia" was inhabited by the White-Huns: *ephtalitae.*[59] As a matter of fact, a fifth century abridgement of a saint's life refers to a bishop of the Huns who, at that time, lived north of the Caucasus.[60]

The idea that the Huns played a key role in the realm of the Bulgarians may be confirmed by the Byzantine chroniclers who speak of as Huns those Bulgarians who, upon the destruction of their realm by the Khazars, had fled toward the west.[61] The Khazars occupied Bosporus by the end of the 600s; however, the western Crimea remained free of their control until 787, when the Khazars occupied Doros, an outpost of the Byzantine Church in the Crimea.[62] The list dating back to the early eighth century, of the bishops of the Doros metropolitan[63] records the suffragan bishops of the Huns and of the Onogurs respectively, a concrete proof of the presence of the Huns east of the Meotis during the early 700s.[64]

Priscos Rhetor speaks of the Onogurs in connection with their embassies to the Byzantine court of 457 (or 461).[65] Byzantine chroniclers[66] describe the Onogurs as White- and Black-Ugors, perhaps on the grounds of their physical appearance, social structure, and/or geographical location. The White-Ugors lived in a matriarchial social structure and entered, during the reign of Emperor Heraclitus, the mid-Danube region. They were to be known as Pseudo-Avars because they moved into an area that previously belonged to the Avars.[67]

The *Russian Primary Chronicle* says that the Black-Ugors had passed by Kiev *en route* to "Hungary" across the Magyar Moutain.[68] The Ugors are mentioned by the author of the *Vita Constantini,* who records that Cyril of Thessalonica had met with some of them.[69] Their king, so the *Vita Methodii* reports, wished to see Methodius, the brother of Cyril: "Cum vero rex Ugrorum in regiones Danubii venisset, videre eum voluit" (But when the king of the Ugors had come into the regions of the [lower] Danube, he wanted to see him [i.e., Methodius] .)[70] He spoke with him in a manner as was proper for such men to hold a conversation: "Collocutus sum eo, quemadmodum tales viros decuit sermones habere."[71]

It may have some significance that, during the meeting, the Ugor king not only requested the prayers of the missionary, but that the "barbarian" was on his best behavior toward the missionary—the king received him in a manner as befits a prince: "ut principem decet, sic excepit eum." [72]

CHAPTER I

FROM GEZA TO ANDREW

The Hungarians have lived in their country from the time when Árpád the Conqueror occupied the Hungarian plains in about 896.[1] Originally, the Hungarians (Magyars) were a branch of the Ural and Altaic stocks. The Ural stock consisted of the Finno-Ugrians, and the Altaic stock, of the Turkish races and the Mongols. As the Finno-Ugraians were separated into the Finns and the Manseri groups—*Man'si* meaning men, alias fighting men, warriors—so the Turkish races were, in due times, separated into the Western and Eastern Turks with the Ogurs being the descendants of the western Turkish race. Hungarian historians are inclined to accept the above mentioned *Manseri* as the Proto-Magyars, a group of peoples that were united so to speak with the Ogurs of the Turkish family. Out of the crossbreed of races the Magyar tribes were born, tribes, seven in number, which led a semi-independent existence under Turkish-Khazar rule east of the Black Sea.[2]

Around 830 to 899 these tribes moved and lived on the plains between the Don and Dnieper rivers, an area called Levedia from the name of one of their chieftains. From there they migrated suddenly to what are called today, the upper Rumanian lowlands between the Pruth and Dniester rivers, but then known as Atelcosu from "etel" meaning river, and "cosu" [köz], plain in between.

It was in Atelcosu [Etelköz] that the seven tribes, or rather their chieftains, elected Árpád the son of Álmos, chieftain of the strongest and most numerous Magyari tribe, as their leader in war and peace. Three small Khazar tribes also joined the united Magyars.[3] By this time, the Magyars (Hungarians) were well known to the Byzantine court circles, who referred to them as Turks, Scythae, or Onogurs, hence the name Ungarus, Hungarus, Ungar, etc. It may be worth mentioning that before 899, a smaller Hungarian group, probably a separate tribe, did not follow the majority going westward, but turned east and settled in the lower Volga region. As late as the 1230s, four Hungarian Dominican friars were sent to locate this tribe and found it before it finally disappeared in the Tartar invasion of the 1240s.[4]

From Atelcosu the united Magyars (Hungarians) entered the Carpathian basin, and apparently the conquest took several years. Árpád died in 907, and his successors were unable to maintain practical authority over the various tribal chiefs, who in turn undertook the direction of their regional affairs. The tribes settled in the southeastern regions, attacked the Balkans continually until the 960s.

In the battles near Riad, 933, and Augsburg, 955, the German kings put an end to Hungarian raids. But it should be noted at this point that in 955, for instance, it was not the whole Hungarian armed force, dispatched by an almost unknown Magyar "national" leader to raid the west, but only two tribal armies that suffered a crushing defeat at the hands of the Germans.[5] As the main Hungarian force remained intact and Hungarian territory free from foreign invasions, the new Hungarian ruler, Duke Géza (970-97), Árpád's fifth direct successor, successfully reestablished centralized rule over the entire Hungarian people. In 973, the third year of his rule, he felt strong enough formally to request peace and missionaries from emperor Otto I.[6] From this act of Géza, known as the Quedlinburg mission and resulting in the Quedlinburg Agreement, dates the real beginnings of western Hungarian history, the history of Hungarian *kingship* that was to commence in the year 1000 and last through the centuries until 1946.

There was never a doubt of Stephen's succession to his father's heritage as elected leader of the country. Duke Géza had carefully prepared the way for his son's assumption of authority and thoughtfully assured Stephen's ascendancy to power by obtaining the consent of the national council to his election. A mid-twelfth century source informs us of the unwritten Hungarian custom of selection of an Árpád scion from the direct line of Álmos, the father of Árpád, provided that the heir was publicly acknowledged and elected by a council made up of the leading personages, "principales persone communi et vero consilio, libera voluntate et communi consensu." Accordingly, when Duke Géza died in 997, his son Vajk, previously baptized as Stephen, took up the reigns of authority in the country with the full approval of the council.[7]

As the sources vary in explaining the exact meaning of the term, council, and fail to give a clear description of the council's activity, it does not seem correct to refer to this council as the "constitutional" or "national" assembly, even though, during the first half of the ninth century, the assembled national leaders exercised *de facto* constitutional rights over the heads of the elected leaders of their country. That Stephen's succession followed smoothly might have had much to do with Géza's strong handed policy in directing both the domestic and foreign affairs of his people in the twenty-five years of personal rule. For at that time only a clear sighted ruler could have averted destruction, perhaps complete annihilation, of his people by the better organized and then more civilized inhabitants of western Europe.[8]

As early as the 970s, Duke Géza had tried unsuccessfully to convert his followers to the accepted political and religio-cultural practices of his western neighbors. But this policy was rudely interrupted by the council of the elders. Géza, fearing civil war and worse, retreated gracefully, though it seems clear from the records that he had no choice but to submit to the pressure of the "council".[9] It was left to his successor to realize his design, and Stephen succeeded in putting into force his father's policy.[10]

A careful examination of all the sources reveals that Stephen had more cooperative forces at his disposal. They were not, however, Hungarian. As a matter of fact, no Hungarian gave a helping hand to the ruler in preparing his country's future destiny. The Hungarians, at least those who were in responsible positions at the time, hardly realized the unique and highly dangerous political position of their own people surrounded by hostile and suspicious inhabitants of the West, North and the South. They were unable to see that without acclimatization to continental principles and without maintaining friendly relations with the West, the Hungarians were in danger of disappearing from the historical scene, as their predecessors, the Huns or the Avars before them. Consequently, Stephen, the young ruler, who had ample opportunity to observe the domestic scene and the inadequate machinery of domestic politics from his father's court, entertained no vain hopes as regards to his own compatriots' understanding of the "nation's" future. Fortunately for him—and for the Hungarians—there were forces in his country, foreign *hospites,* who were willing to go along with the ruler's politics and offered him armed assistance should the need arise.[11]

The need, in fact, did arise soon after Stephen's election. Interestingly, it was not the much feared council, but Stephen's rival for the reins of power, Koppány, the head of another Hungarian tribe, who revolted against Stephen's rule and the new policy. It is possible that Koppány took up arms and led his tribal forces to depose Géza's successor out of purely personal consideration. A synthesis of the available source material points, however, to an entirely different factor which may have played a decisive role in Koppány's warring efforts. This new factor was religion.[12] In other words, the reorganization of the country along western institutions and lines of religious thought was fully foreign and, therefore, suspect, to any Hungarian chieftain who had never before in his life maintained contact with different nationals or spent any time thinking out political relations and obligations among his own kindred. It was this latter fact, indeed, that forced Duke Stephen to accept foreign military help from the armed *hospites* living at his court, and to rely upon the advice of the foreign born clerics, mostly Benedictine monks from Rome active at the dukal court or in missionary efforts throughout the country.[13]

There remains the question who these armed foreign guests were. And how did it come about that Frankish and Roman missionaries were active among the Magyars at a time when the Hungarians had no contacts with the outside world, except their German neighbors?[14] This will be discussed more fully in a later chapter. Suffice it to state here that the foreign military aiding the cause of Stephen in Hungary consisted of German warriors who presumably were members of the entourage of Stephen's Bavarian-born wife, the Princess Gisela.[15] At the time of Gisela's marriage to Stephen, in the late 990s, her father, Henry the Quarrelsome, had fallen into political disfavor with the imperial court, therefore the marriage of a German speaking princess to the Hungarian duke presented no immediate political danger to the latter's country. On the other hand, the clerical missionaries were recruited from countries other than the Germanies for political reasons. For example, in the 970s, Bishop Pilgrim of Passau, with the imperial court's full approval, launched such an ambitious missionary policy in western Hungarian territories that the Magyar court thought it advisable to counteract the bishop's designs be reverting directly to the traditional national institutions, that is pagan religion. In fact, it is entirely possible that Géza's "westernizing" policy, initiated with imperial help in 973 broke down as a consequence of Bishop Pilgrim's thoughtless and ill-considered behavior.[16]

Stephen learned from the mistakes made by Géza not to trust the religio-political policies of the Ottonian court and turned to non-German speaking missionaries instead.[17] He successfully established contact with the northern religious centers of the Frankish kingdom. In addition he was unexpectedly able to secure the help of monks of a Roman monastery who were originally destined to help the missionary cause in Bohemia.[18]

What is particularly important here is the timing of Koppány's attack on Stephen's newly developing institutions.[19] All records agree that the "revolution" took place while Stephen was still a duke (*tunc duce*). But even his personal biographer, Bishop Hartvic, fails to inform us whether such a revolt coincided with the hostile and distrubing activities of Stephen's uncle, the lord of the Transylvanian region. Hartvic explained in detail, however, that Stephen completely defeated all the dissidents before his royal coronation. And the incomplete record left by Keza indicates that Stephen's coronation took place after he successfully subdued all his enemies.[20] We may assume, therefore, that Duke Stephen fought his decisive struggle with Koppány in the late 990s, perhaps as late as 999, and that this victory gave him a free hand in realizing his lofty designs: making Hungary a full fledged member of the western religious and political body.[21] The entry in the *Annales Hildesheimenses,* faithfully echoed by a late Hungarian source, that Stephen made the successful attempt to arrest his arrogant uncle, Gyula of Transylvania, only in 1003, need not be considered too seriously.[22] The German chronicler possessed little information regarding political events in Hungary.[23] Had he been better informed, he would not have failed to report the coronation of Stephen as king of Hungary.

More important is the identity of another opposition leader mentioned by name in the chronicles.[24] It seems that Kean and Ajtony, who governed the southern Hungarian territories claimed by Stephen's court as parts of the Arpadian realm were actually one person.[25] The earliest available source is very obscure on this,[26] and even Hartvic deemed it unnecessary— or was unable—to give detailed information. Only a later chronicler provided ample information on the deeds of Kean.[27] Nevertheless, since the late fourteenth century *Life,* known today as the "second" *Life* of Bishop Gerard gives so detailed and interesting a report on the Ajtony *Legenda* it is necessary to investigate this further.[28]

At first, it seems highly improbable indeed that these two personages mentioned by two distinct narratives, should be identical with one another.

The role played by Kean was that of a Bulgarian chieftain, who held strong ties and family connections with territories that came under Hungarian rule in the late ninth century. The chronicler only noted that Kean rebelled against Stephen's rule, though a keen observer will notice that exactly the same remark was passed on the role held by Gyula of Transylvania prior to his forced submittal to Stephen's authority.[29] To complicate the matter further, the record splits on the chronological data of the events. According to the earlier but fragmentary narrative, Kean's submission occurred after the coronation of Stephen in 1000.[30] This chronology is supported by Hartvic. The later narrative source, comprising elements of the national *gesta*, gave no exact reckoning, though stated that the defeat of Koppány and Gyula's forced conversion occurred before Stephen's coronation and that only afterwards (*per haec*) did Stephen make war on Kean.[31] However, our source indicates that Kean's defeat occurred in the later part (years) of Stephen's reign, possibly in the 1020s. This attitude was also taken by the later biographer of Bishop Gerard, whose author mentioned the event just before the actual establishment of the episcopal see of Csanád following the warring between the royal forces headed by Duke Csanád and Ajtony.

Both Kean and Ajtony were killed in the battle, both of them died under similar circumstances, and, what a coincidence!—both Kean and Ajtony were under the direct influence of the Byzantine court. The similarities between the two persons are striking indeed. Further the tautological narrative concerning the manner of life and the authority actually exercised by Ajtony bears a strong resemblance to the description of Gyula's prerogatives before the latter's deportation from the Transylvanian headship.[32] Stephen's uncle was to be replaced by the ruler's granduncle, a very old former tribal duke himself, Zoltan by name. In the case of Ajtony, it was another trustworthy military *dux*, Csanád, who actually succeeded the rebellious Ajtony in order to promote both the political and religious interests of the central court in Ajtony's former territorial possessions.[33]

Whatever the interpretation of these events, there is no doubt that several well organized uprisings were directed against the centralizing policy of Stephen. That one of these reported rebellious movements took place in the later years of King Stephen's reign is quite understandable. The real issue, therefore, is not the identity of names of personages who played their allotted roles within the still undefined borders of the recently arrived Magyars in the western community. The issue is the safe-keeping of the occupied territories, and in this regard Stephen was to meet every challenge—even in his later years.[34]

Stephen's success in obtaining recognition of his own position as ruler of an independent people resulted also from his favorable relations with two western institutions, the empire and the papacy. For he was given a crown by the pope and simultaneously obtained the emperor's tacit acknowledgment of the papal act. The conditions under which the relations were established must be explained further.

Stephen knew from his father's experimentation with western institutions in the country that he needed foreign aid if he really wanted to carry out his designs aimed at gaining continental citizenship for his nation.[35] The rebellious behavior of the rival leaders in the country showed him clearly that the national elders[36] fully disapproved of his policy for fear lest the traditional institutions be submerged in new and foreign establishments.

Whether personal rivalry influenced the decisions taken by a Koppány or Gyula, to mention only two regional leaders whose appointment to office dated back to the times of Stephen's father, is really immaterial to our purpose. But the records, scant as they are, do indicate that it was the national council[37] elders which played a decisive role in determining the form the government was to take.[38] Moreover, Stephen when making up his mind concerning his policy, habitually avoided this institution.[39] It seems safe to conclude, therefore, that the heart of the opposition lay in the council.[40]

Several factors reinforce this hypothesis. First, when preparing himself for the life-or-death struggle with Koppány—quite understandably since victory or defeat meant continuation or decline for the ruling family— Stephen not only relied upon heavenly aid, but made sure that he obtained the assistance of the armed and trained military forces headed by one of his German guests.[41] The chronicler noticed that it was Stephen's military commander who actually defeated and killed Koppány in single combat.[42] The sources also indicate, however, that in later years Stephen had no need to rely upon the military aid of his German guests. It was Duke Csanád, for instance, who headed the royal Hungarian army when fighting Ajtony, and it was the royal military commander of the forces stationed in the attached Transylvanian territories who received orders to fight off the invading enemy in the later years of King Stephen's reign.[43]

Another important factor is the cooperation of the ecclesiastics at the Hungarian court directed against the pagan national interests held and defended by the council. It has been said according to the record that all the first religious co-workers of Stephen were foreigners. But, as a careful synthesis of all the available records indicates with certainty, these clerics active in the territories of Stephen were not necessarily German speaking missionaries. The majority of the clerics engaged in missionary work in Hungary were, as was pointed out above, from the West, and monks from Rome whose leaders, naturally, exercised no small influence on the religious politics of Stephen. It was these foreign speaking religious who influenced the Hungarian ruler to start negotiations with the papacy soon after his succession to the reigns of power.[44]

It is not clear whether Koppáany's seemingly unexpected military reaction was the answer to such negotiations with the papacy—if one may speak of establishing relations with the papacy at a time when the German emperor claimed actual headship of all Latin Christendom[45]—or just a timely reminder to the dukal court of the increasing foreign military aid in the country. Since the German military belonged to the entourage of Gisela,[46] and as they spoke a different language, they had little contact with the country's military leaders. There must have been a tremendous cultural difference in civilization between these guests and the natural leaders of the host country, though, in this instance, too, Stephen and later on his son, Emery, formed exceptions to this rule. Through their mere presence at the central court, the German speaking knights must have evoked envious hostility in the country. The point is that Koppány's attack preceded Stephen's coronation as king of Hungary by only a short time.[47]

Hartvic is our only source for the first Hungarian move toward a monarchy supported by the pope. From him we know that Stephen sent his trusted friend and advisor, Abbot Astric of Pécsvárad, to Rome to negotiate for papal recognition of himself as king of the country. It is to be noted that the Hungarian delegation was directed to Rome and that the favorable answer was given by Rome without imperial interference.

The coronation took place on Christmas day, 1000, at Stephen's court, in the presence of the spiritual lords, and their clergy, the trustworthy royal stewards, and the people.[48] It is further to be noted that the record made no mention of the secular lords, that is, the members of the council, as participants in the coronation ceremony.[49] This is not, however, an accidental omisssion by the chroniclers, but a clear indication of the view suggested above that Stephen became king without the consent of the national elders.

There are two principal reasons why the new king felt himself forced to act without the council's assent. First, from the constitutional viewpoint, Stephen's headship of the people had been assured three years before, when, upon his father's death, the council unanimously elected him as Géza's successor. Second, the domestic atmosphere created by the armed opposition of Koppány and Gyula to the ruler's policies must have been anything but propitious for calling a meeting of the tribal chiefs and national leaders to witness a Christian, and, therefore, western, ceremony. Had the council met in the presence of Stephen, it would have been as witnesses. It is doubtful whether the council would have felt satisfied with such a passive role.

It must, as a consequence, be concluded that it was the ruler's intimate ecclesiastical advisors who favored contacts with Rome. Astric, who may have been a boyhood friend of Pope Sylvester II,[50] and who knew of the feverish political intrigues and activities of the "urbs aeterna," must have assured his Hungarian master of the absolute necessity of gaining recognition from what was at the time the only permanent capital of the western world.[51] The domestic conditions were also favorable for the making of this decision. After the two serious defeats suffered by the national opposition, the rest of the formal tribal chiefs would have thought twice before attacking anew in the court of Stephen. No further attacks, therefore, were expected.

Since the continental clerics played such an important role in arranging for Stephen's coronation, it is interesting to determine who actually performed the ceremony. Obviously, it made little difference to the chroniclers, as they failed to note the name of the officiating prelate.[52] From Hartvic's text, however, it is clear that Stephen's coronation coincided with the rapid formation of the church in the realm. The head of this expanding formal organization was to become the archbishop of Esztergom, at the seat of the royal court, and it was probably Sebastian, the first archbishop of Esztergom who crowned Stephen king.[53]

It is not possible to take seriously the assertions of Hartvic that the policy initiated by King Stephen became highly successful. There is no doubt that Stephen did achieve his immediate goal; and through the gaining of western recognition of his position as ruler of a free people, he also secured domestic peace on his home front. Having defeated his immediate enemies within the realm and through reliance upon western contacts presented and maintained by the clerical party at the *curia*, he was capable and that he held the necessary military backing to carry out his design.[54]

The council did not delay long with its approval. In 1000, soon after the coronation, the council, together with the bishops, met in the presence of the king to discuss public needs which arose from the introduction of new manners and institutions in the realm. This will be discussed in detail in the following chapter. Here it is necessary only to stress the point that the meeting of the council and of the more intimate private group of counselors surrounding the king's person followed after, although not immediately upon, the great event on Christmas day, 1000. It is, therefore, tantamount to an acceptance of the fact of coronation and bears witness to the personal triumph of Stephen over his numerous adversaries.

The triumph of the king did not, however, mean the full victory of his western oriented policy. On the contrary, the sources suggest that the council met and approved Stephen's politics for fear of something worse: a public rebellion against the ruler's strong-handed policy which he had initiated and carried out without questioning or seeking the approval of those who were called upon to direct the affairs of the country.

The 1018 campaign of King Stephen in alliance with Basil II of Byzantium[52] may prove the strength of the Hungarian monarchy, but it also could exemplify the desire of King Stephen to divert the attention of the nobility from domestic trouble making.

The situation in 1001, or at least in the early 1000s, was very similar to the conditions of the 970s, when Géza, himself dissatisfied with the behavior of the imperial missionaries and under heavy pressure by the council which feared a rebellion, compromised his principles and submitted to the wish of the councilors. In the case of Stephen exactly the opposite happened. This time it was the councilors who surrendered to the will of the determined king. The attitude of the council, however, rested on compromise only, and no compromise presents a real solution. In less than forty-five years, the suppressed feelings of the national opposition were manifested with ferocious vitality during the uprisings of 1046. Had it not been for the self-sacrificing determination of Bishop Gerard and the tactful understanding of the new Arpad ruler, Andrew I, Christianity would have been wiped out in less than half a century upon its commencement in Hungary.[56]

King Stephen, however, deserves the credit for having introduced western and Christian principles into his country, and having thereby secured the means for national survival of the Hungarians on the European scene.[57] Despite their faults, the legislative acts of the king and his council present a surprisingly well thought out and adaptable program that was actually realized during the four decades of Stephen's rule. The main weakness of this program is that it was conceived and arranged by the ecclesiastical advisors, who were still, and remained for decades to come, foreigners, foreigners by birth and feeling living among the native population. Stephen undoubtedly sought to remedy the situation by creating a corps of voluntary helpers of whose fidelity he was sure.[58] These men were the royal stewards taken from the lower ranks of early eleventh century Hungarian society, a social stratum that formed the conquered element of the population. This "conquered" element represented the remains of the old Pannonian-Roman inhabitants in the western sections of the realm, while in eastern Transylvania, too, it was the "local" element that proved to be the most loyal to the King and his policies.[59]

The native inhabitants, who by the eleventh century had learned the conquerors' tongue and were accustomed to their manners, came to form a balancing factor between the Magyars and the foreign-born clergy. It was probably this conquered element of the Hungarian population that first entered the ranks of the clergy and helped to spread the new doctrine among the populace.[60] Whether Stephen, by relying so heavily on the lower social strata of the inhabitants, committed an error in the realization of his political designs, remains questionable. His stewards and personal appointees to responsible public offices, previously held by the tribal nobles, were unpopular among the national strata of the population so much so that in the 1046 uprising the royal appointees were, together with the bishops, among the first victims of the rebellion. It is further known from the record that the teachings of Christianity were received with contempt by the majority of the inhabitants, and the use of naked military force in converting the people had highly superficial results.[61]

King Stephen made the difficult start during his reign, and the Magyars were fortunate enough to have capable leaders who succeeded him, who carried further and slowly accomplished Stephen's design.[62] King Andrew I, who ascended to the throne in later 1046, was a true Árpád scion who understood fully the importance of a western oriented Magyar policy.[63] It was only Stephen's two direct successors, neither of them of the Árpád line, who caused delay in accomplishing, what may be called, the Árpádian policy of Hungary's Europeanization.[64] As a consequence of the unfortunate regulation by Stephen of royal succession, formulated, it seems, under the growing influence of Queen Gisela, the Venetian-born Peter, the queen's nephew, inherited the throne upon Stephen's death in 1038. The national council, whose members intended to regain some of their regalian rights after the king's departure, approved of Peter's succession. But the hierarchy resented Peter—or rather the circumstances surrounding Peter's election—and refused to crown him king.[65]

Naturally, from the council's point of view, the approval of Peter fulfilled the constitutional requirements of his rule in the negative sense, therefore, the council in 1038 still disapproved publicly of the western institution of Christian kingship! Less than three years afterward, the council asserted its right to depose Peter on grounds of his incapacity.[66] In 1041, it was the council that elected his successor, this time a royal steward of the conquered part of the population, whose sole qualification for an election consisted of his being the son-in-law of the deceased King Stephen.[67] Aba, the new king, saw to it that his election was also recognized by the ecclesiastical party, though the royal coronation sealed the fate of this upstart three years later. Aba, who with the churchmen's support sought to continue Stephen's policy, lacked both the social and personal prestige of his great predecessor.[68] In 1044, when the German emperor following the invitation extended to him by the deposed Peter, invaded Hungary, the royal Magyar forces left their king in the lurch in the decisive battle at Ménfő. Western Hungary came under German occupation, while King Aba was murdered by the adherents of the national party shortly after the battle.[69]

What was the real purpose of the council in letting King Aba perish is not known. Even if Aba called down upon himself the councilors' wrath by his ecclesiastical coronation, the council must have been aware of the consequences of an imperial victory over Hungary at the time.

For the victorious Henry III not only reinstated Peter as king of Hungary, but made certain his coronation by the episcopal college of the realm by attending it, in the presence of the secular lords.[70] Thus, Hungary became in imperial fief. By 1046, full anarchy prevailed in the imperially controlled country. It was then that Bishop Gerard of Csanád decided to enter into public politics, and convinced the council of the necessity of restoring the realm to the Árpádian rule.

CHAPTER II

STEPHEN THE SAINT

---

1. The King's Best Known Co-worker: Gerard of Venice

Egressus itaque de cognatione sua tendebat ad orientem,
ubi Habraam dives ac pater multarum gentium factus est.

Vita minor s. Gerardi

No contemporary chronicler paid serious attention to the arrival of
Gerard of Venice in Hungary around 1025. Up to the present, no serious
historian has been willing to look into the question, while today any
researcher concerned with the topic may find himself at a loss as to where
to start digging for the real meaning of the conditions surrounding this
minor event of the year 1025. After all, why should it be so important to
determine the exact date of an unknown cleric's sojourn in the realm, and
how would this help to explain the circumstance of his remaining in the
country? Were there not, in the Hungarian realm, other clerics better
known and more respected than this recently-arrived Venetian monk?
In fact, it is not known for certain whether he was a Benedictine or a
follower of the hermit, Saint Romuald.[1] A picture of the Hungarian scene
around the mid-1020's may serve to clarify the matter.[2]

It is known from the reports of contemporary travelers in the country
that King Stephen made a determined effort to solicit the cooperation of
all possible foreign helpers in his westernizing program in the realm. The
kingdom had expanded by that time well beyond the borders of today's
Hungary, and it included the Transylvanian territories.[3] In this huge and
still rather sparsely populated country the king successfully broke the
old patriarchial system of tribal land holdings and political communities.

Moreover, he was able to carry this out without encountering much resistance since he had so recently dealt harshly with the two greatest and most feared chieftains in the realm, the above-mentioned Koppány and Gyula. It will not escape the attention of the careful observer that the chronicler reporting the events about 1000 made a clear distinction between the two tribal lords, one from the more cultivated and definitely western region of Transdanubia, and the other lord of Transylvania in the east.[4] Apparently, he wanted to emphasize "sicut fideli et veraci relatione tunc temporis viventium," that the rebellion was subdued all over the country.[5] For all practical purposes, this might have been the case except that the outlying fringe sections of the whole Carpathian basin remained for many years to come under non-Magyar rule, the north remained occupied by the Polish prince, Boleslaw, and in the south-east a huge chunk of land was actually ruled over by Ajtony, who had close contact with the Greek imperial court in Constantinople.[6] After Stephen had suppressed further Bulgarian efforts to regain parts of the Hungarian countryside formerly held by Bulgaria, the territory of Ajtony came to be an integral part of the Hungarian kingdom.[7] The seat of both local government and missionary episcopate first called Marosvár, it was called, after 1030, Csanád.

In 1030, the west Hungarian border came under attack from the German emperor, Conrad II.[8] There is no evidence to indicate that there was any kind of cooperation between the attacking Germans and the Bulgarians; the *practical* cause of Conrad's action was the refusal of King Stephen to let the German agents sent to Constantinople pass through his realm.[9] The very fact that the Magyars stood up as one man to fight off the German invader shows how the ruling monarch was able to count on the solidarity of his countrymen. By 1030, the chroniclers mention no German auxiliary force fighting on the side of the Hungarian king; it was the king with Hungarian troops who drove the imperial armies from the Hungarian territories.[10]

It was during these somewhat chaotic mid-1020's that Gerard went to Hungary. He did not go alone, and arrived without the faintest idea of remaining there. If we are to believe this late fourteenth century chronicler, Gerard went to Hungary to resume his interrupted journey to the Holy Land after a shipwreck on the Adriatic near Zara.[11] Hungary was a favored route for pilgrims on the way to Jerusalem.[12] It is much more likely, however, that, as the earlier and certainly far more trustworthy narrator of Gerard's *Vita minor* made it clear, Gerard's travels to and through the land were merly incidental.[13] That he was presented to the King only corresponded to the prevailing custom, and it is only natural to assume that the king asked him to stay and work in his kingdom.[14]

Why was it so natural? Did Stephen of Hungary ask any foreign sojourner to remain and work for the Christian cause in his realm? The record indicates that he had many distinguished and noble visitors calling at the royal court,[15] —the *Vita minor* makes no mention of the annual field day, the gathering of the nobles, when depicting the meeting of Gerard with King Stephen. Consequently, in spite of the narrative of the later chronicler, the meeting probably took place at the royal court.[16] Since the sources speak only scantily of the qualifications of the Venetian monk, it is necessary to turn to his own writings in order to gain more information.[18] It is quite reasonable to suppose that anyone asked to stay and work in the kingdom had to possess certain qualifications.[19] The record simply says that Gerard was a learned hermit who went to Hungary and remained with King Stephen. He himself, however, says that he spent a good deal of time travelling in search of learning before becoming a monk,[20] and suggests that he was valuable to the king for both his learning and foreign contacts of an ecclesiastical and political nature. This reason alone may have caused both Stephen and his immediate advisors to prevent the Venetian's departure from their midst, and there is evidence to show that one of the court clerics, perhaps another Italian, persuaded Gerard to stay.[21]

The date of his arrival may have been the summer of 1026, the time of the visit of Richard, abbot of Verdun, at King Stephen's court.[22] The date is important for the reason that it excludes various unfounded assumptions regarding his real function in the Hungarian realm before the actual establishment of the bishopric in 1030.[23]

It was once held, for example, that Gerard, born earlier, entered Hungarian territory as early as the first decade of the eleventh century; that he was asked to stay in order to become the tutor of Prince Emery, a son to King Stephen, that he tutored the prince for seven years, then spent another seven years at a hermitage near Bél.[24] Thus, it was only after fourteen years of sojourn in the realm that Gerard was, all of a sudden, called to head the bishopric of Csanád. Since the defeat of Ajtony did not take place until the very late 1020's and the missionary territory itself was hardly organized before 1030, this would place Gerard's arrival in Hungary around 1016 or even earlier. On the other hand, if Gerard went to the Hungarian court as late as 1025, he had no time, nor was there any need, for his educating Prince Emery, as the prince was then about 28 years of age.[25] Further, Gerard has not become the bishop-nominee to the see of Marosvár, then not yet established, during the first meeting with the king.[26] For the record says that he was to receive the bishop's dignity only after careful examination by the king of his personal qualifications included in educational brotherhood, religious disposition[27] and ability to participate in domestic and foreign missions as well as to play a role in the royal council.[28]

As a matter of fact, we do not know the exact date of birth of the Venetian, nor do we have knowledge of the occasion that led him to the monastic life. His *Vitae* report that he was an "oblate" in an abbey at Venice, and that he was elected abbot of the same community.[29] If he was a monk following the rule of St. Benedict, he was bound to stability. If a monk was found worthy of being sent to another monastery or a place offering higher instruction in the arts, he was supposedly to remain at that place in those years of study and return thereafter to his home community. The self-revealing passage by Gerard contradicts such a peaceful picture, the more so as Gerard—in the same opus, but in a somewhat different context or frame of mind—disapproved on various occasions of both the manner of living and the private morals of his confreres and fellow bishops who were also of the Benedictine rule in Hungary.[30]

Although both the *vitae* and the text of his work indicate that he led a religious community life in Hungary after his accession to the bishopric[31]—a way of living that was certainly[32] in sharp contrast with the community ideal of the Benedictines. Although Prof. Endres concluded from Gerard's writing that the Venetain was actually a member of the fellowship of St. Romuald, such a view is, however, open to objection. As Endres himself said, the followers of the latter saint were a very rustic group.[33] It is doubtful whether Gerard, a learned cleric, would have had much liking for joining St. Romuald's fellowhip. It should be noted here that St. Romuald himself intended to go to Hungary and suffer martyrdom among the heathen Magyars, although Romuald's project has usually been dated around the year 1001.[34] But the passage in Romuald's biography relating the events shows clearly that simple ignorant clerics desiring only the crown of martyrdom were unwelcome at Stephen's court, partly for the reason that they would have created bad propaganda for the king, partly also because the "westernizing" royal court had no use for unschooled *ignorami*, clerics though they were.[35]

In discussing Gerard's arrival at King Stephen's court, it is noteworthy that the *Vita* makes the unusual comment that only Gerard was actually retained at the court, while his companions were secretely dismissed.[36] Were the others dismissed because they may have been ignorant religious men travelling without a serious purpose eastward? Or were the "socios . . . qui mecum in Danubio descendunt" asked to go without Gerard, who obviously was the leader of the small group, because their presence did not fit into the scheme of Hungarian "westernizing" policies?[37]

The mystery of Gerard's early religious affiliation lies somewhere else. He probably entered religious life early, but remained in minor orders for many years and, as a tonsured cleric, he roamed the continent. The remark by the *Vita minor* that "a pueritia cepit Domino . . . devotus existere et evangelicis documentis peromnia patere," may or may not mean that he was offered as an oblate at the age of five, and it is more likely that Gerard was a free lance cleric when entering the Hungary of Stephen in 1025. According to his own writings, he was already an ordained priest. It is more plausible, therefore, to place his date of birth about the year 990. Accordingly, he would have been around thirty-five when beginning the real and purposeful phase of his life after many years spent in countless wanderings. During the years immediately following his arrival, the Venetian spent his days in the solitude of a hermitage near Bél, with only the saintly Maurus keeping his companionship.[38] His daily schedule consisted of his mortifying practices and writing. Even in the later days, he expressed certain longing for the hermit's way of life that he led at Bél, and during his busy years as bishop he wished for the silence of his monastic abode where he was able to pursue his beloved studies.[39]

The appointment of Gerard to the see of Csanád presents a further case for study. Both the circumstances of the nomination and the fact that he was named by the Hungarian king to head a Hungarian bishopric that was to be established over the territory held until then under Byzantine jurisdiction raises various and interesting problems. Contrary to the statement of his *Vita major*,[40] Gerard did not become a bishop-nominee immediately upon his arrival in the realm. The conditions within the kingdom were not favorable for such a quick advancement. For it would be questionable whether Stephen, who was so cautious with foreign clergymen and so painfully correct in observing canonical regulations in filling leading church posts over the country, would have appointed an entirely unknown cleric, a newcomer, to a responsible and representative position.

The episcopal office in Hungary during the whole Árpádian age remained highly important from the political as well as an ecclesiastical view point. Bishops were expected to carry full secular responsibility within their ecclesiastical territories.[41] Thus, the early *Vita* of Gerard did not elaborate on the circumstances of Gerard's nomination to, and actual acquirement of, the missionary territory, but asserted simply that after a few years spent amidst various duties in the realm, and since political conditions permitted, he was called upon to become the ordinary of Csanád.[42]

The Hungarian ruler held the right to appoint bishops or clerics in general to leading church positions in his realm rests mainly upon the authorization of the Holy See.[43] It was the Hungarian medievalist, Prof. P. Váczy, however, who called attention to the high ecclesiastical privileges attributed to King Stephen, and noted the interesting fact that Stephen exercised his rights as *rex* and not as *sacerdos*.[44] Unfortunately, we have no direct access to the papal bull conferring the prerogatives upon the person of the first Magyar King, for the so-called "Sylvester-Bull" was proven a forgery many a year ago.[45] On the other hand, that such a papal writ existed is clear from the statements of the *Vita major* and Hartvic.[46] Moreover, it is unlikely that a young king of a new Christian kingdom would have dared to misuse his authority in church matters without proper approval.

If Stephen received authorization from the papal court to act in church matters within the borders of his realm, the question arises whether he thereby lost prestige in the eyes of his countrymen. The answer to this question is probably in the negative. As I have pointed out above, the king was surrounded by ecclesiastical advisors, whose public position had actually been secured by law.[47] This left little initiative indeed for opposition by anyone.[48] Such opposition remained subdued until the death of King Stephen.

What must be emphasized, however, is that the first Hungarian King making appointments to church positions in his realm never thought of himself as a priest,[49] and nowhere does the record indicate that he ever undertook action on the church's behalf without proper consultation with his ecclesiastical advisors. Thus, Gerard's nomination to the bishopric or missionary territory of Csanád did occur with the approval of the royal ecclesiastical advisors, though it was the king who had the last word in the matter. The action taken by Stephen followed in full accord with his authority as the first Christian ruler of Hungary, and authority based upon papal approval.[50]

The *Vita major* noted that Gerard remained in his retreat at Bél until, on the proper occasion, he was called away by the king to head an episcopal see.[51] The wording of the text leaves no doubt that Gerard's promotion to the episcopal dignity was directly related to the formation of the Csanád missionary territory, that it may have followed the actual defeat of Ajtony; too, his appointment by the king came as a well-deserved recognition of his services to the crown and of his personal qualifications as a spiritual leader.[52] Consequently, so it seems, Gerard must have gained acknowledgment of his public services to the king, who, in turn, was promoting the religious and political welfare of his people.[53]

What commissions may, however, have been undertaken by Gerard in behalf of the king? As it was mentioned before, Gerard's foreign contacts seemed impressive to the king. If, for instance, Gerard began his stay in Hungary in the year Richard of Verdun visited with King Stephen, and Gerard greeted the famous churchman there at the royal court, then it seems more than likely that the future bishop of Csanád knew the abbot beforehand.[54]

The record also informs us that Stephen was a very difficult person to get along with, a perfectionist, who only trusted a few people, and usually performed the minutest detals of his various offices himself.[55] That he gave Gerard recognition for his services by entrusting to him an important bishopric in the southeastern part of the country—until 1030 under "foreign" control—shows only that the bishop was one of the few selected and fortunate members of the royal household, who was able to serve the king with utmost loyalty.

In his new capacity as the ordinarius of the Csanád territory, Gerard might have continued in serving his king in various capacities: for one, he may have undertaken missions abroad on the king's behalf, or, not unlike Bonipert of Pécs, to remain in touch with the outside world.[56] Second, he may have helped to plan the new missionary policy of Stephen aimed at the *full* Christianization of Hungary in the future. Moreover, the fact that Gerard, a foreigner by birth,[57] was no scion of an importamt and noble family, nor did he represent outside political and mercantile interests, endeared him to the heart of King Stephen.[58]

Gerard was, whether a monk or merely a secular cleric arriving accidentally in Hungary—and being retained there by force while enroute to the Holy Land—a learned cleric and the type of a person who willingly collaborated with secular authorities, as long as they, these autorities, were willing to collaborate with the Church in carrying on with general public interests. From Gerard, the king had no need to fear disloyalty, and the king could always entrust him with important missions.[59] The fortunate factor that Gerard was an educated ecclesiastic who knew about the European continent from his own personal experiences, made him simply an ideal type for such a royal ambassadorship, domestic and foreign. A faithful servant he was, who never betrayed his royal master.[60]

2. The King's Reign

Pervenit itaque ad partes Pannonie, quarum habenam tunc christianissimus rex Stephanus gubernabat.

Gerard of Csanád's *Vita Minor*

The *Chronicom pictum* gives little information on the reign of King Stephen. Besides Stephen's struggles with his domestic opponents and the somewhat lengthy description of the establishment of the church dedicated to saints Peter and Paul at Óbuda to commemorate Stephen's victory over the Bulgarians in 1018, the chronicler reported only on the circumstances surrounding the blinding of Vazul, Stephen's cousin. Vazul was obviously next in line of succession after the death of Emery in 1031.

The chronicler, however, failed to report anything about the conditions surrounding the death of the prince, and it is necessary to turn to German and Polish annalists for further inforamtion. The chronicler devoted one more short paragraph to the death of Stephen, and gave the account of the King's death incorrectly. The reader today gains the impression that the chronicler glossed over this period of Hungarian history in too much of a hurry; his silence raises doubts and calls for further investigation of the subject.[1]

Unfortunately, too, the royal biographer, Hartvic, writing about seven decades after Stephen's death, furnished only scanty information on this subject. Still, from Hartvic we gain interesting and valuable details on Stephen's mission to Rome, and he does explain the reason why the Hungarian nobles were so conspicuously absent from the coronation rite. Hartvic also gave a brief description of the first legislative statutes of the new king. Yet, the long reign of the king is in the main treated briefly. Some relevant details are given, but many are less important. Thus, for instance, Hartvic's characterization of the king's behavior toward the clergy is given only in general terms based upon second hand information and devoid of precise data. A trustworthy and informative source of the period is Stephen's *Vita minor*. The reign of Stephen must, therefore, be pieced together from several bits of scattered information.[2]

The reign of the king may be divided into three phases. The first phase comprises the first decade of his rule between 997 and 1007 when he decided to send Astric to attend the Frankfurt Synod.[3] The second phase consists of the years from 1007 to 1029 and this period may be significant for three reasons: one, the warfare of the king with the Bulgarians, fought in alliance with the Byzantine court; two, the king's victory over the Petchenegs in Transylvania—a victory which strengthened the king's hold over the eastern portion of his realm; three, progress made in constitutional matters including the centralization of the royal court.

Concerning this second phase, two further observations are to be made. First, Stephen carried the day over his nobles by supporting the Greeks in their defeat of the Bulgarians. This aid he had to render to the Byzantine court because he needed a trusted neighbor on the southeastern borderline at a time when the Germans formed a unified and prospectively dangerous force in the west. Second, the king's humane treatment of the Bulgarian prisoners of war was prompted by political consideration for the future, and not by Christian charity alone. Indeed, by the end of the 1020s, the king needed Bulgarian sympathy during his attack on Ajtony at Marosvár.[4]

The third and final phase of the king's reign lasted for the eight remaining years of his life, years filled with domestic problems caused by the royal relatives at court; the attempt made on his life; the struggle to ensure a worthy successor in the face of German opposition culminating in his rather unwilling designation of Peter Orseolo to succeed him on the throne.

Stephen had to make a quick decision in nominating the new successor by 1031, a question that had to be settled because of opposition by the German sympathizers at the court. Yet, reason had to prevail so as not to awaken the suspicions of the pagan branch of the Árpád family. Stephen the scion of Árpád had to avoid the charge that he was sacrificing "national" interests to the imperial designs of the family of his Bavarian born queen, Gisela.[5]

The picture we gain, therefore, is highly colorful, though one still wishes that in the person of Hartvic might be found a counterpart to Suger of St. Denis who wrote such an accurate biography of his royal master, Louis VI the Fat. Nevertheless, although the king of Hungary had no Suger to write his biography, he had in the person of Gerard a Suger-type ecclesiastic who felt responsible to care for the troubles of the government in Hungary.[6] Gerard's *Vita* ia a source of information on this, an authority that affords a fair picture of not only Gerard's actions and behavior, but also of the background of the times in Hungary. The *Vita* asserts that, for example, the Csanád bishop stood in the service of the king, and that he acted thus out of his own free will, for the love of the people and the monarch, whose cause he found just enough to aid.[7]

Gerard's occupations in the service of Stephen included missions on behalf of the ruler, be they foreign in nature.[8] In the domestic field, Gerard might have been asked to concentrate his attention as royal advisor on the development of Christianization,[9] and judged by the remarks of his *Deliberatio,* Gerard complied with the requests of his master.[10] As royal advisor Gerard gained influence with the king in determining policy dealing with the slowly moving work of Christian missions in the heathen countryside.[11]

The problem, as Gerard saw it, was threefold. First, the work of conversion had to be very thorough, and no good work could be done without conscientious missionaries, clerics dedicated to their vocation in the field. The missionaries available for such a project were neither too numerous nor were all capable of learning sufficient Hungarian to make their work really fruitful. To remedy the situation, Gerard proposed the training of a Hungarian born clergy to carry on with the work of conversion. By relying on Hungarian born and speaking clerics, the king could make his policy work by making it more acceptable and also more understandable to the conquering population. Because, as Gerard saw it, the greatest handicap to the royal policy consisted of the fact that hitherto the missionaries had been foreigners whose foreign tongue and customs could not gain the trust of the proud conqueror caste. Furthermore, by training the Hungarian-born clerics the king also trained a potential administrative personnel for himself in the sense that the native clergy would also become the eyes and ears of the court on regional administrative matters.[12] Gerard who was much in favor of full separation of ecclesiastical and political interests, was willing to grant an exception, at least on a temporary basis, to his master to assure the latter's political hold over the realm.[13]

The predominance of the foreign born missionaries active in Hungary cuased a real disruption of the royal policy—to introduce Hungary to the western world—as the self-conscious conquering "Magyar" element refused to submit to the royal summons to take a new religion,—to adopt a new god, as they put it. It was never made clear to the heathen Hungarians that by submitting to the service of the "new god" they were merely changing external forms of worship of the God, the same Whom they adored both privately and publicly, before their nominal conversion to the tenets of the Christian religion. Consequently, in the foreign speaking clerical element the Hungarians saw only the representatives of outside interests—that meant unaccustomed and unfair administration to them.[14]

Gerard could claim as he did somewhat later, that this policy was entirely misunderstood by the members of the Council. It was only in the 1030s at Csanád that, for instance, Gerard was able to organize his diocese and to gain the aid and confidence of the regional lords.[15]

The second problem Gerard had to face as the king's advisor was the lack of cooperation between the foreign missionary element and the earliest Hungarian speaking missionaries who were trained on the job by foreigners. The "Hungarian" clergy, no doubt, originated from poor families, the subdued, lower social stratum of the then existing population of the realm.[16] It is possible that some of the educated foreigners looked with contempt upon this native clerical element, although the "natives" were staunch co-workers of their foreign born colleagues.[17]

Such a misunderstanding may have been, of course, due to the fact that the native clerical element usually served in the capacity of interpreters in missionary enterprises. In Hungary in particular there was a need for such interpreters as only a handful of clerics knew the Hungarians' tongue. These Hungarian speaking men were ordained priests without much educational backgroud, and yet, they had to be accepted as fully fledged clerical companions by the rest of the clergy. Such acceptance was forced upon the foreigners by royal command, and the proud westerners were, naturally, disinclined to accept their undertrained Hungarian speaking colleagues as equals.[18]

This misunderstanding may have been responsible for the slow progress made in the missionary-spiritual field, or for the disruption, in the 1040s, of missionary work in the realm. It is important to note at this point that even Gerard preached through an interpreter—as late as 1044.[19] The record shows that the interpreter of his "famous" Easter sermon was an ordained clergyman.[20]

The third problem confronting Gerard, therefore, was the establishment of schools in Hungary for the education of the future native and educated clergy that was to be called upon to take over from the foreign missionaries the burden of Christianizing the land. This he proposed to the king, whether in the council or out of the council in private conversation with Stephen is unimportant as it was the king who had the last word.

Whether Gerard was the first cleric to propose such a solution to the problem of clerical education in Hungary cannot be proven. It seems certain, however, that the Csanád bishop was the first to set up a cathedral school in Hungary with the understanding that the first teachers of his cathedral school at Csanád should be clerics from other places, perhaps from Pannonhalma. That the abbey of Pannonhalma, founded about 1000, had its own monastic school is evident from the record.[21] The saintly Maurus, the second bishop of Pécs, was among its first graduates, and Maurus is known also on account of his literary activities in Hungary.[22]

That the plan of Gerard to form centers of education for the future Hungarian clergy suffered some defeat, or at least, caused much misunderstanding, is clear from the remarks of the bishop himself who in his critical statements referring to the days of Peter acknowledged the inability of the first Hungarian school to produce a strong, trained clerical body in the kingdom.[23] On the other hand, there exists a document pertaining to the reign of King Andrew I that indicates the fairly high level of learning among the leading members of the Hungarian hierarchy of that age.[24]

In "foreign politics" Gerard might have been active as Stephen's representative outside of Hungary. Vilmos Fraknói made some interesting observations on Stephen's relations with Rome.[25] Although there is no evidence to indicate the participation of Gerard in the ceremonies of dedication of the Hungarian religous homes established by King Stephen in Rome or in Ravenna,[26] János Karácsonyi's thesis that Gerard had his share in the planning of these houses abroad for Hungarian pilgrims during the first half of the eleventh century, is still tenable.[27] That at least one of these places, the house in Rome, served a purpose and maintained a cultural designation might be concluded from a 1058 papal bull, which survived in a seventeenth century transcript of a 1347 document.[28]

The king acted in good fauth in establishing these religious houses for his subjects visiting abroad. However, the houses had more than mere religious purpose. Following Hartvic's description of the Hungarian house in Rome, it might have served as the "embassy" of the Hungarian kings in the papal capital—the only permanent "capital" in the then known European world: *caput mundi,* to strengthen relations between the Hungarian court and the papal curia.[29]

After the death of Stephen in 1038, Gerard held strictly correct relations along purely ecclesiastical lines with both kings Peter and Aba as both rulers took measures to undermine the influence of the Church in the kingdom. Only in 1046 did Gerard again try his hand in Hungarian politics, and probably saved Hungary both from civil war and of disintegration. The experiment cost him his life. Obviously, he was well known in the realm and had far too many enemies. When the political order broke down by the mid-1040s and Gerard organized his group of conspriators to prepare for the return of the exiled Árpád scions to Stephen's throne, his whereabouts were known in advance by his political adversaries.[30] He was killed at the moment when he was about to meet face to face Andrew, the future king, whose return to the throne and country the bishop so eagerly supported.[31]

Something, finally, should be said of Gerard as a person. He was and remained the withdrawn, shy type, too preoccupied in his free moments with his personal problems. He worked hard to overcome the weakness of the flesh that so frequently disturbed him. His later years and behavior prove that he was a lonely man and unable to get along with others. He disliked life at the royal court and took refuge from the affairs of the world as soon as he possibly could in his nearby hermitage at Bél.[32] This particular location was not far from the royal headquarters at Székes-fehérvár so that he was available whenever the king desired his presence.[33]

It is remarkable that Gerard, shy and choleric as he was by nature, was able to accomplish so much as a bishop. That there were many in the episcopal college who disliked him for personal reasons is evident from his writings. That many of his religious confreres especially those at Csanád hated his strict adherence to the regulations is revealed by his own remarks in the *Deliberatio*.[34] The good bishop was a driver of men, nervous and in many instances rather insecure and, one might say, inconsistent.[35] That he and King Stephen got along well might have been due to the fact that both men were similar in personality, and both were able to respect each other's position and duties. To the king, Gerard was not only the valuable foreign emissary, but also a personal friend who could speak his mind to him.[36] As an administrator, Gerard faced a diocese comprising the then perhaps most insecure political areas of Stephen's realm.[37]

He evidently spoke his mind in the presence of his monks and episcopal colleagues. The results here were less encouraging. The reason may have been that the German oriented and Latin speaking bishops were skeptical of, disagreeable to the ideas of Gerard, rather jealous of the influence and capabilities of this Venetian.[38] Also, disagreeable to the German ecclesiastics was the fact that Gerard sometimes took issue with the Hungarians. He honestly disapproved of politics of both the pro-German and anti-German parties.[39]

Gerard considered the Hungarians a primitive but honest people.[40] And yet, he deplored the inconsiderate and uncivilized attitude of the Hungarian nobility.[41] The bishop's remark that the Hungarian nobles preferred horses and stables to learning might be characteristic of a learned westerner's contempt for the uncivilized conditions in Hungary. The bishop worried in fact about the immediate future of the Church in the kingdom,[42] not because the forthcoming revolution would end many priestly lives, but because the revolution would be the result of poorly done missionary work.[43]

Neither was Gerard in favor of the dominant behavior of the "Magyars" in the countryside. The bishop's concern, as evidenced by the "singing-girl episode," for the vanquished stratum of the population was real.[44] He saw that the "Magyars" were too lacking in numbers to achieve lasting results in the country without the cooperation of their recently subdued subjects. No such cooperation could have been forthcoming, however, until the social and religious barriers between the conquerors and conquered were broken down.[45] The king, too, saw the problem, though to his royal mind, force was the only answer. Stephen was an Árpád who knew his people. The prefatory note to his Laws, or the remark of his *Vita* that Stephen "secundum ecclesiasticam doctrinam instituens, iugum et legem disciplinae subpositis cervicubus adhibuit, omnesque immunditias malorum prorsus destruxit,"[46] support such an assumption. The Hungarian monarch stood not alone in this regard; his contemporaries in England, for instance, had to follow a similar policy.[47]

Was it the bishop's personal tragedy, or was it an early Hungarian national tragedy that Gerard's contemporaries were unable to comprehend his ideas?

3. Establishment of the Csanad bishopric: a Political Necessity

The bishopric of Csanad had peculiar beginnings. Although located in an area of former Byzantine interests, the diocese was founded by King Stephen[1] —and not by the Byzantine Patriarch,[2] —at a time when the latter was still in communion with Rome.[3] Furthermore, the Hungarian King must have had in mind the establishment of the bishopric in this region as early as the beginnings of his reign when this area formed no part as yet of the kingdom.[4] For, at that time, the institution of a diocese was bound to render support to the political, secular organization of the area and strengthen its ties with the Hungarian realm.

That the King was very much concerned about the religious-political future of the Marosvar region is evident from the narrative by Hartvic which states how welcome the arrival of Gerard in Hungary was to the King, and explains how after deep consideration,[5] he decided to give the new bishopric to Gerard of Venice for two reasons: first, because the bishop-designate knew the language and customs of the inhabitants of the area;[6] second, on grounds that Gerard possessed the needed qualities of a born leader, both religious and secular,[7] who could carry full responsibility in his difficult obligations as the spiritual ordinary of the newest Hungarian frontier region, or march, on the Hungaro-Byzantine border.[8]

That the Csanád bishopric was not among the original ten dioceses formed by King Stephen in about 999 is evident from the text of Hartvic.[9] On the other hand, the King had the foundation of twelve dioceses in mind when he undertook the organization of the Church in the realm, and, evidently, he had to leave aside the establishment of bishoprics in regions which, though they belonged, geographically speaking, to the central Carpathian basin: the mid-Danube area, were not yet under direct Hungarian control.[10]

The takeover of the Marosvár region by 1030 through military force is described in detail by the chroniclers. Since the sources also mention the attack of Emperor Conrad II on Hungary in 1030,[11] it may be assumed that there was a certain relationship between the two occurances: the attacking Germans from the west, and the rebellious Greco-Hungarians living within the nominal framework of Stephen's realm.[12] Various explanations suggest themselves, but the following hypothesis seems to be far more reasonable than any other, because it is based upon the record. First, there must have been an imperial plan at Conrad's court to form a political and military connection with the Greek court of the Southeast in Constantinople as early as the later half of the 1020s.[13] However, such a "contact" between the West and the Southeast would have included Stephen's kingdom, either as a "buffer" zone between the two empires, or, as a secondary goal, Hungary's elimination from the continental map to become a German vassal state in the late 1020s.[14]

Second, the military conquest of the Hungarian realm had to be more practical prospect for the Germans, as the newly gained regions in the mid-Danube section would have served as a permanent type of military march between the Byzantine and Ottonian empires of the 1030s. Thirdly, because evidence is lacking it is impossible to say whether the sudden German attack originated without deeper planning on the part of the German military, or that the suddenness of this move might have been caused by rumors of rebellion in Hungary at the time. It may, indeed, be reasonable to assume that the Hungarian kingdom at the time seemed a sure prey to the German military. In other words, the Germans did not think it was worthwhile to make arrangements in preparing their attack. As a consequence, it can be concluded that there was no cooperation between the attacking Germans and the rebellion of Ajtony in the Marosvár area.[15]

Last, and it seems highly important, upon the unexpectedly quick victory of the royal Hungarian force over the Germans, King Stephen made use of both the victorious war psychology[16] and of the fact that he had the whole Hungarian armed force at his disposal[17] when he suddenly attacked Ajtony, and did away with this petty prince of the southern Hungarian regions on the Danube. In such a way, Stephen first gained military and political control of the southern region on the lower Danube, and, second, he succeeded in establishing a firmly entrenched Hungaro-Byzantine border directly over the lower Danube region.[18]

Therefore, the foundation of the Csanád bishopric occured under martial conditions. It followed immediately upon a military conquest caused by and undertaken for reasons of political necessity.[19] In a sense, it formed the last portion of the conquest of the 890s, although at that early date the region around the lower Maros river may already have been part of the Árpádian holdings gained and distributed among the seven conquering tribes. It was only during the chaotic decades of the tenth century, under the weak rule of the Árpádian court, that certain chieftains of the Maros region were able to establish themselves as semi-independent petty kings in their area; and only King Stephen had the strength and determination to put an end to these secessionist tendencies of the Maros region dukes by defeating them and reattaching their holdings to the Árpádian realm.[20]

The religious side of the Maros area strife also had political consequences, namely that the Maros dukes, in order to strengthen their political position and their separation from the court of Stephen, supported the Byzantine Church of their region and counted on Byzantine ecclesiastical cooperation in their policies.[21] In their point of view, the Maros region was far enough away from the Greek court, safely to seek Byzantine alliance at the expense of the nearby Hungarian court.[22] That the Byzantines, however, were not really interested in Ajtony's political fate never really entered the mind of the latter. When the showdown came in 1030, it was Ajtony who lost his game without Byzantium's having lifted a finger in defense of its ally.[23]

The defeat of Ajtony and the establishment of the new Hungarian bishopric on the Byzantine border had, in fact, far reaching complications. For, by forming a new ecclesiastic administrative unit, Stephen also established a new region within his secular organization.[24] As a result, this new regional unit came under the headship of two persons: the churchman Gerard of Csanád, and the royal steward, Csanád by name, the victor of Marosvár.[25] We have no record of personal directives issued by King Stephen to his regional stewards of the kingdom except a few royal statutes preserved in Stephen's Code of Laws.[26]

From these latter acts it seems plausible that the royal stewards, and bishops as well, proved to be the most loyal supporters of royal authority in the countryside,[27] and that it was through the vigilance of the regional ecclesiastics that the authority of the central court slowly gained stability in the realm.[28]

It was a slow process, however. In Csanád it took the bishop and the count years to assure themselves of the willing cooperation of the local nobles. Surprisingly, it was the bishop who made the first step by opening up a school at his cathedral at Csanád.[29] To his cathedral school he invited the offspring of the local nobles to gain an education and indoctrination in contemporary politics. Such an education had to render some definite goal in return.[30] Therefore, in perhaps an unduly short period of time and with far too inadequate education, the new graduates of the school were quickly advanced in clerical orders and given appointments to ecclesiastical prebends within the diocese. Whether Gerard wanted to secure thereby the loyalty of the noble fathers by making prelates out of their sons is a problem none of the sources go into, though, from the writings of Gerard it appears that the bshiop felt compelled to undertake such a step in order to secure certain trustworthy Hungarian nobles for his new ecclesiastical administration.[31]

In order to understand properly these new Hungarian ecclesiastics, it is necessary to show that around the 1030s Hungary was inhabited by two social strata. One consisted of the conquering (Magyar) element[32] that still continued to live off the countryside. The work of Bishop Gerard makes the reader unwittingly think of the Frankish Merovingian Gaul in the sixth century.[33] The other social stratum consisted of the earlier inhabitants, the "conquered" peoples who did all the work and formed the foundations for any organized common life. In the Csanád region it was this lower social element that provided the bishop with a framework on which to build Christian communities.[34]

There is another curious characteristic of this conquered social stratum in the Csanád area. They lived in towns, in small communities:[35] while it was only the still heathen or only nominally baptized Hungarians who lived in or rather "off" the countryside. It is a pity that we know so little about the Hungarian towns and town-life of this period. We know only that towns were in existence in the realm populated mostly by non-Hungarian speaking inhabitants engaged in trade and commerce.[36] The Danube and its tributaires provided the kingdom with commercial routes, as we know, for instance, that as early as the 990s, salt was mined and taken down on the Maros river.[37]

That the town population had its share in royal favor is evident from the representative session[s] held by King Béla I in 1060, when the King called upon two elected representatives of each Hungarian *villa*[38] (a lower unit of the administration of the realm, possibly equivalent to the English Hundred[39]), to attend his public meeting that dealt with common "national" interests so that he might assure himself of the solidarity of the lower element in the realm and against the then very active German party supporting the cause of the emperor and opposing the rights of the Hungarian Árpád king. In fact, by 1060, the German party consisted almost entirely of Hungarian and German nobles who had settled in Hungary,[40] and the King, Béla I, felt compelled to call upon the lower nobles and the non-Hungarian town-population to support his cause.

There are certain rules laid down in the royal statutes of King Stephen concerning public relations between the court and the non-noble inhabitants of the kingdom, the population of towns. Those regulations are short and deal mainly with the security and personal rights of the non-nobles against the all powerful local potentates.[41] From these scanty statutory laws it seems clear that Stephen realized in time the potential political usefulness of the non-noble element that lived as yet without any personal prerogatives. Finding himself in special need of royal protection, this element was in turn willing to render any aid to the King should the need arise.[42]

This double victory of King Stephen must have aroused fierce jealousy on the home front, however; the King had improved his own position tremendously at the court, while a psychologically prepared and recently proved armed force stood ready at his personal command.[43] The national Chronicle reports that by this time the King wished to withdraw from the care of worldly business to make room for his son, Prince Emery, on the royal throne.[44] Nevertheless, Stephen missed the appropriate moment for reaching such a decision. For as soon as he announced his irrevocable decision to withdraw, the Prince mysteriously died in a hunting accident,[45] and an Árpád conspiracy was formed against the life of the aged, sickly King.[46]

Under such circumstances only a person like Gerard could fill the troublesome position in the new diocese. Certainly, the Venetian's knowledge of Greek[47] and earlier experience with the eastern world[48] proved positive factors in his choice for the new post.[49] The bishop realized that the new administrative region formed, both from the secular as well as from the religious view point, a very important link between the Hungarian court and the Southeast: Byzantium.[50]

Regardless of the fact that King Stephen and his predecessor had chosen the West for political as well as cultural alliances as the sole means of political survival of their nation,[51] Gerard knew that Greek contacts and Byzantine influence in Hungarian politics, if the term can be used at such an early date, played an increasingly important role. After all, as early as the late 1040s, the Byzantine court sent a royal crown (diadem) to Andrew I of Hungary during the period of strained political relations with the German emperor, Henry III; another Byzantine diadem was sent by the Byzantine emperors to Hungarian king Géza I in about 1075,[52] when the Hungarian court found it impossible to deal with its western neighbor.[53]

The Byzantines were right there on the new Hungaro-Byzantine border, and King Stephen maintained an "embassy" [home for Hungarian pilgrims on their way to Jerusalem] for the frequent Hungarian political envoys to stay in Byzantium.[54] Moreover, the Hungarian court needed trustworthy secular and spiritual officials[55] in charge of the new regional

unit of administration, and yet, both of these leaders had to be know-
ledgable about Byzantine ways and conditions in order to take effective
charge of their territory. The ease with which Gerard took up his abode
in the monastery of the Byzantine monks at Csanád, while the monks
were persuaded by Count Csanád himself to move to a nearby new location at Oroszlányos, and to keep up with their liturgical religious services,
illustrates Gerard's competence and Csanád's.[56]

The basic population of the area, Gerard's new diocese, consisted of
Byzantinized Bulgarian elements, Christian at least in name, and culturally
an element which also maintained strong commercial ties with the southern regions, and, to a limited extent, with the West as well. Although the
record presents only a sparse documentation of permanent town settlements, historical research has succeeded in establishing proof for their
existence.[57] These cultural and business centers were small markets,
where because the population was settled permanently, earlier missionaries
had tried to form small religious nuclei for organized ecclesiastical life.[58]
The missionaries active in this area before the time of Gerard, were,
however, Byzantines. It is known that Methodius, for instance, upon his
second expulsion from the Moravian region, found refuge and a place for
his evangelizing activity amidst the populace of this region, which, according to its political beliefs belonged to the then Bulgarian realm of Tsar
Simeon and came under the ecclesiastical jurisdiction of the Byzantine
Church.[59]

Our evidence in this regard is scanty indeed, and its interpretation is
rather confusing. Slavic scholars try to prove the predominance of the
Cyril-Methodius missionary undertaking in the region to establish evidence for their theories of earlier Greek interests in the area; Hungarian
scholarship, on the other hand, going by limited but solid source evidence,
takes pains to prove its hypothesis by the final victory of the western
type: Roman religious element over the region, the southeastern portion
of Stephen's kingdom.[60]

One thing is certain: earlier religious settlements did exist in the Csanád
region before Gerard took over the spiritual governorship of the area
and the new bishop made remarkably rapid progress with his new subjects.
This result is the more remarkable, because, Gerard said, he used careful
cathecising before actually converting his flock to the teaching of the
western Chruch. He gives the impression of a man who felt compelled to

do a careful job in his field because of the Byzantine indoctrination and possible existence of heretical sects in the region. The fact that he used Hungarian speaking missionaries, and that he himself relied on an interpreter when preaching to his new converts,[61] shows that he skillfully counterbalanced the influence of the Byzantine Church. Although his services were held in the Latin rite, he stressed the need for sermons in the vernacular, which, as the example of the "singing girl" episode proves, need not necessarily be in Hungarian.[62]

4. The King's Ecclesiastical Policy

In contrast with King Stephen, and in spite of the fact that there were two *vitae* recording his story, the life and activities of Gerard of Csanád remained obscure. The controversy concerning his *vitae*, as, for example, the possible influence his *Vita minor* had upon the composition of the *Vita maior*, is still strong; the dating of both "lives" still a matter of controversy.

It may not be a useless idea to revive here the nearly eighty year old theory of Henrik Marczali, who said that, essentially, both of Gerard's *vitae* date back to the eleventh century.[1] The shorter Life could have, as a documentation piece, been prepared for the canonization of Gerard of Csanád in 1083;[2] its compiler might have based his report on eyewitness accounts from people who knew the bishop well. It is the opinion of Marczali that although the later *Vita maior* contained a good deal of intelligence on eleventh century events, its fourteenth century MS is, regardless of the 1381 entry it carries, only a transcript of some earlier text.[3] Consequently, the *Vita* is, in its present form, not an original composition. C.A. Macartney added to this observation of Marczali the remark that the narrative of the *Vita maior* was based upon matieral covered by the *Vita minor,* and the compiler/author of the earlier *Vita* made use of additional data.[4]

There are, in fact, some similarities between the *Vita maior* and some passages recorded in the fourteenth century Chronicle; these similarities prove that the author of the *Vita* had some information, taken from the already available text of the Chronicle, at his disposal; however, in

Marczali's view, it was the compiler of the Chronicle, who took his information from Gerard's *Vita maior* because the material covered by *Vita*
was already in existence by the fourteenth century.[5]

In an attempt to determine the date and status of the "lives", and the
sojourn of Gerard in Hungary, two difficulties ought to be eliminated
from the way. One is that though King Stephen relied upon the support
of many qualified people, such as Abbot Astric or Adalbert of Prague,
in his diplomatic and missionary efforts,[6] the lives and achievements of the
king's trusted advisors were not preserved for posterity in writing. No
writer commemorated the life of, and only very recently had the learned
György Györffy pieced together the scattered information available on,
Astric;[7] the lives of Adalbert contain little references to his activites
in Hungary.[8] Yet, there were two *vitae* written on Gerard.

Did Gerard deserve two lives (two even if the "major" were only a
strongly beefed up version of the "minor") because he, together with
King Stephen and Prince Emery, became one of the first three Hungarians
to be canonized as saints? Were episcopal "lives" (in which the political
activities of the bishops were stressed at the expense of the sanctity of
their lives) not in overabundance in Germany at the same period?[9]

The second difficulty is that there is too little known about Gerard.
His year of birth is unknown; the time of his arrival in Hungary is uncertain—except perhaps for the reference he made to Richard of Verdun,
who travelled through Hungary in 1026.[10] The date of his death is unknown, too; most probably, he died in February, 1046 or 1047.[11] It is
known from the *Vita* that Stephen had Gerard held back by force but
let his companions continue their journey to the Holy Land;[12] on the
other hand, the statement of his *Vita minor* that Gerard, upon his being
retained in Hungary,[13] served for seven years as a tutor to Prince Emery,
lacks counterreference.[14] The prince was dead by 1031.[15]

Macartney noted that the author of the *Vita minor,* who in Macartney's
view provided information for the *Vita maior,* had transcribed a then
already extant text, and made his orignial "contribution" by adding an
introduction and conclusion to the piece.[16] It is, however, exactly the
beginning of Gerard's narrative (Gerard was born in Venice to well-to-do
parents; lost his father at an early age when he failed to return from a
pilgrimage to the Near East; he was offered as an oblate to a Venetian
monastery; because of his great intelligence, —and perhaps family

background—he was permitted to receive an education in the monastery)[17], that failed to provide information as to the whereabouts of Gerard in his early years.

When really did he enter and what monastery? Was he an oblate? Did he enter on his own, after the completion of his studies? Where did he continue his work? There is a reference in the *Deliberatio* about his student days, to the effect that he had roamed all over the continent.[18] Did he "roam" as a monk? His boast that he knew everything, "nil lectionis me effugere potest," may become a wayward monk of the eleventh century.[19] The narrative only emphasized that upon return to his monastery, Gerard immediately was elected an abbot;[20] however, being dissatisfied with his manner of life, he decided to go to the Holy Land. He made this decision because he wished to follow in his father's footsteps, and because he was much interested in scriptural studies.[21]

The early, hard-core portion of the *Vita*[22] reports that Gerard was unable to carry out his resolution. He not only suffered a shipwreck on the Adriatic near Zara, and was diverted from his original route by being persuaded to travel through Hungary, but that Bishop Maurus of Pécs presented him to King Stephen; the king was so impressed with the sermon of this learned foreigner that he prevented him from reaching Jerusalem.[23]

Among the early Hungarian chroniclers Hartvic alone reported that Gerard was called upon by King Stephen to take charge of the Csanád bishopric because of his intellectual and spiritual qualifications for the sacred office. The episcopal biographer of King Stephen took pains to point out that Stephen, though he needed trustworthy persons to head the episcopal sees in his realm, examined first of all the spiritual qualifications of his nominees for office. Hartvic also emphasized that Gerard, through his attendance on the king, during the last seven years of the reign of Stephen, had been carefully prepared for his role as spiritual head of the latest and perhaps the then largest Hungarian ecclesiastical administrative unit.

That the king's precaution in selecting trustworthy persons was not without foundation was proven by the turbulent times following his death in 1038, when under the weak reign of Stephen's successors, the still semi-Christianized and little cultured Magyars came close to extinguishing entirely the recently founded western institutions in the kingdom.

According to the Chronicle, it was Gerard's chief merit that, by his interference in secular politics, he saved the Hungarian monarchy in 1046.
No little wonder then that the Hungarian chroniclers gave Gerard the
royal treatment in their narratives of the Árpádian age.[24]

Little is known about the organization of the new bishopric, or about
the organization of the Church in the realm in general.[25] From the remarks of the national record, supported to a limited extent by the *Annales
Altahenses* and the *Annales Hirschenfeldenses,* it seems that Stephen
followed the Ottonian policy regarding church matters by making full
use of the episcopal college in secular policies. As the bishops in Stephen's
time were without exception foreign born churchmen, such a policy,
to the great consternation of the Hungarian population, must have been
relatively easy.

No Hungarians were appointed to higher ecclesiastical positions in the
kingdom. The first Hungarian speaking bishops came to play a role by the
early 1040s in the days of King Peter only, and these later churchmen
must have caused more embarrassment than real help to the Hungarian
king. They were little educated, and their main qualifications for the
priesthood and leading church prebends must have consisted of their
personal devotion to the successors of Stephen.

Stephen's *Vita minor* spoke of "sancta Dei ecclesia in pace collocata
et ex Romana auctoritate iuste ordinata."[26] The *Vita maior* (Hartvic's
major source) carried more information: "princeps christianissimus, aliquando communiter cum omnibus, aliquando singillatim cum uno quoque
eorum colloquium habens provincias in decem partibus est episcopatus,
Strigoniensem ecclesiam metropolim at magistram per consensum et
subscriptionem Romanae sedis apostolici ceterarum fore constituens."[27]
The quoted text calls for a two-fold observation. (1) The King did not
make such a decision alone, but in the Council, *colloquium habens.*
(It is of some interest to note that both, the early twelfth century Rein
MS 69, f. 30', and the thirteenth century Lilienfeld MS 60, f. 164'a,
carry the term: "colloquium habens."[28] (2) Only a general plan had been
drawn up for the establishment of ten dioceses without any specifications;
this plan had to be ready before the coronation of Stephen. The delegation
dispatched by Stephen to Rome was to report to Pope Sylvester II that
the Church in Hungary was already a functioning reality.

Stephen, before sending his delegate to Rome, had summoned a meeting of the *Concilium magnum* to discuss this important step he was about to take with the elders. Yet, such a discussion had to take place at two levels: (a) in a Common Assembly, *aliquando communiter cum omnibus;* and (b) on an individual basis, *aliquando singillatim cum uno-quoque eorum*—assuming, of course, that "singillatim" means *sigillatim.* Evidently, Stephen expected every member of the Council to speak out and to render his personal approval (or, for that matter, disapproval) of his plan.[29]

The point to remember is that Stephen placed as yet little trust in the Hungarian speaking and native clergy; they were men of good will but with scanty education and, consequently, very low moral standards. They were mostly ignorant as yet of the higher calling of the clergy, and were simply incapable of celibacy or spiritual leadership. As late as 1055, the royal chancellor under Andrew I, Nicholas, the Hungarian born and educated bishop of Veszprém, proved incapable to prepare, to draw up in good Latin a simple document, the founding charter of the abbey of Tihany.[30]

Although it is known from the *vitae* of Gerard that he had several Magyar speaking missionaries at his disposal in his new diocese, it is rather probable that even these missionaries were foreign born, or that they came from the conquered, native stratum of the population in Hungary. The singing girl episode makes it clear that though the cleric who accompanied Gerard on his journey knew Hungarian, he had trouble explaining to the bishop the subject matter of the girl's song. But the bishop's remarks that happy were those sons and daughters of the race that in their daily grind were able to keep their joyful spirit, clearly show that the girl did not sing in Hungarian.[31]

This singing girl episode plus the fact that Gerard had only a few Magyar speaking missionaries under his jurisdiction at Csanád proves that the bulk of the new region's inhabitants consisted of already baptized people. The circumstances explain also the rapidity in completing the diocesan organization and its smooth functioning administration. What is surprising, however, is the fact that, with the exception of Maurus of Pécs,[32] no native advanced to church prebends, at least the record made no mention of this.

The little educated Magyar noble scions were the ones who were nominated to church positions as soon as they gained ordination to holy orders. How they, these unlearned rustics, were able to discharge their ecclesiastical obligations remains a mystery to the modern historian, unless it can be assumed that at least the minority of the recently ordained Hungarian clergy consisted of the descendants of the native families, the low social stratum of the conquered population, or, that the "natives" were placed in lower church positions, but were actually running the entire operation.[33]

This last is a highly probable hypothesis; namely, it was the conquered social element that provided the king with the trusted regional stewards in charge of the royal domain, territories comprising previously unoccupied lands all over the country. It is the royal legal statutes that afford a clue in this regard. The lowly born royal local representatives were given proper legal protection—a protective high *wergeld*—against the encroachments of the regional lords, descendants of the conquerors.[34]

The bishop's *vitae* say, and Gerard's writing confirms the truth of the matter, that actually it was these nobles who were in need of evangelization, forced conversion to western principles. Hence the need for Magyar speaking missionaries. These nobles lived in and off the countryside, and the bishop took care that before they were baptized, they were properly instructed in the elements of the faith. Gerard personally supervised the spiritual upbringing of his proteges, though, naturally, he had to rely upon interpreters when speaking to them. The bishop, however, could not bring himself to like the irresponsible conquering element in Hungarian society; he made the most cutting remarks about the nobles, and the results of a decade and a half of constant missionary work among them had but little to show. Although they gained baptism by royal command, no episcopal zeal for the souls could convince them of the importance of sprirtual values.

This must have been the sign of the times. In Bohemia, where Christianity had far deeper roots among the native nobility, the latter continued to live like pagans as the *Vita* of Adalbert of Prague brings out.[35]

It also remains a possiblity, however, and the record supports such a hypothesis, that Gerard in the 1030s was frequently called to attend secular business at the court of King Stephen. As a matter of fact, from the *Deliberatio* one might conclude that Gerard was almost constantly

en route. He travelled back and forth in the realm. The curious coincidence that his unfinished *opus,* the *Deliberatio,* was addressed to Isingrim,
a member of the Benedictine community at Salzburg, proves beyond
doubt that Gerard did maintain contacts with the outside world as well.
It is highly unlikely that Gerard felt a lost stranger outside of Hungary;
his writings plus his private and public behavior present the figure of a
remarkably mature European.

Isingrim, the addressee of Gerard's *Deliberatio* might have been a
clerical resident of Salzburg, who, according to Jean Mabillion[36] could
be identified with Isingrim the monk at St. Peter's in Salzburg. Gerard's
description of him, "demonstratur. . .nostro in fratre diuini collegii
isimgrino,"[37] does imply that both Gerard and Isingrim were confreres
following the Rule of St. Benedict; that Gerard was a monk is evident
from his *Vita minor,* "nam religonis habitum puer accepit,"[38] or, from
a side remark he made in his Deliberatio, "nos hora expectante nona
faciat."[39] Isingrim of Salzburg–Admont died in 1091. The abbey of
Admont did play a role in eleventh century Hungarian politics, Keza
said,[40] and the earliest known version of King Stephen's Laws survived
in Admont MS 712, ff. 119-126'.[41] Knowing Gerard's vanity about his
association with the scholarly world, Isingrim had to be a person living
in the cultured west, with whom Gerard attempted to maintain scholarly
contact. The *Deliberatio* itself is no practical handbook of theology.
It rather reminds this writer, for one, of a *Fleissübung* of a frustrated
scholar who vehemently tried to remain in the circle of western cultural
exchange.

The religious organization of the new, huge diocese took years to
complete; the slowness in this process was due to its size and the lack of
qualified clergymen. Clerics were and remained a permanent problem,
and, at least in the first years of its existence, the new diocese had to be
supplied with poorly trained priests, mostly sons of noble families who
were sent to Gerard's cathedral school by their parents, often for want
of some other and more promising occupation.[43]

The problem was further complicated by the fact that the Csanád
region comprised several townships with mercantile inhabitants and
craftsmen both mostly of foreign origin. Judged by the record, they
must have been Greeks, or of Byzantine and oriental origin. This town
population had also been already christianized by the Greek Church.

Therefore, although no formal religious schism then existed, the new bishop faced a new problem and had to work hard to gain the confidence of his new religious flock as well as their political adherence to the cause of the Hungarian king.[43]

That the secular authority, the quick handed steward, Count Csanád, took chances with the Greek populace is evident from his handling the expulsion of the Greek monks of the Marosvár monastery in order to make the house ready for the new Roman Bishop. Gerard, however, was more than a mere secular authority. As the spiritual ruler of these Greek initiated faithful he felt responsible for their religious welfare and political trustworthiness. The sole solution he could find was frequent visitation of the diocese, especially of the townships; obviously, on these visits the heathen Hungarians living in the countryside presented the real problem. Their spiritual care was entrusted to the seven Hungarian speaking companions of the bishop, while later the first graduates of the cathedral school were placed in charge of the religious needs of the conquering Magyar element.[44] Whether Gerard wanted to make use of the opportunity to attach the conquering Magyar to the ecclesiastical organization of his bishopric is a question which cannot be answered because supporting evidence is lacking. It remains, however, a plausible hypothesis.[45]

The bishop's remarks also show that he considered the new region very important for the future development of the Hungarian kingdom. And yet, it was quite obvious to the learned bishop that an uneducated noblility was incapable of playing a leading role among the more advanced and cultured town element, and the bishop grew furious when the first graduate of his cathedral school likewise failed to understand!

The bishop desired a close cooperation between the Magyar nobles and the inhabitants of the boroughs,[46] a cooperation destined to cement political and cultural relations between the Hungarian and Byzantine courts.[47] Perhaps he even hoped to foster a future alliance between Szefesfehérvár and Constantinople to make Hungary more acceptable to the Greeks, more capable of defending its own against the German danger in the West. Either the bishop was too advanced for his time, or the Hungarian element in the realm was far too backward to appreciate the real opportunities arising from a closer cooperation between the conquerors and the conquered.

Evidently, the Magyars by the 1030s were unable as yet to perceive that the conditions of the old fashioned conquest applied to the peoples of the mid-Danube region by their own forefathers more than 150 years before could no longer be imposed. The inhabitants of the Csanád region, especially the town population were not political cattle; those merchants and craftsmen should have been treated on an equal basis, if not socially, then at least politically.[48] The Hungarian court failed to heed the warning of the Csanág bishop, and missed a marvellous chance which never recurred.

The warning of Gerard was not without foundation. Gerard saw, and so did Stephen, that the later regional addition to the Hungarian kingdom created a direct frontier with the Bulgarian holdings of the Greek empire, and that Byzantium was the seat of eastern culture and political influence. There was no doubt in the bishop's mind that his king had decided three decades before, in 1000, that the Hungarian political future in Europe had to be western oriented, and yet, as the bishop said, the west showed no real political interest nor concern for the future of the Hungarian kingdom. Consequently, occassional Greek contacts on a friendly basis would have served the Hungarians in diplomatic dealings with the West.[49]

The Byzantine emperors were more than willing to lend a helping hand to the Hungarian monarchs. Hungarian relations with the West at this particular time meant only the German empire as the papacy was too deeply involved with its own inner problems to wield much influence, while the kings of France in the eleventh century were themselves helpless figures on the chessboard of their own politics. The German empire, however, remained dangerous, and the expansionist designs of the imperial court toward the East remained unchanged. To the Greeks, relations with Hungary would have thus provided, first, a buffer type zone between their own territories and that of Germany, and second, an alliance with a strong centralized Hungary would have protected the Greeks from future and immediate German attacks.[50] At this time, southern Italy was still under Greek control, and the German court had real interests in the Italian peninsula.[51]

The sense for *Realpolitik* prompted the old Hungarian king to advocate the succession of Peter Orseolo to the Hungarian throne after 1031, assuming that the Italian duke, whose father had to flee his Venetian possessions on account of German intrigues, would assume a more forceful anti-German policy in defending Magyar interests.[52] It seems also that Gerard himself, a compatriot of Peter Orseolo, was of a similar opinion. When, however, Peter turned out to be more German than some of the Bavarian entourage, including Queen Gisela, his royal aunt, Gerard, in the early 1040s bitterly denounced the king's relations with King Peter. The policy was all right; only the person thus selected, Peter, was the wrong one for the role![53]

Gerard was afraid to act without strong royal support behind him. He could expect such support from the royal house only, the Árpád family, because only the Árpáds were qualified to lead their nation or to make decisions concerning its political and religious future.[54] Gerard had not been in vain a royal councillor; he, too, knew of the prerogatives of the royal family just as he realized that neither Peter, a foreigner, nor Aba, a social upstart, were qualified, in either political or social sense of the term, to lead the nation. This, in turn, explains Gerard's conspiracy against the two kings so that the Árpád dynasty could be restored in Hungary.[55] Only under the national dynasty could the Church flourish, because only the national dynasty would be willing to defend the Church within its realm. In short, here is the "clue" in the matter, if the dynasty approved of the Church, then the nobles, too, tolerated it, accepted its existence in their midst. Without royal support the Church in Hungary could not survive.[56]

And yet, the question remains: did the Church remain a foreign body within the political framework of the nation?—or, to be more exact, with the Magyars? How was it that the Church, the source of major support for the monarchies in the West, needed royal support in Hungary for its mere survival? The answer is, once again, given by Gerard. First, there was no direct personal contact; second, the clergy were unable or unwilling to compromise. Finally, the Church was short of native clergy to spread the faith. The fact that the educated, proud westerners were unwilling to accept their native colleagues as equals proved disasterous in the 1046 uprising.[57]

It is a characteristic and even more unfortunate factor that Gerard, who was there and who knew about the situation, did not propose a remedy. Gerard, though well trained and intelligent, was too absent-minded a priest and too much of a dreamer as a person to be able to evaluate the conditions adequately. As long as the old king was alive, Gerard functioned normally as a bishop; the palace stood behind him. With Stephen gone, Gerard's inabilities became all too apparent. It was not his fault. And yet, it may well be asked whether Stephen had not made a mistake in appointing his scholarly protege to a post the filling of which required presence of mind and the ability to make practical decisions in a time of need.

CHAPTER III

THE POLITICS OF KING STEPHEN AS ILLUSTRATED BY BISHOP GERARD'S *DELIBERATIO*

Haec adhuc iniquitas in toto orbe dominatur terrarum, uspiamque non dormit.

Gerard of Csanád

S.R. Maitland pointed out in his medieval essays more than a hundred
years ago how easily the writings of medieval authors were lost through
negligence, fire, warfare, floods, bad weather conditions in the region, etc.
The observations of this remarkable medievalist could readily be applied
to the case of Gerard of Csanád, for this man, the author of various
religious and political treatises in the first half of the eleventh century,
is practically unknown to the world today.[1]

Although what is possibly Gerard's major work, the *Deliberatio supra
cantum trium puerorum,* a theological essay on the Song of Daniel, Daniel
3:57ff., did survive in a late eleventh century manuscript,—the author died
in 1046—, the work is incomplete. Whether it is the work that is incomplete, or the late eleventh century manuscript which contains it, is a question
that cannot be decided. The MS preserved in the Munich State Library contains eight books of the work, and it seems that this should be the complete
Gerardian opus. Apparently, the work was not finished because Gerard was
prevented from completing it by his sudden death in the 1046 Hungarian uprising. It can be assumed that Isingrim to whom Gerard addressed his writing, the Salzburg Benedictine who later became the head of the new Admont community, had the work copied into one codex, the codex of 167
folios known today as MS 6211 of the Munich Staatsbiliothek. As a result,

the codex should be complete, containing all the chapters alias "books" sent piecemeal by Gerard to his younger and yet illustrious confrère at Salzburg.[2]

The codex of the *Deliberatio* was copied by various hands, though all of the same school, and the opus itself was evidently intended to be a *reader* for the monks of the Freising community. The question remains, of course, whether the codex had been copied at Freising, where it was found,[3] or somewhere else, to be used at a different monastic community. Also, was this codex the only one that survived the times, or was it one of several copies made, it may be assumed, under orders from Isingrim? The available MS was annotated by a different hand (perhaps that of the proof-reader, corrector) in short marginal notes as if to summarize some of the seemingly more difficult passages for the reader.

The *Deliberatio* makes difficult reading for various reasons. One reason would be that Gerard evidently had no time to write a well edited opus: "non quippe secuti sumus oratorum mormures, et rethorum debachationes, qui tantum uenustatem eloquiorum et non uirtutem misteriorum inmitantur."[4] Gerard himself sensed that he could not express himself well in composition; ". . . disputans secundum mediocritatem meam in primo capitulo epistole pauli ad hebreos."[5] This could be another reason. Finally, the third reason would be that Gerard used Greek terms in Latin: Gerard "gehört zu den eigenartigsten Schriftstellern des 11 Jahrhunderts sowohl nach dem Inhalt wie nach der Form seines Werkes."[6]

Though he himself made some reference to an "opere demonstratum reliqui,"[7] a seemingly unknown work of his, he did mention three of his previous dissertations. (1) A commentary of St. Paul's letter to the Hebrews;[8] (2) An explanation of the First letter of St. John. "Quondam reor me ex hoc ipso satis et copetenter (sic) dixisse quam libet ingratum licet non ingratum disputans circum mediocritatem meam ubi loquitur coelestis dialecticus iohannes."[9] (3) A dogmatic treatise he sent to Andrew, a priest, "quem nuperrime in tabellis solius ad andream diuinum fratrem exemplicaui,"[10] and afterwards to Richard, abbot of Verdun.[11] Presumably, Gerard made contact with Abbot Richard when the latter passed through Hungary on his way to Byzantium, in 1025 or in 1026.[12] Since he knew Greek, he did use in the original the writings of Pseudo-Dionysisus Areopagita;[13] he relied upon the *Etymologiae* of Isidore of Seville, and he knew of the existing heresies in Europe in his time. An entire page, f. 124, is devoted to the enumeration of heresies, "in illis sic quidem potentantur qui magis diligunt tenebras quam lucem."[14]

The bishop of Csanád was a biblical scholar—as far as one may speak of a "biblical scholar" in the mid-eleventh century—who knew his Vulgate by heart, was well acquainted with the works of the church fathers, Greek and Latin, and who travelled to the Holy Land with the serious intention of making a lifelong study of the Bible in a faithful imitation of Saint Jerome of the early fifth century. Gerard was deeply impressed by Jerome, both Jerome the biblical authority, and Jerome the letter writer. Gerard even imitated the vanity (is there a true scholar without vanity?) and bad temper of Jerome.

Although it is probable that, besides these theological treatises, Gerard also left two political writings: compilations, behind;—one of these was the legal statutes, *Leges,* of King Stephen of Hungary; the other a royal *Libellus de institutione morum* of Stephen addressed to his prospective heir(s) on the Hungarian throne,[15]—on grounds that, first, Gerard was the, and only known, writer of capacity active in Hungary in the days of King Stephen who could have undertaken an enterprise that required not only skill but also learning and familiarity with secular politics;[16] second, that in both instances, in the *Leges* and in the *Libellus,* Gerard wrote as a compiler, and as a compiler he had to know the mind of the king. In fact, there were very few persons in Hungary in the times of Stephen who could and did know the reasoning of the monarch;[17] third, that the awkward terminology plus the disorderly fashion of both legal works are reminiscent of the writing technique of Gerard in his *Delibera-tio,*[18]—the hypothesis remains, due to the lack of concrete evidence, hypothetical.

The *Deliberatio* is a piece of good writing, but it is the product of a frustrated scholar who was prevented from further scholarly work by everyday religious and political obligations, and who felt cut off from the rest of the cultured world by being active in Hungary, that semi-civilized land on the eastern border of Europe at the time. It is also, however, a most disorganized work.[19]

Actually, it was these two factors: the incomplete MS material, and the half finished condition of the writing that make it hard if not imposs-ible for the researcher to reconstruct the works of the Csanád bishop back in the early 1040s. Although the Munich MS is, or seems to be, a complete version of all that Gerard had written of the *Deliberatio,* it stands all by itself. To this day, there are no other copies, no other MSS around that carry the work, even incomplete, of Gerard. Consequently, it is not possible to reconstruct a "critical" text of the opus. The MSS of the *Leges* plus the *Libellus,* on the other hand, did not survive in early MSS, but only in later versions. Needless to say, all of these later versions are incomplete. Moreover, an unfinished MS may not reflect badly on the author whose work the MS carries, but on the scribe who copied the manuscript from an earlier, probably already corrupt copy.[20]

The same holds true for the Munich MS of the *Deliberatio.* If it is assumed that this MS had been copied from Gerard's own work, it should be a clear, uncorrupt MS version of the original. What, however, can be presumed if the MS is not a direct variation of the Gerardian work? And a second question that naturally comes to mind, is the question whether the work was sent by Gerard—and presumably both composed and written down by him—in a final, polished shape, or was it only a hastily written "draft," a first draft, that needed reworking? From the remarks of Gerard, it may be concluded that the latter was the case. The Csanád bishop had no time to write carefully, and had even less time left for "editing" his opus. Could it be that Isingrim was Gerard's editor? —and addressee alike? Isingrim, though much younger in years, was advanced in learning, lived in a peaceful monastery, and presumably had time for leisurely editing of religious dissertations. It is a most likely possiblity.[21]

Here we are concerned with the *Delibertio* alone. The work can be studied from both its relgous and "political" contents, political in the sense that the side-remarks of the noble bishop made in the angry moments of his choleric nature, cast a deep and highly significant shadow over the Hungarian scene. The religious, theological interpretation of the opus has already been truly done by Hungarian scholars and theologians, A. Bodor, Dom. Irén Zoltvány, Dom. T. Hajdú, and Endre von Ivánka, to mention the more prominent names. Although two decades ago János Horváth commented in his usual expert manner on the literary-historical merits of the opus, the historical-political meaning of the work is still little touched upon.[22]

From the point of view of the historian, the work is significant for two reasons. First, it is a gold mine of historical observations on an age of early Hungarian history where sources are few. Second, it is a running commentary of the Csanád bishop on King Stephen's policy of "westernization" (a kind of cultural policy), and helps answer the questions: was the cultural policy of King Stephen good? Did it accomplish much? As was indicated earlier, Gerard took a rather skeptical view of Stephen's religious-cultural policy.[23]

What then was the king's policy? Was it simple "westernization" of the Magyar people, the conquering element in Stephen's Hungarian society of the early eleventh century, or was it something more, the preparation of the Hungarians, Magyars and conquered non-Magyars alike, to enter the continental body politic?[24]

What actually constituted the *corpus politicum Europae* around the year 1000? Was it a functioning political organization of all continental peoples, kingdoms, systems, under one head, or was it merely a name, a term applicable to the peoples that populated western Europe at the time? From the Hungarian viewpoint, three contemporary authorities may have provided some answer to the problem; Widukind, the Saxon historian, Thietmar of Merseburg, the well known chronicler, and the author of a document of Otto III addressed to Pope Sylvester II, and known as the Imperial Diploma, dated January 23, 1001.[25]

The first two historians depicted their hero, Otto the Great of Germany of the previous century, as the lord of Europe, acting for, fighting for the European cause. The imperial document of Otto III by that name described the emperor as the master of that particular European world,— "Romam caput mundi profitemur, Romanam ecclesiam matrem omnium ecclesiarum testamur,"[26]—a lord so powerful that he had earlier selected and made his former tutor, Gerbert as pope to the Holy See. "Domnum Silvestrum magistrum nostrum papam elegimus et Deo volent ipsum serenissimum ordinavimus et creavimus."[27]

It is highly probable that the Hungarian court at the time made no distinction between the secular and spiritual rights and prerogatives of the German emperor. But people at the court knew about such a distinction: *Roma caput mundi*, Hartvic noted,[28] and, as the record indicates,[29] tried hard to please the secular ruler: the emperor of the west, for strictly political reasons. Further, the popes at that time were not able to exercise any significant political influence. In other words, Stephen of Hungary following the example of his father, Géza, a contemporary of Otto the Great,[30] in order to make himself and his people, meaning the Magyars and not necessarily the non-Magyars of Hungary at this time, acceptable to the continental, European community of peoples, whose headship the German emperors claimed to have.[31]

Judged by the words and deeds of Stephen, however, this "westernizing" process had to have a far deeper meaning than mere politics, to please the emperor. It had to be a religious-cultural undertaking because the new Hungarian realm would not otherwise had a chance to survive in its new political and religious surroundings, and it had to be a project pleasing to God.

That memebers of the royal court, including Stephen, knew about the imperial claims is evident from the report of Hartvic, c. 9, that Stephen's delegate to Rome was sent "ad limina apostolorum, ut a successore sancti Petri, principis apostolorum postularet" the threefold request of Stephen: (a) "Novellae christianitati in partibus Pannoniae largam benedictionem porrigeret;" (b) "Strigoniensem ecclesiam in metropolim suae subscriptionis sanciret, et reliquos episcopatus sua benedictione muniret;" (c) "regio etiam dignaretur ipsum diademate roborare, ut eo fultus honore coepta per Dei gratiam posset solidius stabilire."[32] In other words, the pope was in the eyes of the Hungarian court, not the vicar of Christ but the humble successor of the Apostle Peter—not an imperial nominee. And when the Hungarian delegation received a favorable hearing: "quibus audistis valde gavisus Romanus pontifex, cuncta, prout fuerant postulata, benigne concessit,"[33] the religious issue: conversion to the western, Roman Catholic Church, became to the mind of Stephen and his court, the means of entry into the western world.[34] It may not be unimportant to mention it here that this entire passage is a Hartvic "original;" it is not mentioned in the *Vita maior*—Hartvic's chief source of information,—nor does the *Vita minor* carry the information.[35]

The religious issue was carefully supported by the political marriage of Stephen to Gisela of the imperial family. The marriage took place, so the *Vita minor* reports,[36] before Stephen applied for a crown to Rome.[37]

Both king and his Csanád bishop agreed on such a policy—Gerard the more so as the policy was already being realized by the time he arrived in Hungary. The bishop also understood that this religious-cultural process arrangement had to be pro-Rome and anti-German, for despite the political and moral weakness of the papacy at the time, the German empire meant political danger: possible takeover of the territory of the new realm in a form of religious-political vassalage to the German imperial court. Further, the fact that the papacy was weak after Sylvester II meant that there was less danger of papal interference in the religious affairs of the Hungarian realm, for two reasons. One, King Stephen as the head of the state and the protector of the Church, who also nominated bishops and established dioceses with Rome's formal approval could use the Church in his kingdom to extend royal authority along political lines; two, as long as the king remained in charge of the Church, as its chief protector, the Magyar noble element was willing to go along with it. There were German missionaries and foreign born bishops in Stephen's realm, but they were there by the will and authority of the king, and as long as the king tolerated them, the nobles, too, would tolerate them.[38]

The problem with such a policy, however, was that the Church did become a tool in Magyar domestic politics, not a helper, as in Germany or in France at the same period, but a tool, the means to be used to gain political stability and to strengthen the centralized authority of the royal court in the kingdom. And here, at this point, the Csanád bishop began to object. Evidently, he did not get too far with King Stephen. But with the successors of Stephen, though only because the two immediate successors of the great king were worthless political creatures themselves who actually used the organization of the Church for their own, selfish, personal political needs, Gerard, though perhaps not too successful, was far more emphatic. Judged by the writings of Gerard and by the sources, the policy of Stephen was not a success. It failed to achieve its objective as it used naked force to convert the people.[39]

What was Gerard's objective? And how is it that the Church in Hungary, became after all, a factor in Hungarian politics, and between 1046 and 1106 the country was literally turned into a theocracy?

The bishop wished for a simple thing, both religious and political in its implication: a thorough indoctrination of the Hungarian nobility, the Magyars—hence his school policy. For indoctrination needed no force of arms—only the force of the intellect and good royal example,—hence his adherence to King Peter's cause as late as 1044. To Gerard's mind, religious indoctrination also meant introduction to the political scene, and such an introduction had to come through the sheer personal superiority, intellectual ability of the one who did the introducing. No arms, no naked force![40]

Three and only three items in Gerard's writings can be mentioned that pertain to the political scene of the Hungarian early 1040s. The first of these was investiture, the "sale" of church prebends for political reasons to religiously unqualified persons. Added to this was the lack of education of the new Hungarian clergy, and finally the lack of cooperation of the Magyar element of the Hungarian society, a lack of cooperation that led to a disaster for both church and realm by 1046 and afterwards.[41] What the bishop meant was this: without a strong secular authority to enforce religious ordinances, those ordinances were useless. This in turn showed not only that the Church was still young and it needed support, but also that in spite of the nearly eight decades of religious missionary activities among the population,[42] it never became deeply rooted among the Magyars.

The problem of investitures mentioned by Gerard indicates a strange condition in Hungary in the 1040s. Presumably under German influence, the appointment of political personages to ecclesiastical positions became customary in the realm during the reigns of Peter. "Igitur rex idem (i.e. Aba, Peter's successor), habito sinodico concilio, cum cummuni episcoporum et principum omnia decreta rescindi statuit, quae Petrus iniuste secundum libitum suum disposuit, episcopis duobus pontificia vi sublata reddere voluit, sed quia alii ordinati erant, hoc Romani praesulis iudicio reservandum censuit."[43] Although both Conrad II and Henry III of Germany supported the renewal movement within the Church, the emperors also used the episcopate for secular, political situations, and King Peter, the imperial protege, must have had similar designs in mind for the Hungarian hierarchy. It is not surprising, however, that the old foreign bishops, all appointed by King Stephen, failed to sympathize with Peter—hence, the advancement of the young Magyar clerics to responsible church prebends. It is also very interesting to note that King Aba, though he badly needed political support within the realm, broke with this type of church policy. King Aba did not manipulate episcopal appointments, nor did he interfere in ecclesiastical business. Nor did he tolerate church interference in royal politics.[44]

The investiture problem plus church control of education, especially in the 1040s, might indicate another aspect of church-state relations in Hungary at the time. Gerard may have tried hard for an ecclesiastical assumption of power, just as the Council sought to regain its lost authority in secular matters. Gerard, although he spoke of separation between

Church and State, favored religious predominance in secular matters: theocracy based upon what has been called "political Augustinianism." He did this not because he wanted the Church to predominate completely in the realm, but because of his personal conviction that the realm as such still needed the support of the Church to maintain its position on the continental chessboard of secular politics.[45]

Investiture points, furthermore, toward the question of growing German cultural influence in the new kingdom in this particular decade. It was the queen's German oriented party that elected Peter Orseolo king in 1038; it was the same party that aided Peter to regain his throne in 1044. It was this same party that requested the imperial coronation of Peter, and evidently witnessed the coronation performed by Henry III. But it is important to observe that this party was not acting for good reasons; the party was selfish in its objectives of securing its predominance in Hungarian politics and eventually preparing the road for a German takeover (*Anschluss*?) of the mid-Danube region.[46]

It is quite obvious that the Church in Hungary proved to be an obstacle to such a plan; consequently, this ecclesiastical opposition had to be overcome. This plan had to be executed in two ways. One, infiltration of the ranks with less educated, less dedicated, more naive and more willing to cooperate young clergymen. Two, removal of the old leaders. Judged by the chronicler's remarks concerning Aba's action rescinding all previous acts of his immediate predecessor as soon as he, Aba, came to power, I conclude that by 1041, Peter had already greatly facilitated such a German takeover.

This is also one of the reasons why Peter had to go. Gerard, the countryman of Peter and trusted advisor of Stephen, councillor, who also boasted of Greek contacts, could not be removed so easily, however. Although there is no direct evidence, there is good reason to believe that Vata was in the pay of the German party to kill Gerard. The haste and clearly desperate attack on the bishop, just when he was about to meet Andrew and his party, is a clear proof for this.[47] Gerard had to be removed from the scene before he could join forces with Andrew. The rather submissive attitude of King Andrew I to the German imperial court shows further that Andrew could have used a councillor trained to deal with westerners, and that there was no other Gerard of Csanád around either in learning, or in experience, to fill the vacuum.

Why Gerard in his religious treatise emphasized politics so much is a hard question to answer. Evidently, he, as a member of the council, was aware of the failures of missionary efforts in Hungary. Moreover, since he himself never learned Magyar and failed to establish direct contact with the Magyar speaking part of the population, he may well have experienced a certain feeling of guilt.

There was, however, another reason, a far deeper one: the fact that he, though a foreigner himself, could not get along with other foreigners.[48] In other words, he suffered a great deal of personal frustration. Gerard had to admit that he made progress only along two far less important lines. First, he made headway with the old king, whose councillor he became, and who elevated him to the high dignity of the Csanád bishopric. In this capacity he certainly wore two hats: that of the bishop and of the royal *missus* who together with the regional royal steward administered the diocese. And secondly, the bishop got along fairly well with the non-Magyar part of the inhabitants in Hungary, principally because they already knew his language and at least could talk to him, and they were already Christians. To them the bishop could be patronizing.

Gerard, though he was a saint, was also a very difficult personality and certainly did not believe in social equality. On paper, he strove for equality. When it came to realities, however, he was a different person. It was the trend of the times, and Gerard, too, was a product of his age.

CHAPTER IV

THE INTERREGNUM, 1038-46

---

1. Bishop Gerard the Politician

Ubi itaque divinae intelligentiae spiritus non est, et notionis omnia transcendentis scientia, ibi asinorum procul dubio spiritus regnat.

Gerard of Csanád

Hungarian historians usually refer to the eight year period immediately following the reign of King Stephen as the "interregnum." The designation is correct. It is true that no direct Árpád scion succeeded to King Stephen's inheritance until 1046. Nevertheless, the Council intervened by electing and deposing two Hungarian kings during this period. The first ruler to suffer such a discouraging fate was Peter Orseolo, the nephew of King Stephen. The Orseolo was the son of Stephen's sister who had married Peter Orseolo, the then deposed duke of Venice.[1]

That the council upon the death of King Stephen suddenly played a decisive role in Hungarian public affairs can be easily explained. Its members felt an unexpected relief from the dominating personality of the old king, and they wished to restore as much authority as possible to themselves, the degraded and humiliated Greater Council. They recalled this time that Stephen, too, was "made" a ruler, elected by them. Stephen's coronation, on the other hand, had been unnecessary by their standards. As a consequence, in 1038, Stephen's widow, Queen Gisela, finding herself in a fearfully weak constitutional position, determined to assure the succession of her closest relative living in Hungary, Peter, to her dead husband's inheritance. Since Stephen died mid August,[2] a date when according to the decree of Andrew II, the annual Great Council usually held its meetings,[3] the widowed queen might have decided to push through her nephew's succession in the meeting of the Council. She distrusted the more intimate royal council, and she was aware of the bishop's hostility toward Peter, the Venetian, as king of Hungary.

Unfortunately, the brief annual assembly of the Great Council of the more distant nobles of the realm failed to secure Peter's legal claims to the throne. The chroniclers stressed the point that Peter was elected king under pressure and was not given the proper royal annointing.[4]

The question is, of course, whether the Council was identical with the assembly mentioned by Anonymus? Keza implied[5] that the election of Peter—not the coronation!—occured with the approval of, or through the *consilio iniquorum.* Evidently, churchmen and members of the King's advisory group were opposed to Stephen's choice of the Orseolo for two reasons: (1) Stephen acted, when making his choice, under pressure from the queen,[6] and presumably after the assassination attempt made at his life;[7] (2) the Orseolo was not *idoneus regnare.*[8] He was not an Árpád by birth, and only members of the Árpád dynasty were to be called upon to rule in Hungary.[9]

The Council: *consilium regale,* was not identical with the *senatus;* in this writer's opinion, the Council: *consilium, concilium,* denoted the actual meetings of the King with his trusted advisors, a "curia regis" type of an institution.[10] The Senate, especially the gathering of the "whole senate:" *totius senatus,* mentioned in art. II:2 of Stephen's Laws,[11] meant the meeting of the Greater Council of the nobles: "principes, baroni, comites, milites," to quote from art. IV of Stephen's Admonitions,[12] a Council not always in session. The Council: *consilium,* meeting more frequently, played a greater role: without it, (1) royal election; (2) the realm's government; (3) the country's defenses and military affairs; (4) its foreign policy, and (5) domestic policy could not be maintained, nor directed. "Consilio enim constituuntur reges; determinantur regna; defenditur patria, componitur prelia; appellantur amici, propellantur inimici; civitates construuntur, et castra adversariorum destruuntur."[13]

It was essential, therefore, that only mature persons were to be included among the members of the Council; "a stultis, et arrogantibus, ac mediocribus non valent componi," though young men were not, just because of their inexperience, excluded from its ranks. The bishops, whether in the Council or outside of it, represented a strong political force in governmental circles. "Si illorum benevolentiam habebis, neminem adversariorum timebis;"[14] they represented a strong religious and political force in *consilio*—"sine enim illis non constituuntur reges nec principatus,"[15] and had strength as an episcopal body as judged by art. I:2 of Stephen's Laws.[16]

Considering the circumstances of the nomination as King Stephen's successor of Peter Orseolo, it may be assumed that, under given conditions, the bishops had in fact asserted more power than the Council itself—so Stephen's *Vita maior* recorded.

The problem with King Aba, on the other hand, was different. He was elected immediately after the dethronement of Peter, and was crowned king, "regio more rex est coronatus." Whether Gerard of Csanád participated in the coronation of Aba is uncertain, though I assume that he did. Hence the rather sharp rebuke of King Aba by Gerard on Easter Sunday, 1044, a public humiliation of the monarch which, incidentally, caused the king's military and political downfall. In fact, although the bishop participated in "making Aba king," he later undertook the initiative in dethroning him, when the latter proved to be unworthy of the royal dignity. At least, judging by the text of his famous sermon, Gerard used the unworthiness of the king to justify his deposition.

Perhaps this is also the reason why Gerard took no part in the 1041 election of King Aba; at least he was not mentioned directly by the chroniclers. Such an omission may be due to the lack of a fully restored text of the narrative, or, more probably, Keza took the presence of Gerard for granted in the gathering of spiritual and secular lords. The point is, however, that, in describing the events of 1046, the chroniclers went into detail on Gerard's participation in all public meetings held for the sake of restoration of the Árpáds and summarized at length Gerard's sermon against Aba on Easter, 1044.

From the condensed text of this fateful Easter homily it is clear that Gerard looked upon Aba as an uneducated savage, a man unfit to reign in the realm of King Stephen. There is no doubt that the bishop seized the opportunity rendered by the king himself who had meted out drastic punishment to forty noblemen forming a conspiracy against him. It must be remembered, however, that even the laws of King Stephen had ordered the strictest punishment of conspirators against the king, and from a strict legal viewpoint King Aba was only acting in spirit of the law. In 1044, the domestic situation and the foreign danger, the possibility of military interference in Hungary by a foreign power on account of King Peter's flight to the German imperial court upon his dethornement, permitted no slackening of royal authority. King Aba knew that he had to form a common front against the aspirations of King Peter and his followers, who, through the efforts of the imperial court, succeeded in gaining sympathy of the Holy See.[17]

Although there is no reference to it in the papal register, according to the *Annales Altahenses,* Hungary was placed under a papal interdict for deposing the rightful monarch in the kingdom.[18] It is extremely doubtful that any papal anathema would have had any real effect on the Hungarian lords, both secular and spiritual, at that time. Pope Benedict IX was a weakling elected at eighteen years of age to the papal see, subject to the imperial schemes of Conrad II or even Henry III. From such a man a detailed knowledge of Hungarian conditions could hardly have been expected. Probably, he was forced or asked by the German court to undertake a punitive move toward Hungary in order to present an official pretext to Henry III for subsequent interference in the affairs of the Hungarian kingdom.[19]

A careful reading of Gerard's work offers, however, a different version of the situation; namely, that as it is known, the Hungarian clergy of his time maintained contacts with the West; consequently, Gerard, too, must have known in detail of both the political conditions of the papacy and the situation in the German empire. Presumably, he wanted to prevent a full scale deterioration of Hungarian domestic conditions by pushing Aba out of the public scene and supporting, if indirectly, the claims of Peter.[20]

How Gerard tried to explain away the coronation of King Aba is another problem. The record tells us that the *election* of Aba was based on a compromise—a temporary solution only to relieve tension. That the compromise envisioned the coronation act to make the royal elect's ruling rights acceptable to the nation is questionable since it was the nobles who murdered Aba within a few weeks upon the remarkable Easter sermon of Gerard.[21]

It is quite clear, therfore, that after the reign of King Stephen, the council regained the authority it held before in the realm.

The event is given in detail by the German imperial chroniclers. Since they described in such minute detail the campaigns or the very presence of Henry III on Hungarian soil, it is difficult not to interpret this as the awakened interest of the imperial court directed at the political incorporation of the Hungarian territories in the empire, a scheme that, in the event, did not work too well for the imperial planners.

King Peter reigned from 1038 through 1041, and from 1044 through 1046. He was deposed twice by the Council, with the full approval of the bishops. Between 1041 and 1044, there reigned King Samuel Aba, whom the record depicted as a "comes" who had married another sister of the deceased King Stephen.[22] The record indicates nowhere that Peter was ever crowned king in 1038 or afterwards. Indeed, all available information seems to confirm the fact that Peter's succession resulted from the intrigues of Stephen's Bavarian born queen, Gisela, who showed no particular liking toward the Hungarians after her husband's death. It seems likely that the assassination attempts in the Árpád family in the early 1030s made a lasting impression on the queen. Thus, in 1038, when the council assembled to choose his successor, it was the dowager queen who intervened and secured the succession of her nephew, Peter, to the crown.

The queen was unable, however, to promote her will completely. For the bishops did not comply with her wish that the elected king be anointed. As a consequence, somewhat as the Merovingians in Gaul, he lacked the dignity of an anointed ruler and fell an easy prey to the designs of the bishops and the council in 1041.[23] The reason for the bishops' opposition to Peter and his reign is evident from Gerard's writings. The good bishop did not cease to complain that ecclesiastical conditions in the realm had deteriorated after the peaceful years of Peter's predecessor.[24]

As was mentioned above, between 1041 and 1044, Aba ruled Hungary. It is probable that not only was King Aba not a member of the Árpád family, but that he was a non-Magyar by birth, having originated from the stratum of the conquered population. His marriage into the Árpád dynasty must have served both dynastic interests and the cause of domestic peace, for both the position of the house of Árpád was enhanced, and the domestic tranquility promoted by permitting a powerful non-Magyar noble to marry into the conquerors' family.

In spite of the fact that he was legally elected and was the anointed, crowned ruler by 1041, the Hungarians looked upon King Aba as a political upstart. Three years later he died a miserable death, apparently killed by his own kindred.

Interestingly, in 1041, Aba was elected and anointed by the council's bishops upon the deposition of Peter. In 1044, King Peter was reinstated as ruler of Hungary by his imperial protector, Henry III of Germany, who went to Hungary and personally crowned Peter king at the ancient capital of King Stephen. The newly crowned king imitated the imperial policies by appointing clerics and even laymen to clerical positions in order to assure that only "trustworthy" persons in leading positions were in charge of the ecclesiastical affairs of the kingdom. This further substantiates the thesis mentioned above that Peter remembered the lesson of 1038, when the bishops of the realm, then all appointees of King Stephen, refused to cooperate with him, as a matter of fact, refused to crown him king.

Both Gerard and the Chronicle in their narratives keep referring to King Peter's immoral living and the consequent deterioration of public morals in the realm. Moral misconduct on the part of the ruler may well have endangered the prestige of the monarchy. Certainly, Peter's appointees to the episcopal sees were poorly trained, ill equipped clerics, young Hungarians, who possessed neither the education nor the conviction to speak out freely against the secular misuse of church institutions in the kingdom.[25]

Peter's election, as we have seen, was accepted as valid, but his kingship remained in doubt during his entire reign. In fact, it is remarkable that a ruler elected king by the national council was refused coronation with the crown of Stephen and anointing by the nation's bishops. Since he was more than eager to accept the crown from the hands of the German emperor, it is doubtful that Peter himself would have refused coronation by the archbishop of Esztergom.

The record makes very clear, however, the attitude of the council toward the reign of Peter. It seems certain that, by electing Peter, the councillors wished to gain time. By delaying his anointing, they maintained a free hand, so to say, until such time as they felt free to restore an Árpád monarch to Stephen's throne.

After 1044 Peter was and remained deeply conscious of his unsupportable position as king chosen and crowned not by the Hungarian episcopal body, but by the German emperor, a foreigner that is, who in ecclesiastical theory held no authority to make or depose kings. Accordingly, he sought by nominating to leading church and secular positions men personally devoted to him to secure his own constitutional position within the country. He failed, however, to accomplish this, and fell, once again, from power. This second fall was largely due to the concentrated efforts of the old members of the Hungarian episcopate. These bishops, under the leadership of Gerard of Csanád, a countryman of King Peter by birth, revolted against such a personal, high-handed, and autocratic policy, and called upon the exiled Árpád scions to return to the realm and take over the reigns of power.[26]

These short eight years were the time when the political training of the Csanád bishop, a training he gained through the hard schooling of King Stephen, by participating in the decision makings of the royal council, stood him in good stead. Gerard, or course, could not remain inactive during the three years of King Aba's rule. Thus, since Gerard engineered the opposition to both the tyrannical reign of Peter and "terror" of King Aba's rule, as well as the restoration of the lawful Árpád heirs,[27] one may consider the Csanád bishop as the king-maker in the immediate post-Stephen era. Judged by his own writings and the official records of his life, Gerard never acted for selfish, personal reasons, but always for the common good, be it that of the realm as a whole or of the Church as part of it.[28]   The bishop was a fighter for justice, to whom the highest cause was to prevail for the sake of the Church and the kingdom in spite of all adversities.[29]

At this point, it is important to consider Gerard's work, the *Deliberatio supra cantum trium puerorum,* which he was prevented from completing by his sudden murder in 1046. Presumably, the work itself was in the process of composition in the late mid-1040s, an important date to remember, for Gerard continued to play an outstanding role in Hungarian affairs.[30] That he enjoyed the full cooperation of the ecclesiastical and secular elements in the kingdom is evident from his major work. Although he never personally showed disrespect toward the Venetian, it is evident that he wholly disapproved of Peter's interference in church matters. The church synods held under the short reign of King Aba proved also to have no lasting effects.

During the critical years of the early 1040s, the attention of Gerard remained focused on both political and religious matters. What most disturbed the bishop was the trend among the "nationalists" to regard the Church and her priests as a hostile foreign element which must be uprooted from the country in order that the traditional identity of Hungarian institutions might be preserved. Gerard was never favorably impressed by the religious attitude of the Magyars, nor by the religious tendencies of the royal courtiers. He warned of a reaction among the country population to the manner of living at the central court. He feared a kind of heathen reaction clothed in the appearance of resurgent traditionalism, if it is possible to use the term in an early eleventh century context, to the teaching of the Church, the life of her priests, and to western institutions in general. And yet, no one paid serious attention to him.[31]

When Gerard noted that the Magyar nobles paid little concern to religious matters and discussed politics all day long or listened to the songs of the native bards, he wished only to point out how strongly "eastern" the Magyars still were after more than four decades of missionary work among them. Such eastern, almost Asiatic motives that displayed so strong an interesting matters of common concern, did not diminish, but rather grew during the following century. For example, in the 1140s, Otto of Freising, the well known historian, noted among his personal experiences gathered in Hungary, how public minded the Magyars were. The Hungarian nobles of the reign of Géza II, 1141-1161, despised the luxuries of life, but kept a sharp eye on the deeds of their king and all constitutional matters governing the public good of the kingdom.[32] The same attitude is evident in the deeds of the council regulating the affairs of the realm in the early 1040s.[33]

The circumstances of the murder of King Aba and the return of Peter to the throne of Stephen call for more attention, however. The text shows that Aba was murdered by the nobles, by men who suffered persecution under his reign. In other words, personal enemies or political opponents had removed him from their way. Kéza also deemed it important enough to mention that Aba's potential murderers felt encouraged to act by Gerard's sermon and by his personal attitude toward the king.[34]

If we are to believe the emphasis laid by the Chronicle on the direct blood relationship within the royal family as the sole right to royal succession, it seems that Peter actually possessed a weaker claim to the throne than Aba did. For Aba came, as far as can be determined from the record, from the lower social stratum of the population. He might have been a known leader in a given area of the conquered inhabitants. His sole right to succeed to Stephen's inheritance rested on his marriage into the royal family. But this was scarcely a reason to strengthen his position over the Hungarian nobility. In fact, the Hungarian nobles completely disregarded his claims.

The Chronicle made the point that Aba's kingship rested on both his election and coronation. But such an argument had little appeal to Gerard since he made rather unflattering comments on both the king and his colleagues in the episcopal college. Whether his references concerning his fellow bishops who dared not open their mouths in the defense of truth should be related to Peter's appointees participating in the political administration of the realm, or should be interpreted in a purely ecclesiastical context, remains an open question. It seems, however, that Gerard was very disappointed with the new members of the episcopal body in Hungary. If this is the case, then it becomes clear why Gerard opposed Aba's rule so much. Aba presented a danger to the political and co stitutional independence of the recently established kingdom.[35]

The situation with Peter was different. He was reinstated by imperial military force on the throne of King Stephen. By receiving the realm from the hands of the German emperor Peter made himself a *vassus* of Henry III, while his kindgom became an imperial fief. The accidental factor that the Germans lost a substantial number of their military in their campaign in Hungary only confirmed the emperor in his conviction that he had to preserve, as much as possible, the constitutionality of Peter's rule by having him crowned king of Hungary with the royal insignia of King Stephen. Further, the Hungarian chroniclers failed to note, although the German annalists expressed the matter in detail, that Peter's coronation occurred before the full assembly of the nation's dignitaries.[36] Of course, it is not entirely clear what the Germans understood by a "congregatio principum?" It is certainly possible that the meeting may have consisted of the men of the German oriented party only. In fact, the sources report that upon Peter's coronation, Henry III made the Magyars comply with the imperial legal usage.[37] It is immaterial that the Hungarian annalist, in depicting this part of the event, implied that the emperor graciously permitted the Hungarians to retain their own traditional customs, etc. The early and contemporary German text, from which a chronicler must have taken his information, gives a contrary interpretation.[38]

The formal acceptance by Henry III of Hungary as an imperial fief did not occur until Easter, 1045.[39] A letter written three decades later by pope Gregory VII to King Solomon of Hungary—Solomon being another imperial protege on the Hungraian throne—states that upon Aba's defeat and Peter's coronation in 1044, Stephen's crown and a "holy" lance were returned by the emperor to the Holy See as the place of origin of the Hungarian crown.[40] In view of the fact that in 1044 the Germano-phile Benedict IX occupied the see of St. Peter, and that in 1046 the emperor Henry III had to intervene in Roman politics, one had until recently assumed, despite the rather skeptical attitude of certain Hungarian historians, the truth of such an assertion.[41] Further, although the account of Peter's coronation did mention the insignia of King Stephen, no such description was given by the record reporting the corornation of Andrew I in 1046, regardless of the fact that Andrew was crowned by the three surviving Hungarian bishops.[42]

Gerard could not live long enough to see the results of his planning. He died shortly before Andrew I could secure the reigns of power over the land. Presumably, the bishop and his entourage were murdered by some rustics whose sole reason for hatred toward the bishop and the western faith consisted of blind opposition to anybody and anything "western," anything different from the established way of life. It is remarkable, however, that the name of the gang-leader, a certain Vata, was given by the chronicler as if to imply that more than simple-minded personal dislike lay behind the uprising that broke out in full force in 1046.[43]

That the entire uprising was a natural reaction against foreign elements in the country, especially foreigners in leading positions, seems clear. And it is significant that the uprising broke out only eight years after the death of King Stephen. Peace and relative prosperity kept the administration of the realm going during the years following Stephen's death, although both Peter and Aba had a hard time keeping the state organism functioning. It remains unclear, however, why the uprising broke out with such vehemence in 1046. And why exactly in that year? Had the sojourn of the emperor at Rome something to do with it? True, King Peter was murdered in that year. Was it possible that with the royal authority vanished from the public scene, all public order and respect for authority disappeared in the realm amidst the "national" opposition hostile to anything foreign?—and few quarrelsome nobles took matters into their own hands?[44]

The opposition must have been a strong one indeed, as it was the pagan "national" party that planned the murder of King Stephn, and it cannot be doubted for a moment that the sudden death of the heir apparent, Prince Emery in 1031, resulted from the decisions of the same opposition party.[45] When Gerard wrote disapprovingly about the manners of his confreres and the Hungarian nobles in general, he obviously referred to this opposition.

The chief difficulty, and the bishop's major political problem, was that the Árpád heirs, Levente, Andrew, and Béla, displayed at first no clear intentions as to whose side they were on, or what sort of attitude they would assume toward religious and cultural matters when they gained the royal authority. In 1046, Gerard still did not know which of the three brothers was going to obtain the throne. Levente was a pagan. The second eldest, Andrew, seemed to be a good Christian, however, and supported in public the cause of the Church. Nevertheless, until he actually possessed full authority in the realm, even Andrew seemed hesitant. Upon his coronation, however, he followed in the footsteps of King Stephen.[46] The three bishops who alone survived the blood bath of 1046, anointed Andrew, as his election had occurred earlier.[47]

It would be interesting to find out who the other bishops were. As the record mentioned by name only five bishops who joined the cause of Gerard, we may assume that the rest were the political apointees of Peter and Aba, bishops who did not even try to face up to the new situation. Probably, the five were the nominees of King Stephen, though all of them were elected by normal canonical procedure. Gerard also seemed to have realized that the brunt of hatred in the uprising was directed mainly against foreigners and not necessarily against priests, most of whom were Germans and Latins as the chroniclers put it,[48] and who held higher or lower executive offices in the realm. Thus, while in the 990s the wrath of Koppány had been directed against the "westernizing" tendencies of Stephen, in the 1040s the opposition aimed at the office holders of non-Magyar origin, and succeeded in exterminating them.[49]

When, in 1061, King Béla I made up his mind to oppose, by politics and military force, the attempts of the German party to make Hungary, once again, a German satellite, he relied on the direct support of the locally elected representatives of the smallest administrative units in the kingdom.[50] When, in the same year, a second uprising broke out against "westerners" in Hungary, it was the king who suppressed it—by the force of arms—having taken counsel with his local representatives.[51]

The Csanád bishop had no such representatives at his disposal, but he had the esteem of the people in his diocese.[52] As the major opus of the bishop, the *Deliberatio,* was written around the mid-1040s, it can be assumed that Peter's second reign reached its zenith in both ruthless severity and cruelty at that time. The writing presents convincing evidence of the passive resistance of Gerard and some of his clergy to the policies and personal behavior of the monarch.[53]

Gerard's major problem was that he, too, was isolated from the rest of the Hungarian population. Although he served the royal court, he withdrew to his private cell whenever his mission was fulfilled; though he attended the meetings of the royal council, he left immediately—in the middle of the night—to return to his lonely hermitage at Bél or the bishopric of Csanád.[54] He was out of touch with reality, with real people. He avoided real people when making or playing politics. He also criticized the behavior of his fellow bishops. That the bishops were Germans or Italians by birth and feeling, and could not speak the Hungarians' tongue. That they kept no close contact with their flocks. That they failed to educate properly the faithful in matters of religion.[55] Gerard forgot to mention, however, that he himself never learned proper Hungarian. That after two full decades spent in Hungary he still had to preach through an interpreter.[56]

The bishop could only sense the hostility of the Hungarians toward himself and toward organized religion. He, in turn, despised the ignorant Hungarian nobles.[57] With good reason, too. And yet, Gerard, the spiritual leader and master of the Csanád region could not even talk to those nobles. He could not converse with them directly, and when he called upon his personal interpreter, the personal contact was gone.

The western educated bishop failed to comprehend that the simple, I might say primitive, mind of the Hungarian nobility the bishop's ignorance of their language meant only one thing: that this bishop—and the other proud high ecclesiastics as well—was not really interested in their spiritual fate, or in Hungarian life, everyday problems, etc.[58] Had Gerard tried to learn at least some Hungarian, and spoken to the Hungarian nobles in broken Magyar, the bishop would have earned their respect, would have won a full victory for his cause, the "westernization" of the Hungarian kingdom.[59]

Without possessing the real and only means of communication, however, Gerard remained a stranger among the people, the "Magyar" segment of the population whose fate he really cared about.[60] By 1046, the results were not exactly encouraging.

To the bishop's mind the clergy was mainly responsible for the "westernization" of the Hungarian realm. After Stephen's death it was his, and the bishops' and their clerics' duty to provide qualified political as well as spiritual leadership for the realm to help it through its political crisis by placing it safely into the hands of the new generation of the Árpádian princes. As the bishop pointed out to his spiritual colleagues and to the clergy, they could not afford to fail in the political crisis; they must proceed in spite of the failures of the nobility. To the nobles, Hungary was their own country, but the clergy had to live there, or die with it.[61]

2. The Martyrdom of Gerard: A Political Murder

Coniuratio in Ungarico regno contra Petrum regem oritur.

Annales Altahenses, a. 1046

When the national council met at Csanád in 1046 to recall from exile three Árpád princes, Levente, Andrew and Béla,[1] the sons of Vazul, the council was aware of the consequences of its forthcoming decision. "Tunc in Chenad [sic] omnes in unum convenerunt consilioque habito communiter pro filiis Zarladislai transmittunt" (They gathered in one body to have a council session at Csanád [at which they decided] to send for the sons of Ladislas Szár [requesting their return].)[2] The invitation of the council to the three Árpáds meant that it had taken the government of the realm into its hands and that it regarded the king, Peter Orseolo, the nephew of Gisela, King Stephen's queen, unfit to retain the throne.[3]

The reports of the chroniclers, including that of the compiler of the *Vita maior* of Bishop Gerard, speak of the 1046 meeting of the council at Csanád as a convention of princes and nobles of the realm and mention the bishops' purely auxiliary role at the convention.[4] The chroniclers describe the bishops as a body of churchmen who had approved in principle of the contemplated change(s), but refused to take action toward their fulfillment. It may be that the hierarchy, threatened in its existence by the princes and nobles, had approved, under pressure and for the sake of its own survival, the resolutions passed by the council, as if identify itself with the work of the council. The hierarchy may have been acting in such a manner in the hope of gaining the sympathy of the new Árpád monarch for the interests of the Church.[5] "Infelix terra, que inter deum et hominem discordiam operatur" (Unhappy [are the people of] the land that [who] causes discord between God and man), writes Bishop Gerard in his *Deliberatio,*[6] as if to underline his determination to leave, together with some of his episcopal colleagues, the meeting of the council at Csanád, the participants of which, incidentally, decided to transfer their assembly to Székesfehérvár.[7] It is possible that Gerard, a close co-worker of the deceased King Stephen, had attempted to establish some personal contact with the princes before the Árpád princes would meet with the "princes and nobles" of the council newly convened at Székesfehérvár.[8] As it is evident from his writing, the bishop had little confidence in the nobles; he had, in fact, a rather low opinion of them: "ut de his autem, sic de ceteris, quibus securitas nulla in mundo est" ([to be free of the hands of] of those, and the others, who make everything insecure in the [this] world).[9]

It is important that Gerard's *Vita maior* speaks of an "universa multitudo Ungarorum" that had greeted the returning Árpád princes in the "town of Pest," on the left-hand side of the Danube. It was the same multitude, and not the princes and nobles of the council now gathering at Székesfehérvár, that revived national pagan institutions and murdered bishops, priests, and abbots; and, with the foreknowledge and approval of the returning Prince Andrew,[10] the same multitude did its best to extirpate Christianity from the entire country.[11] The bishop sensed that he, the co-worker of King Stephen and perhaps the senior member of the Hungarian episcopate, had to inform the returning Árpáds of the condition of the Church and religion in the realm in order to convince Prince Andrew of the need to join the cause of the Church, instead of persecuting it.[12]

The bishop's plan to meet face to face with Andrew failed to materialize. Perhaps not so unexpectedly, there appeared on the right-hand side of the Danube across from the town of Pest, pagan leader Vata and his group of followers who prevented the meeting between the bishop and the prince. The *Chronicon pictum* makes it clear that the attack by Vata upon Gerard and his party occured according to a plan: "cumque ad predictum portum venissent, ecce viri impii, scilicet Vatha et conplices sui, . . . irruerunt in episcopos" (as soon as they [Gerard and his party] arrived at the ferry [previously agreed upon], there immediately appeared the rascals, that is, Vata and his men, who rushed on the bishops.)[13]

The statement by the compiler of Gerard's *Vita maior* that the bishop and three of his episcopal colleagues, accompanied by a *comes* Zonug, were en-route to Buda to render an honorable reception to princes Levente and Andrew; and the compiler's remark that Gerard had been aware of the danger involved in his personal undertaking, stress the nature of the entire mission.[14] The bishop knew that it might cost him his life to meet with the prince(s).[15] But he also knew, according to the dream he had, that if he not succeded in meeting the prince(s), his colleague, Bishop Beneta, would accomplish the mission of meeting and informing Andrew about conditions in the realm.[16]

Gerard thought that he might be able in a personal interview to convince the prince(s) of the need for the Church in the country, and thereby end the persecution that seemed to have the support of the prince(s),[17] which enabled the pagan forces to gain the upper hand in the realm. Andrew himself delivered the bishop Beneta, who alone among the four bishops had survived the attack, from the hands of the Vata group.[18] It was Beneta who, in turn, provided Andrew with the necessary intelligence concerning the stiuation of the Church and politics in general in the realm in 1046. It may be assumed that the bishop persuaded Prince Andrew to complete the program of Christianization and to fulfill the policies of King Stephen.[19]

King Andrew I, who had been crowned king by the three bishops who had survived the bloodbath of 1046,[20] was described by the *Chronicon pictum* as the "Catholic King;"[21] the *Constitutio ecclesiastica* issued by Andrew I in 1047 is proof of his Christian convictions and belief in Christian kingship. "Ut quicunque Ungarus, seu peregrinus in Ungaria, . . . ac sacram legem a divo rege Stephano traditam non reciperet, capite et bonis multaretur" (If any Hungarian [i.e., any inhabitant of Hungary], or someone in transit in [passing through] Hungary, . . . will not accept the sacred laws issued by the sublime King Stephen, he will be fined in person and in his goods.)[22]

The anti-Orseolo behavior of the "princes and nobles," supported by the bishops, resulted in the restoration of the Árpáds to the Hungarain throne and led to a Christian victory that, in no little extent, was due to the self-sacrifice of Gerard of Csanád.[23] The Árpád monarch now decided to eliminate paganism in the country during his reign and to assure the continuity of the Christian-European policy of King Stephen.[24]

CHAPTER V

STRUGGLE FOR THE THRONE

Coniuratio in Ungarico regno contra Petrum regem oritur.

Annales altahenses, a. 1046

The period from 1046 to 1077, covering the reigns of kings Andrew I (1046-60), Bela I (1060-63), Salomon (1063-74), and the unrecognized Geza I (1074-77), all of whom had to struggle to gain access to and to remain on the Hungarian throne, could be characterized by three major events. (1) Andrew I, elected to the throne and a successful restorer of law and order in the realm of King Stephen, failed to obtain recognition from the German court as a sovereign monarch until he agreed to have his five-year old son, Salomon, crowned king in order to make him eligible to marry the daughter of Henry III. (2) Discouraged by this open foreign intervention in Hungarian affairs, Bela I attempted to ensure successsion to the throne for himself, on grounds that he was the younger brother of the ruling monarch; however, the German imperial court objected to this, and Bela I died suddenly during his campaign to halt German invasion of his country. (3) Salomon, who became king upon the death of his uncle Bela, abused royal authority; although the Hungarian bishops negotiated a truce between Salomon and the two sons of Bela I, Salomon breached the truce and turned against the princes who, acting in self-defense, defeated Salomon by 1074. The bishops who were supported by the armed forces, now crowned Geza, the elder son of Bela I, king; and yet, Geza I had misgivings about the coronation and tried to negotiate peace with Salomon, but died before the talks were completed.

1. Andrew I Seeks Recognition

There seems to be little doubt that the 1046 uprising in Hungary was caused by German interference in Hungarian politics. In 1044, after the coronation of Peter Orseolo, Emperor Henry III promulgated German laws for the Hungarian subjects of Peter Orseolo,[1] who blindly ignored the laws issued by his uncle and predecessor, King Stephen,[2] and handed over the realm as a fief to the German court.[3] A German chronicler had access to a Hungarian intelligence report and records that the friends and associates of Orseolo misled him and invited Andrew, the exiled nephew of King Stephen, to enter the realm with troops to restore it to the Árpád family.[4] The Hungarians revolted against Peter Orseolo, the German chronicler reports, captured and blinded him because they did not want him again to request military aid from the German court.[5]

Andrew at first supported the anti-Orseolo uprising,[6] that, it seems, may have resulted from a well planned conspiracy to eliminate the Orseolo and German influence from the country.[7] The rebellion was organized by Vata, the pagan leader who had assassinated Bishop Gerard of Csanád in 1046 before the bishop had a chance to meet with Andrew, to inform him about political reality in the country.

Orseolo did not surrender without a fight; he was captured, tortured, and killed by his captors, it was reported, because Andrew intervened too late to save his life. Andrew was only able to assure that the body of Orseolo was given a decent Christian burial at Saint Peter's basilica in Pecs.[8] Andrew enjoyed immense popularity among the people of his realm and his reign was quite successful. He forbade, under pain of death, the practice of pagan cults and religion by ordering every inhabitant of the realm to return to the faith of Christ;[9] and he restored the Laws of King Stephen.[10] A statement of the *Chronicon pictum* is contained in the articles of the *Constitutio ecclesiastica* which Andrew I issued in 1047;[11] it is an important statement because it records the monarch's resolution to return to the Christian and European policy of King Stephen, and to restore thereby the validity of the Hungarian code of law. Andrew rescinded the German laws that had been issued by Henry III in 1044 and thereby eliminated the grievance that caused the revolt of 1046.[12] Andrew I's Christian and European policy was aimed at Hungarian interests:

"prophanas et Scythicas ceremonias falsosque deos abrogarent. Et simu-
lacra demolirentur" (they have abandoned pagan and Scythian rites,
together with [the cult of] false deities; and they destroyed the images
[of those deities] .)[13] This may be why the chronicler calls Andrew the
"White-King" and the "Catholic Monarch."[14] Andrew was determined
to conduct a policy leaning toward Rome.[15]

Andrew, being childless at the time, also persuaded his younger brother,
Bela, to return to Hungary to be in line as heir to the throne upon his
death.[16] Ioannes Cinnamus, a twelfth century Byzantine chronicler,
says that it was Hungarian custom to let the ruling monarch's younger
brother inherit the throne.[17] Bela received *partem tertium principis:*
the princely-one-third of the realm's territory, for his upkeep and to serve
as his base of operations.[18] His right of succession to the throne was not
weakened by the marriage of Andrew I to Anastasia of Kiev, by whom
Andrew begot two sons, Salomon and David. The chronicler stresses the
point that, in spite of this, Andrew I and his brother lived peacefully
with each other.[19]

The chronicler says that Andrew established a monastery at Tihany
in honor of the Mother of God and of Saint Anianus;[20] Anianus was a
French saint who had defended Orleans from Attila the Hun,[21] —an
interesting coincidence in view of the fact that the sister of Andrew's
queen was the wife of the king of France.[22] The inhabitants of the Tihany
religious community were Byzantine monks.[23] To appreciate the importance of this monastery it will be necessary to examine the Hungaro-
German political background of the 1050s. The *Annales Altahenses*
and the *Chronicon pictum,* whose compiler bases his report upon the
historical annotations of contemporary eyewitness of events, Bishop
Nicholas of Veszprem and chancellor of Andrew I,[24] provide information.

It was at this time that the German emperor, Henry III, wishing to
avenge the death of Orseolo, attempted to occupy Fort Pozsony on the
Hungaro-German frontier, and laid siege to it.[25] During the siege, a Hungarian diver, Botond by name, sank the German ships on the Danube.[26]
After some eight weeks Henry III abandoned the siege, but invaded
Hungary again in the following year.[27] Andrew I developed a two-pronged
system of defense. He scorched the contryside where the German attack
was expected to occur to prevent the Germans from having any access to
food supplies;[28] he cutoff communications between the German army led
by the emperor himself and the German supply ships on the Danube,[29] and

forced Bishop Gebhardt, commander of the ships, to return to German waters. At night, Andrew I's troops harrassed the Germans, forcing Henry III soon to request an armistice. The emperor asked for free-withdrawal from Hungary and for food to feed his hungry troops. In turn Henry III promised not to attack Andrew and/or his successors. Cursed be he who would dare to attack Hungary in the future![30]

The chronicler of these events[31] says, in a curt statement in which he misquotes the name of the princess, that although the emperor had promised the French court that his daughter would marry the son of their king, Henry III now offered the hand of his daughter in marriage to the son of Andrew I.[32] The German source reports, however, that Salomon and Judith were married in 1058, after the death of Henry III, on the Morava river that formed the Hungaro-German border at that time. In 1058, Audrew I and Henry IV, Salomon's brother-in-law, signed a new treaty.[33]

There may be another view of this arrangement. It seems that the Hungarian chronicler fuses into one narrative the records of various German military campaigns in Hungary in the early 1050s, and provides his own interpretation of these events. The German sources report that the siege of Pozsony occured in 1052, and that the emperor broke off the siege because of the personal intervention of Pope Leo IX when Andrew I promised the pontiff that if the Germans were to lift the siege, he would be happy to meet all of their demands.[34] The Pope first dispatched Odilo of Cluny to investigate matters at the Hungarian court,[35] after which he went himself to visit the emperor at his camp near Pozsony.[36] Henry III agreed to accept the offer of Andrew I; however, the German annalist reports that after Henry III left Pozsony, Andrew changed his mind and denied everything.[37] The remark made by Wibert, the biographer of Pope Leo IX, that the intervention of Rome caused the curia to lose face in the field of international politics, may be interpreted in this context.[38] The German sources report that peace was reached with the Hungarian court only upon the death of Henry III, after several requests were made by Andrew of Hungary. The advisiors of Henry IV of Germany agreed to the marriage of Judith to Salomon under one condition: that is, Salomon must be crowned king during his father's lifetime, prior to his marriage to King Henry IV's sister.[39]

These were acceptable to Andrew's court; both he and Bela, and the sons of Bela, together with the Hungarian nobility agreed to the terms set by the German court. As Andrew I must have viewed the situation, his son's unexpected coronation as king of Hungary would not endanger the succession of his brother to the throne. During a discussion he had with his brother at the hunting lodge at Varkony, Andrew I told Bela that he had his son crowned king in the interests of a peace treaty he planned to conclude with the imperial court.[49] The Hungarian chronicler emphasizes that Bela, acting out of fear that he would be assassinated by his brother's henchmen, agreed to his brother's proposal;[41] yet, the chronicler says, Andrew, seeking his brother's willingness to cooperate, was so overcome with surprise and joy that he, the king, bowed deeply before Bela, and thanked him.[42] The chronicler may express a somewhat biased opinion, and his report should be understood accordingly.

Bela fled the country for the court of his Polish father-in-law, and returned to Hungary with three Polish army divisions.[43] Andrew I now requested military advisors from the German court.[44] Probably, what happened was that Bela went to Poland to stay away from politics at home; he did not want to get involved in the new Hungaro-German political situation that must have been very much in flux at this time. And yet, he wished to be prepared for any possible German reaction and political-military development in Hungary.[45] Upon his return home, Bela remained in his own territory, the princely-one-third, with the Polish forces under his direct command. It may have been no coincidence that during his absence from the court of Andrew the representatives of the German court tried to persuade Andrew to leave the country with his family, and to go to Bavaria.[46]

The German chroniclers report that the imperial court had little liking for Andrew I. Hermann Contractus barely mentions his coronation as king of Hungary. To the German court, the coronation of 1058 of Salomon, son of Andrew I, had already served its purpose; it assured the succession of Salomon to the Hungarian throne and, through Salomon's German queen, actually confirmed German predominance of the country.[47] After signing the second treaty on the Morava river in 1058, the German court had no further need for Andrew I; it wanted him out of the country. It may have been this attempt by the German court to force the removal of Andrew I from Hungary that prompted Bela to seek

Polish aid, and to prevent Andrew's removal with his Polish divisions. Bela attacked the imperial forces that were practically in charge of the abduction of Andrew I on the Hungaro-German border, and attempted to free his brother from their hands.[48]

A Hungarian source reports that Bela defeated both William and Potho, German advisors to Andrew I, at the Tisza river, and thereby caused the German sympathizers of Andrew I to join ranks with Bela's forces.[49] Although the chronicler says that Andrew I died "negligenter detentus" at Zirc, the German annalist claim that Andrew I had been trampled to death by the wagons and horses of his military (alias German horses and wagons) and had not been given proper miedical care after the accident. The truth of the matter is that Bela arrived too late on the scene to save his brother's life. He could only assure a Christian burial at Tihany abbey for the deceased's remains.[50] The intervention of Bela voided the German dream of a political take-over in Hungary and made Bela the scapegoat before the Germans. The plan of Henry III to incorporate Hungary into his empire was abruptly shattered by the deposition of the Orseolo in 1046; the same plan, later revived by the advisors of Henry IV, was again shattered thanks to the intelligence and foresight of Bela.[51]

The German chroniclers could not know that Bela I had understood the political aims of his deceased brother. He had Andrew I buried at Tihany Abbey, the monastery inhabited by Byzantine monks, which his brother had established in 1055 with the consent of the nobles and of the higher clergy.[52] It was through these monks that Andrew I hoped to create a permanent contact with the Byzantine Patriarch in Constantinople, in order to prepare himself for the confrontation he expected to have with the growth of German political pressure at his court.[53] He established Tihany in 1055, the year after the breach occurred between Rome and the Byzantine Patriarch.[54] The breach undermined the prestige of the Byzantine emperor, Monomachos IX, who had shown strong sympathy toward Rome. Through his reliance upon the German-oriented papal curia, Emperor Monomachos IX hoped to counteract the political pressures of Patriarch Kerullarios.[55] Considering the Patriarch enjoyed the support of the monks in Constantinople,[56] Andrew I hoped, by developing a Byzantine monastic community at Tihany,[57] to create an alliance with the Patriarch in order to assert pressure upon the Roman curia of the German popes,[58] during whose pontificates the curia had strong ties with the German imperial court.[59] Through the manner in which he dated his correspondence, Pope Leo IX sought to stress his independence of German influence.[60] Wibert, the papal biographer, claims the election of Leo IX in 1049 was financed by the German court, and that the new pontiff was surrounded by German advisors.[61] It may be assumed that, instead of war, Andrew I wished to rely upon an alliance with the Byzantine patriarch to keep the Germans in check through the Roman curia,[62] and, at the same time, to continue with his Christian policy, the cornerstone of which was his working relationship with the Roman See.[63]

2. To-Be or Not-To-Be: Bela I and Salomon

The reign of Béla I (1060-63) is given different interpretations by Hungarian and German chroniclers. The compiler of the *Annales Alta-henses* tells of the Germans' dissatisfaction with Béla I in a sense that Béla I failed to attend in person the signing ceremony of the peace treaty of 1058 on the Morava river.[1] He states that the assembly of German nobles included the advisors of Henry IV who decided, in 1063, to stage a military summer expedition against Béla I; the advisors also decided to ignore the delegates Béla I had sent to the court of Henry IV, on grounds that Béla had no business explaining his constitutional position to them.[2]

It was the understanding of the German court that Béla I had usurped the throne of his brother Andrew I; instead, Béla I accepted the crown of the realm from his bishops and armed forces.[3] And yet, the fact that Béla I believed that he had to explain and defend his situation before the German court, showed irresolution on his part. The consitutional position of Béla was, however, irregular in view of the fact that, though crowned king by the bishops and the armed forces, the nobles of Hungary had not elected him king. The latter did not participate in the elevation of Béla I to the throne. His failure to have the support of the nobles was a weak spot in the position of Béla that may have prompted the German court to ɛttempt to force him to accept Salomon as king, while Béla retained his princely-one-third of the realm's territory.

The conclusions that may be drawn from the assertion of the chronicler are twofold. One, Béla I did not consider his coronation by the armed forces and bishops as an act of official initiation to kingship, the transmission of authority from the nobles and the people. The remark of the chronicler, "tenuit regnum pacifice, sine molestatione hostium et quesivit bona gentis sue" (he reigned peacefully, without being molested [his] enemies, and did his best for the people), may serve as proof of that.[4] Béla was willing to acknowledge Salomon as king. Second, Béla I was, since the death of his brother, *de facto* ruler of the country.[5] It could not be expected that he would surrender his authority to Salomon, unless he retained his portion of the realm's territory that had been conferred upon him by his brother and legitimate predecessor.[6] It was probably Béla's reference to his territorial portion of the realm that caused Salomon to remain aloof and ignore Béla's proposal. He ignored the legates of Béla.[7] The chronicler says that, because Salomon refused to receive the second delegation dispatched to him by Béla, the latter had no other choice but to prepare for war. Béla I expected the Germans to attack him.[8]

The German army occupied Fort Moson on the border,[9] while Béla I and his troops camped nearby where, and when, Béla I unexpectedly died.[10] Béla's sons fled the country upon their father's death, and Henry IV of Germany wasted no time in placing Salomon upon the Hungarian throne without further bloodshed.[11] And yet, Salomon failed to learn from the mistake made by the Orseolo in 1045. In 1063, he gave a feudal banquet in the Hungarian royal city of Székesfehérvár in the honor of the German Henry IV and his nobles.[12]

A Hungarian chronicler summarizes the achievements of Béla under four headings. One, it was Béla I who had introduced new currency into circulation in the realm and thus boosted the economyy. The silver *denarius* was the new monetary unit, and forty *denarii* were worth one golden *pensa*.[13] To support the new currency, the monarch emphasized compulsory price and wage controls, tolerated no inflation and eliminated the black market;[14] "haec est enim causa, que maxime solet populus pauperitatis et inopia periculis obvolvere" (it [i.e., black market] has been the cause of the people's poverty, and their inability to cope with it.)[15] Béla I regulated the holding of weekly markets in the realm on Saturdays, instead of Sundays.[16] Two, the monarch displayed a benevolent attitude toward those who had previously sided with Salomon. He ordered that their wives and children be not molested or harmed, nor their goods and chattel confiscated.[17] Three, he makes it clear that to gain the confidence of, and the approval by, the people for the reforms in the economy and the government of the realm, Béla I had invited the *villae* to send two delegates each to his royal council (*curia regis*) to discuss with him and before the council all public matters relating to the realm.[18] The chronicler says that King Béla wanted to discuss in council with the elected representatives of the people all business of public importance.[19] The economic innovations just mentioned and the attitude he had taken toward those who were siding with Salomon and against him were questions that required decisions to be made at the highest level as the monarch's will. Béla I reached decisions after consultation with the people's representatives, and he kept those decisions. Finally, the chronicler reports that in the field of religious matters, the monarch did his best to preserve the Catholic faith established by King Stephen and restored by King Andrew I in the country. When the mob led by pagan leaders demanded from him the restoration of "national" pagan institutions in the kingdom,[20] Béla I consulted with the representatives of the people, and decided to suppress the pagan revolt at its very roots.[21]

Béla I was small of stature, but possessed high personal qualities of leadership, determination and an iron will.[22] A real Árpád scion he was, a man of flesh and blood, who realized only too well the meaning of his responsibilities. He felt responsible for the defense of the country in the face of German aggression. His military tactics consisted of a sham-withdrawal; for example, he let Moson fall into German hands because he did not think that the defense of the fort was worth the effort and sacrifice.[23] Indeed, the German chroniclers speak of Moson as *urbs:* a fortified town. From the military-strategic point of view, Moson was not significant.[24] It was the strong personality and military readiness of Béla I that made the real difference and gave strength to the country's defenses in the face of renewed German aggression;[25] yet, upon the arrival of German troops at Moson,[26] Béla died nearby at Dömös and his throne collapsed.[27]

Was his death an accident? or, was it regicide? Was it a political assassination? The German chroniclers report nothing.[28] The Hungarian chronicler mentions an accident.[29] And yet, the fact that the body of Béla I was laid to rest at the monastic church he built at Szögszárd, may imply foul-play.[30] Dömös was a part of the royal domain;[31] security around the king there may have been less tight; and immediate medical aid was not even available; "duxeruntque eum seminecem ad rivulum Kynisua propter quasdam regni necessitates et ibi migravit a seculo" (they have taken him [in a] semiconscious [state] to the creek Kinizsa so that he may conduct some [urgent] state-business, where he died.)[32] The victorious German army had little to fear from Béla I's supporters; without the king, they were helpless.[33] Salomon, backed by German troops permitted the public burial of Béla I at the monastic church Bela had built.

The Hungarian chronicler describes at great length the reign of Salomon (1063-74).[34] He says that the German party placed Salomon on the throne of his father in the presence of German nobles, while Géza, the son of Béla I, fled the realm to Poland.[35] The chronicler describes Géza as a man who was "prudens et circumspectus," and who, upon the departure of Henry IV and his troops from Hungary, returned home.[36] It was now Salomon who fled to the German border town of Moson.[37] The new king must have had a bad consicence, the chronicler says, and felt insecure in his position. Acting under the assumption that the sudden succession of Salomon to the Hungarian throne was a Hungarian problem that had to be solved by domestic means, Bishop Desiderius, a member of the Hungarian hierarchy, persuaded Géza to seek reconciliation with Salomon. On January 20, 1064, Géza and Salomon concluded a peace agreement at Győr,[38] and on Easter Sunday, 1064, the king and the prince attended church service together. In front of the Hungarian nobles, Géza crowned Salomon anew in the cathedral of Pécs.[39] It was this third coronation of Salomon that formed the cornerstone of the treaty between himself and the two sons of the deceased Béla I. Instructed by Bishop Desiderius, Salomon made certain that he did not create the impression that he received the crown from the hands of the German monarch; in accordance with the arrangements made in the treaty of 1058, Salomon now succeeded to the throne after the death of his uncle, Béla I. Géza crowned Salomon anew in recognition of the arrangements of 1058, and to honor the truce that he had made with Salomon at Győr. The text of the Győr truce failed to survive. However, the remark of the chronicler that Salomon "per manus Geysa ducis honorabiliter est coronatus" (by the hands of Géza received an honorable coronation), clarifies the agreement they had reached previously.

There are two more assertions in the report of the Hungarian chronicler that carry a similar connotation. One is that the 1064 coronation by Géza

of Salomon occurred "assistentibus regni proceribus," in the presence
of the nobles of the realm.[40] The other statement is that after the coronation, Géza led by hand the crowned monarch "in regiam beati Petri
basilicam" (into the royal basilica [i.e., founded by King Stephen] named
after Saint Peter), as if to emphasize that the coronation was a constitutional act. The Pécs basilica burned down the night after the coronation,
but it was not regarded as arson.[41] The basilica had been built by Peter
Orseolo,[42] but it served the needs of a bishopric that was founded by
King Stephen.[43] The Győr agreement reached by Salomon and Géza may
have included a clause to the effect that, upon the death of Salomon
who had no children, it would be Géza and his brother Ladislas, and the
children of Géza, who would inherit the throne.[44]

For the next nine years, peace prevailed between Salomon and the two
princes.[45] When the Czechs attacked the town of Trencsén, it was Salomon and Géza who revenged the intrusion by invading Bohemia;[46] it was
with the military aid received from both princes that Salomon successfully
defended the realm from the Cuman attack and defeated the Cumans
in the battle of Kerlés.[47] The chronicler, however, remarks that Salomon
behaved with heedless speed during the battle and displayed poor leadership of men and strategy,[49] and Géza's brother, Ladislas, became the true
hero of the occasion.[50] Unfortunately, the chronicler is careless in the
exact dating of events. His chronology is misleading, to say the least.
The battle of Kerlés seems to have taken place in the year 1068 (and not
in 1065). Therefore, the Cuman attack recorded as having occured three
years later,[51] actually took place in 1071. The Cumans crossed the Save
river and ravaged the country north of the river, the chronicler says.

Salomon and Géza had reason to believe that the men of the garrison
at Belgrade, where the Save enters the Danube, behaved treacherously by
letting the Cumans through to ravage Hungarian territory.[52] Salomon
and Géza decided to occupy Belgrade. Salomon dispatched the entire
Hungarian armed force, "universus exercitus Hungarorum," to the south,
across the Save, into Byzantine controlled Bulgaria. This entry of the
Hungarian forces into the region south of the Save was regarded by the
Byzantine-Bulgarian high command as a provocation, and the latter
ordered a counterattack. The Byzantine-Bulgarian forces relied unsuccessfully upon what may be called Greek-fire,[53] to stop the Hungarian ships
used at the Save crossing. There were too many ships, and the "Greeks"

were defeated.[54] The Hungarian army occupied the Byzantine-Bulgarian border by either establishing and maintiaing bridgeheads south of the Save, or by creating a military zone in depth on Bulgarian territory directly south of the river. Salomon and Géza then took personal command of the operations, and began the siege of Belgrade. Because the besieged garrison of Belgrade received aid from the Cumans beyond the siege-zone, Commander Ján of the Sopron division attacked the Cumans and destroyed them. The Cuman-Patzinak prince, Kazár by name, had a devil of a time escaping capture by Ján's forces.[55] Ján's attack upon the Cuman-Patzinaks was not only successful, but it proved to be decisive in the siege of the fort.[56] Belgrade (the town and the lower fort) fell, and Salomon and Géza forced the captured enemy forces to march in front of the upper fort in order to frighten its defenders into surrender. And yet, despite the use of siege machinery by the Hungarians, the upper fort of Belgrade held out for two more months, when, finally, a captive Hungarian woman put fire to Belgrade on a windy day.[57] Commander Niketas of the Byzantine-Bulgarian force made a last ditch attempt to resist, but had to surrender.[58] Salomon and Géza then made arrangements for an armistice, which they confirmed with a handshake; however, Niketas decided to surrender only to Géza because he knew that the prince was a god-fearing man.[59]

Was Niketas playing politics? Did he insist on surrendering to Géza because he wished to cause a split between Salomon and Géza? Had he known that he was playing into the hands of Vid, Salomon's wicked political advisor? Vid had, on previous occasions, cautioned Salomon about Géza; the question is, did Niketas have any previous contact with Vid? The answer to these questions may come from a single incident reported by the chronicler. After the siege of Belgrade, he reports, when the war-booty was divided into three equal parts, of which Géza was entitled to one, the spoils were suddenly divided to four parts, of which Géza and Vid gained one-fourth each, although Vid had no legal claim to any of the booty. The incident was designed to downgrade Géza, who, the chronicler reports, was visibly shaken by the incident: "unde dux valde molestatus est."[60] The incident caused a rift in the working relationship of Salomon with Géza.

In point of fact, Géza was specially perturbed by the probability that Vid had, before or during the siege of Belgrade, established contact with either the Byzantine high command or the Byzantine court. Although this probability is not mentioned by the chronicler, the fact remains that there appeared, before Géza, a Byzantine delegation to pay him a courtesy call: to thank him for the humane attitude he had shown toward the captured Byzantine-Bulgarian prisoners-of-war during the siege of Belgrade.[61]

The Byzantine court may have wished to establish public contact with Géza at the instigation of Vid, Salomon's political and personal advisor.[62] Vid may have had diplomatic and political objectives in persuading the Byzantine court to contact Géza, on grounds that he could now claim that, after all, it was Géza who had played political chess with the Byzantine court; Vid could warn Salomon not to trust Géza again. "Duo gladii acuti in eadem vagina contineri non possent" (two sharp swords cannot be held in one sword-holder), he argued with Salomon, "sic et vos in eodem regno congregare potestis" (just as the two of you cannot rule the same kingdom.)[63]

No where does the record show that Géza had attempted to co-reign (and/or co-rule) with Salomon. The record does show, however, that, in the process of carrying out his duties, Géza gained the love of his subordinates and his former enemies' respect.[64]

3. Geza I, the Unrecognized King

Geysa dux magnus compellentibus Hungaris coronam regni suscepit.

Chronicon pictum, c. 124

Encouraged by Vid's advice, Salomon decided to play a friendly game of political chess with Géza, the chronicler reports, and the game for real power began in earnest.[1] At first, Salomon demanded that Géza accompany him on his Bulgarian expedition to Nis;[2] Géza understood the nature of the plan and, for the time being at least, went along with it. He ordered, for instance, one-half of his armed force to remain behind in his duchy under the command of his brother Ladislas, and took only the lesser half of the force with him to accompany Salomon.[3] Géza was able to see through the plans of Salomon and made certain that he would not fall prey to the conspiracy planned by Vid.[4] Ladislas was dispatched to the Russian court at Kiev to request military aid, if needed, against Salomon; "ut contra machimenta regis sese premuniret."[5] In other words, Géza wished to have a strong force to support negotiations or a reconciliation with Salomon.

Salomon and Géza began to evaluate their political and military positions in the realm and gathered a team of negotiators around themselves. They went to Esztergom and, accompanied by a select team of sixteen men chosen from the hierarchy and from the ranks of the nobles to attend a meeting on a nearby island in the Danube to talk things over and to reach an understanding. From the meeting on the island, Géza returned to his duchy.[6] During the negotiations both parties had asked for guarantors. Vid, Salomon's political advisor, and Ernyei, the royal reeve and, according to the chronicler, a decent man, became the guarantors for Salomon, while Géza designated the bishop of Várad and Vatha, a weak character, to be his guarantors before Salomon.[7] The two parties exchanged guarantors to work out a lasting truce; in fact, Géza sent Vid and Ernyei back to Salomon to negotiate an agreement which was to last from Saint Martin's day (November 11, 1071) through the feast of Saint George (April 23, 1072).[8] Géza needed an agreement to gain time for Ladislas had returned from the Russian court without accomplishing his mission. Also, the Czech Otto, married to Eufema, the sister of Géza and Ladislas, could not be persuaded to render military aid.[8a] The negotiated truce broke down from the lack of good will on both sides; and after both parties withdrew their guarantors, war began.[9]

Vid was unable to receive substantial Byzantine aid for his scheme against Géza and Ladislas and persuaded Salomon to turn to the German court for sympathy and aid. Both Vid and the German duke Marchrat put Salomon under pressure to attack Géza before time had run out; in that particular moment, Géza was "destitutus omni auxilio."[10] They informed Salomon that Géza had repeatedly requested Russian, and more recently Polish, military help, and the time had come to eliminate him from the scene during a hunting party. "Noctis in silencio impetum faciamus super eum, . . . et oculos eius erumus" (At night, silently, we attack him . . . and put out his eyes.)[11] Géza had to be eliminated, they argued, because without him his party supporters would pose no serious threat to Salomon's reign.[12] With Géza removed from the scene, Salomon would have had nothing to fear, suggested Vid,[13] who did not give his advice cheaply. For his services he asked Salomon to confer upon him the duchy (the princely-one-third) of Géza.[14]

The fateful meeting between Salomon, Vid, and, presumbably, the German Marchrat, took place in the abbey of Szőgszárd.[15] The Italian-born abbot of Szőgszárd, William,[16] found out about the conspiracy and notified Géza at once.[17] Vid, however, was a born conspirator; he had already planted an agent in the immediate surroundings of Géza. When the messenger of Abbot William arrived at Géza's court, Géza's advisors, who were paid by Vid, tried hard to downgrade the credibility of the abbot's message: "quia—the chronicler comments—volebant tradere ducem in manus Salomonis" (they wished to deliver the prince into the hands of Salomon.)[18]

Abbot William remained persistent, however. It was Géza's father, Béla I, who had established the abbey of Szögszárd,[19] and he was able to see through the wicked plans of Vid, who, by then, had gained complete mastery over the monarch,[20] went in person to the court of Géza to warn him about the immediate danger.[21] The abbot told Géza that he was outnumbered and unprepared for a showdown battle with Salomon's forces and recommended that Géza negotiated with Salomon. Acting, however, against the abbot's advice, Géza gave battle to Salomon's forces at the church of the Sons-of-Nog, east of the Tisza river, and lost the engagement.[22] Géza lost because of treason, although those who comitted the treason were annihilated by Salomon's army due to a practical misunderstanding.[23]

After his defeat, Géza fled to his brother Ladislas, and the two of them met with their brother-in-law, the Czech Otto, at Vác. Otto had strong forces with him, and Ladislas encouraged Géza to pray to Allmighty God that the former victor be now annihilated![24] The chronicler leaves the impression that, though Géza had the army of his brother-in-law at his disposal, he needed a divine miracle to save his cause. Indeed, Vid dutifully informed Salomon about the escape of Géza and his meeting with Ladislas and Otto at Vác; and, once again, argued for an attack upon Géza without further delay. The troops of Géza were either dead or defeated he reasoned; the army of Otto was useless; this would be the right time to attack and defeat those untrained peasants![25] Ernyei opposed Vid, to no avail.[26]

Salomon now decided to finish off the struggle with Géza. His army quickly occupied a strategic position;[27]however, the combined forces of Géza, Ladislas and Otto had taken up an attacking formation and were ready to meet Salomon's army at Cinkota,[28] where only the hill of Mogyoród separated the two armies from each other.[29] After some hesitation Géza, believing that his cause was just, prayed for divine aid for victory.[30]

At the beginning of the battle of Mogyoród the troops of Otto killed Vid and destroyed Vid's *Bács*-division,[31]while Géza and Ladislas exchanged their standards to confuse Salomon who, seeing the standard of Géza, attacked the troops of Ladislas. When he realized his mistake, it was too late for him to turn around to seek out Géza, and the forces of Géza and Ladislas closed in on Salomon's division and destroyed it. "Cedentur Theutonici fugiunt Latini locumque fuge non inveniunt, et cadunt ante Hungaros, ut boves in macello" (the Germans were cut down, but the Latins, unable to find means of escaping, were slaughtered.)[32] Salomon escaped and fled to join his wife and mother at Moson. His defeat and flight from the battlefield did not undo the havoc he had created. Entire Hungarian army divisions lay dead in the field of Mogyoród.[33] The road was now open for Géza to ascend to the throne and obtain the crown of King Stephen. Yet, the constitutionality of the succession remained in doubt. By fleeing from the battlefiled and seeking safety behind the fortified walls of Moson and Pozsony on the German border, Salomon actually surrendered his claim to the throne, and Géza, "dux magnus compellentibus Hungaris coronam regni suscepit;" forced by his people, accepted the crown of the realm.[34] Géza, *compellentibus Hungaris*, was crowned as the elected king of the realm. Salomon miscalculated and had repeated the mistake made by the Orseolo in 1045. Out of sheer desperation,[35] Salomon now offered his realm as a fief to the German court (of Henry IV).[36] Though born of the royal blood of the Árpáds, Salomon lost his throne in the battle of Mogyoród and forfeited his kingdom by having it turned over as a fief to the German court.[37] The constitutionality of Géza's coronation was already decided by the irresponsible behavior of Salomon, who lost both his crown and his realm.

The papal curia took a dissenting view of the succession of Géza to the Hungarian throne. It is clear from the letters of Pope Gregory VII addressed to both, Salomon (one letter)[39] and Géza (three letters),[40] that Rome objected to the kingship of Géza not because Géza had accepted the crown from the hands of the bishops of Hungary, but because he had not consulted the Roman See on the succession.[41] The papal assumption, on the one hand, that Géza had been crowned by the bishops is clear from the report of the *Chronicon pictum* that says that on Christmas day, 1076,[42] Géza had practically accused the hierarchy of having forced him to usurp the throne of the legitimate monarch who, at that time, was still alive.[43] Géza promised the assembled high ecclesiastics that he intended, in 1076, to restore the crown of the realm to Salomon, but to leave open for himself the line of succession to the throne.[44] On the other hand, the schoolmaster-to-pupil tone of the papal writ, dated March 17, 1074, addressed to Géza as *ducem Hungarorum,*[45] seems a clear indication that the Holy See neither accepted, nor intended to accept Géza's coronation as a valid and established constitutional act. As a matter of fact, Pope Gregory VII wanted Géza to communicate with him indirectly through Margrave Azo, special papal representative sent to his court,[46] in order to show that the pontiff wanted to keep his distance from Géza, whom he regarded as a pretender to the throne, and not its possessor.[47] The Roman See still looked upon Salomon as the legitimate monarch of Hungary, and during the summer of 1074, when the military expedition of the German Henry IV against Géza failed to achieve the desired results, Henry IV decided not to claim Hungary as an imperial fief.[48] His councillors, who were with him during the campaign, advised against continuing the claim: "consulerunt ei, ut reverteretur."[49] Salomon, expecting no further help from the German court, turned to Rome for understanding and support.

Salomon's letter to Pope Gregory VII is lost, but the papal reply to Salomon, addressed as *regem Hungarorum,* survives.[50] Unlike the views of the learned bishop historian Vilmos Fraknói,[51] this writer respectfully voices the opinion that the papal writ is not a tacit, but a warm approval by Pope Gregory of the kingship of Salomon. The pontiff undoubtedly took advantage of the weak political situation of Salomon and claimed Hungary, Salomon's realm, as a papal fief, "a rege Stephano olim Beato Petro cum omni iure et potestate sua oblatum et devote traditum" (once rightfully and devotedly given by King Stephen to blessed Peter.)[52] Papal supremacy over Hungary had been acknowledged by Emperor Henry III, who, the pontiff informs Salomon, sent the crown of the realm back to Rome,[53] "quo principatum dignitatis eius attinere cognovit" ([sending] the insignia of the country to the place of origin of its dignity.)[54] The pontiff called upon Salomon to repent and to recognize the fact that he held his kingdom not as a "royal" (that is, German), but as a papal benefice: "sceptrum regni quod tenes, . . . apostolicae, non regiae, maiestatis beneficium recogniscas."[55] If he, Salomon, were to meet these requirements, he could be assured of the full support of Rome: "et nostram in Christo amicitiam plene habere poteris."[56]

Salomon did not listen to the plea of Pope Gregory; he, once again, requested German aid instead, but failed to receive it.[57] In the meanwhile, Géza's popularity in the realm was rapidly growing. As a matter of fact, Géza stated in his founding charter of the Benedictine abbey near the Garam river, issued in 1075,[58] that he, the former Hungarian duke, was now Hungarian king by the grace of God.[59] Indeed, while Salomon had fully isolated himself in Pozsony, Géza gained firm control of the realm and from this time on Géza was named King Magnus.[60]

He notified the Roman See that he had taken over the government of the country,[61] to which statement Rome responded almost immediately. Gregory VII acknowledged the fact that Géza was *de facto* exercising royal powers in Hungary, but pointed out to Géza the lack of his *de iure* faculties: Géza was in power only because the country's legitimate king had turned his realm into a German fief and had refused to obtain his authority from the Holy See.[62] The pontiff stressed further that although a free country, Hungary was to remain a fief of the Holy See,[63] that regarded its feudal subjects not as slaves, but as its own children.[64] Although the royal powers were in the hands of Géza, and Géza was expected to provide for the protection of the Church and the cause of religion, he would have to receive the special delegate of the Holy See, with obedience.[65] It is, therefore, without any doubt that Rome regarded the "regency" of Géza as temporary in nature, and made the exercise of that regency dependent upon Géza's obedience to the delegate of the Roman See.

The report of the papal delegate to the court of Géza has not survived, but its contents, probably even the recommandations made by the delegate, may be summarized from the April 14, 1075, letter of Gregory VII to Géza.[66] In this writ, the pontiff stresses the argument that peace and unity must be restored between Salomon and Géza; however, on grounds that Salomon had humiliated himself by the handling of his realm, the fief of Saint Peter to the German court, Pope Gregory called upon Géza to take over the reins of power in the realm. "Dominus . . potestatem regni suo ad te iudicio transtulit."[67] The realm was to remain under the authority of the Holy See which would keep the channels of communication open with Géza. "Quapropter si quid vis, . . . nobis confidenter volumus, ut aperias."[68]

In the long run, the recommendations that were made by the papal delegate were gradually implemented by Géza. It is highly probable that the delegate established contact with the Hungarian bishops who, in turn, began to have influence upon Géza. On Christmas day, 1076, Archbishop Desiderius of Esztergom was able to persuade Géza to make peace with Salomon,[69] an indication that the Hungarian episcopate may have been instructed by the papal delegate to seek interaction with Géza.

And yet, the Christmas scene at Szögszárd abbey, 1076, may be viewed differently. The chronicler records that, after High Mass, Géza made, behind closed doors, a confession to the members of the hierarchy.[70] It may be that exactly the opposite happened: Géza openly (but behind closed doors!) accused the bishops of having deliberately misled him by forcing him to accept the crown in 1074. Géza may have bitterly criticised their action and now demanded that they fully cooperate with him and help him to reach some kind of a compromise with Salomon. This assumption is based on the sentence of the chronicler who says that "episcopi vero *letas* [italics mine] Deo gratias agerunt."[71]

It was not the bishops' fault that Salomon failed to respond to the feelers of Géza, and that negotiations between them had bogged down.[72] Whether the bishops themselves participated in those negotiations is not clear; what may be clear, from the letter of Gregory VII to Archbishop Nehemias of Esztergom, dated June 9, 1077,[73] is the fact that after the exchange of letters with Pope Gregory VII in 1075, Géza did not bother to maintain contact with the Roman See.[74] In the June, 1077, writ to the archbishop, the pontiff demanded from Nehemias that he see to it that Ladislas, the younger brother and successor of Géza on the Hungarian throne, partially, at least, during the lifetime of Salomon,[75] establish official relations with the Holy See.[76]

It may be in the nature of politics, though, that the Byzantine court decided to intervene in the Hungaro-papal controversy for temporal reasons of its own. In about 1075, Emperor Michael VII the Dukas sent a diadem to Synadele, the queen of Géza of Hungary and the Byzantine emperor's sister.[77] On one of the enamel plates of this crown there was depicted Géza as "King of Turkia,"[78] as if to point out the semi-official view held by the Byzantine court that, as far as the imperial family was concerned, it regarded the husband of the emperor's sister as the legitimate monarch of Hungary. The gift of the diadem was probably intended to be a house-crown for the queen;[79] and yet, it may have been no coincidence that, about a century later, the enamel plates of this Byzantine diadem were placed on the lower half of the reconstructed Hungarian crown of King Saint Stephen during the reign of Béla III of Hungary (1172-96), who also had a Byzantine queen and maintained a keen interest in Byzantine politics.[80]

CHAPTER VI

LADISLAS THE SAINT

---

1. How To Win the Approval of the Holy See—and Lose It

Qumavis peccator existam, quum cura terrene dignitatis absque grauissimis non potest promoveri criminibus.

King Ladislas to the Abbot
of Montecassino

Géza died on April 15, 1077,[1] after he failed to restore contact with Salomon. He was regarded as a good Catholic, humble before God and truly a Christian prince. Who was buried in the church at Vác[2] which he built to honor the Mother of God.[3]

When the Hungarian nobles learned that Géza was dead, they gathered in a multitude at the court of Ladislas and had him, *communi consensu,* elected regent,[4] and forced Ladislas to accept the election.[5] There are two expressions used in the statement made by the chronicler that call for attention. First, his description of the gathering as a "universa multitudo nobilium," seems to be a repetition of the phrase used by the compiler of the Laws of Lewis the Great of Hungary in 1351.[6] Second, the nobles had not elected a king, but a regent: "ad suscipiendum regni gubernaculum concorditer elegerunt;"[7] Hartvic speaks of Ladislas as the administrator of the Hungarian Christian republic,[8] and Gregory VII writes to Nehemias of Esztergom that the hierarchy did partitipate in the election of Ladislas, creating the impression that although the nobles knew that Géza received no reply from Salomon to his petitions for peace, the nobility did not wish to weaken relations with the curia by electing

Géza's younger brother king at a time when the legitimate monarch was still alive.[9] The chronicler praises Ladislas as regent: Ladislas, the Catholic was regarded as rich in virtues and filled with divine grace and love.[10] Ladislas tolerated no contradiction. Elected against his will, he had not placed the crown of King Stephen upon his head.[11] He wanted peace to return the realm to Salomon, and to regain for himself the duchy, his princely-one-third.[12] He became regent by God's grace and wished to act accordingly,[13] because he knew that, as a ruler, he did not govern but was being governed by a higher authority. A pious successful regent he was, who enlarged the territory of his country, the Hungarian republic.[14] He attached, *iure perpetuo,* Dalmatia and Croatia to Hungary on grounds that his sister was the wife of Zolomer (Zwoinimir), the last king of Croatia,[15] and he had to defend his sister from the enemies of her dead husband. By royal prerogative, he occupied Croatia and claimed the inheritance of his sister's dead husband, who had no children.[16]

Members of the Hungarian hierarchy attempted to arrange for peace between Salomon and Ladislas; Ladislas knew how stubborn Salomon was. Ladislas reached an agreement with Salomon during the fourth year of his regency and granted the king a yearly stipend to provide for the maintenance of his court.[17] The nobles and the bishops, if the term *optimates* means both, as it should, kept a close eye upon the arrangement Ladislas had worked out with Salomon, while they actually prevented Salomon from gaining possession of the realm.[18] Salomon, mistrusting Ladislas, formed a conspiracy against him. The regent, becoming informed about the conspiracy, had Salomon arrested and placed into the Tower of Visegrád.[19] Ladislas knew that Salomon was still regarded as the ruler, even though the legitimacy of his position remained questionable. By fleeing from the battle of Mogyoród, Salomon had surrendered his responsibiliteis as a monarch even if he did not leave the territory of the realm.[20] It may be said with some cynicism that Ladislas only pretended to make peace with Salomon in order to convince the *optimates* that he was forced to reach an agreement with an irresponsible person, unfit to be, or to remain, king. And yet, it may speak well for Ladislas that he had ordered another person, Bados, the son of Bakon, to keep the king company in prison. Ladislas is to have prayed for the king.[21] The regent seemed to be quite eager to return the government of the country to a sane and responsible Salomon.[22]

The continued imprisonment of Salomon by Ladislas hurt the latter's political prestige at home and abroad. The uncompromising Pope Gregory VII expected and received unconditional submission from the Hungarian regent.[23] In fact, Ladislas undertook a surprising step: he rendered military service and aid to Rudolph, the German anti-king and ally of the pontiff against Henry IV.[24] In 1078, Ladislas concluded an alliance with Rudolph of Rheinfeld, the opponent of Henry IV, and married Rudolph's daughter, Adelhaid.[25] Ladislas promised his father-in-law that, out of respect to the Lord and Saint Peter, he would lead an army to aid him against the German king.[26] Gregory VII expected him to protect the Bavarian nobles who, because of their loyalty to Rome, were suffering persecution at the hands of the German court.[27] Consequently, Ladislas provided aid to both the Bavarian nobles and to Leopold of Austria.[28] In turn, as was to be expected, the Holy See permitted the canonization of the first Hungarian saints in 1083.[29]

Hartvic reports that the body of King Stephen could not be moved from its grave even after the customary three days of fasting, because of the feud that existed between Ladislas and Salomon.[30] Only when Salomon had been released from the Tower of Visegrád could the process of canonization take its course.[31] Ladislas ordered the release of Salomon after a *colloquium* with the bishops, nobles and wise men of the country.[32] On grounds that the author of this portion of the *Chronicon pictum* was the Historian-Of-Stephen-III (1162-72),[33] the terminology of "colloquium habere" seems to be predating the usage of the term in early thirteenth century English documents.[34] Salomon remained for a few days with Ladislas, and then fled to the Cuman leader Kutesk, whom he persuaded to lead an army against Ladislas. In return for his services, Salomon promised Kutesk, *iure proprietario,* the territory of Transylvania, and that he, Salomon, would marry Kutesk's daughter. It is understandable why Kutesk "inani spe reductus," invaded Hungary, though in doing so he suffered defeat at the hands of Ladislas.[35] Salomon fled the country with Kutesk, ordered an invasion of the Byzantine-Bulgarian territory south of the Danube, and was defeated again. Thereupon, Salomon disappeared from sight,[36] but some time later was seen briefly at the court of Coloman the Learned of Hungary (1095-1116), when he left to become a wandering hermit.[37] He died at Pola, Istria; his wife and his mother were buried at Admont.[38]

Salomon caused much unnecessary bloodshed and turmoil in the realm and was unfit to be king. As a person, he lacked character and was ready for any compromise. By his irresponsible behavior, he delayed progress in the realm for several decades and caused an almost total breakdown of law and order in the realm. The law codes promulgated by Ladislas may serve as proof of the fact that domestic conditions had deteriorated to a point of no return during the civil wars between Salomon and the princes. Perhaps Andrew I could be blamed for the succession of his incompetent son to the throne at a time when it was the king's younger brother, and not the king's son who inherited the crown, on grounds that Andrew I used the coronation of his son as a political bait to reach an understanding with and to gain diplomatic recognition from the German court of the time. However, one may blame the nobles and the bishops, too, who had for so long tolerated the behavior of Salomon. It might not have been in vain that Pope Gregory VII warned Ladislas that Rome expected him to pay respsects to the Holy See, a vassal paying feudal dues to his overlord, and to take good care of the widows, orphans, the poor and the pilgrims among his people to protect the Church[39] and to keep the promises Ladislas had made in his oath.[40]

Early in his reign, Ladislas issued law codes, which were enacted at the *conuentus* of the *optimates;* i.e., the nobles and the hierarchy of the realm.[41] The new codes were designed to improve law and order. The *optimates* legislated on questions of ecclesiastical and temporal in nature and enacted Draconic measures against theft in the realm. It was stated that anyone who stole anything worth more than the price of a chicken, was to be hanged.[42] The relatives of the accused individual were not permitted to hide him from the law. The suspect could only find refuge in a church.[43] From the resolution of this article, a double conclusion should be drawn. First, conditions in the realm were bad indeed; second, this particular piece of legislation had been enacted by the nobles and the upper clergy who did not exempt themselves from being under this law. In other words, and this is important, the lawmakers stressed the ides of equality before the law.[44] It was not the King, but a body of legislators: *optimates* gathered in a legislative *conuentus,* who enacted this decree. The legislators also decreed that students who were in minor clerical orders, and who were accused and found guilty of minor crimes, were to be beaten with a rod the first time they commited a minor crime.

In the Hungarian society of the late 1070s, the social status of an individual carried certain obligations with it. At this time, the social structure comprised the strata of nobles, free men and freedmen, serfs and/or slaves. If a noble became a thief and, although he escaped from the law, failed to surrender himself to the proper authorities, lost all of his possessions. Members of the noble's family had to pay compensation for the damage the noble caused.[45] One is reminded here of the severity of the Code of Hammurabi. Members of the lesser political-social stratum: free-men, likewise had strict obligations concerning theft.[46] For instance, the law codes of King Stephen ordered the death penalty for any free man,[47] or woman[48] found guilty of theft for the third time. The law-givers of the late 1070s decided to make the first instance of theft of anything that was more valuable than a chicken punishable by death for the thief and enslavement for the children of the thief, who were to lose all of their father's possessions. If, however, a free person stole anything valued at ten *denarii* or less he was only to restore twelfthfold, "duo-decies," the value of the stolen article, and to provide in addition, an ox to the plaintiff.[49]

The third social stratum of servants was given an equally severe punishment concerning theft. If the accused servant was guilty of theft, he was to be hanged; however, if his theft involved something valued at ten *denarii* or less, the thief had to restore the value of the stolen article two-fold to the plaintiff and would have his nose cut-off as a punishment.[50] If the guilty servant were a fugitive from his master, he was to be blinded, so that he could not see and he would have to tell his master what he had done and what he had stolen.[51]

The entire community was held responsible for the maintenance of law and order; it was expected to turn the thief in to the King's itinerant justice when the latter arrived on his rounds of the region.[52] It was held in favor of the individual accused of theft if a relative were the informer.[53] The legislators were expected to provide guidelines for the maintenance of law and order, and to give direction to the royal steward (reeve) in charge of border security to observe the export of cattle and horses across the border.[54] Foreign merchants were ordered to purchase animals only in the presence of the royal reeve and with the written permission of the King in hand.[55] The fact that the legislators insisted that the accused be given a fair court trial,[56] may prove the confidence they placed in judges.[57] The legislators of 1078 also insisted that their decrees be observed at the regional and country markets;[58] merchandise of great value could be purchased or sold only in the presence of witnesses.[59] Only the King could permit the sale of livestock abroad.[60] Since theft had become an ugly past-time at all social levels in the country, the legislators ordered that it be punished at all social levels, and ordered that judges who were found either lenient or too stern with thieves, be punished along with the individuals accused of theft.[61] In contrast with previous legislation, however, the legislators of 1078 ordered more lenient punishment of those who were found guilty of disturbing public peace by unsheathing their swords in public, or by intruding into someone else's home.[62] In the latter instance, the law called for a fine of 55 Byzantine *pensae,* plus the loss of two-thirds of the defendant's chattel to the plaintiff, or to the family of the plaintiff, for anyone found guilty. If the defendant had accomplices, and if they happened to be free men, the accomplices were to redeem themselves by a payment of 55 *byzantii* (Byzantine *pensae*) each; the accompanying servants of the defendant were to share in their master's punishment.[63]

In 1083, in connection with the canonization of the first Hungarian saints,[64] a second legislative assembly was held during the reign of Ladislas.[65] The decrees of this legislation survive only in fragments.[66] The tone of the legislation[67] shows a degree of improvement of conditions in the realm; for example, a thief would not be hanged, but would be sold for the theft he committed.[68] Various decrees of this assembly dealt with servants who were apprehended as thieves.[69] Some of the articles defined the office and functions of the King's justice, *nuncius regis,* to prove that the monarch's itinerant justice was his representative in the field of law and order, and his duties were clearly prescribed by law.[70] Various articles dealt with the method of seeking out thieves, and provided instruction as to what to do when a thief was captured.[71] Some articles spoke of servants who fled their masters;[72] an article described the *joccerydech,* i.e., individuals who formed the "freed" element of the Hungarian society of the 1080s.[73] Some decrees referred to the functions of the *euri; eures, cives,* members of military garrisons in the royal forts,[74] and ordered that the *usucapciones* (chattel acquisitioned by long use) be returned by the new (recent) masters to the previous owner even after a prolonged absence of twenty-five years. The return was to be made at the annual field day of the nobility and of all freemen, held on the feast day of King Stephen.[75]

The fugitive servant—fugitive because of theft and unable of finding employment elsewhere—must return to his previous master.[76] The law implied that members of the ruling element would hire runaway servants thereby increasing their political influence and strength. The law now sought to put an end to such an abuse. On the other hand, was it necessary, one may ask, for a *civis* to flee his place of duty? Had perhaps the *civis* concerned permitted the export of meat animals to a foreign country without the required written approval of the royal court? Or, did he allow a larger than approved number of animals to be taken out of the realm, enriching himself in the process?[77] Stolen goods and captured runaway servants were to be retained in the royal forts, for the reason that the regional royal reeve was in a far better position to keep an eye on happenings in his county than the royal court.[78]

The legislators of this session determined the *status-quo* of the itinerant royal justice. He was expected to obtain the report of the assembled officials of the *civitates* (*civitas*: fortified place; fort and/or town), the inhabitants of which were known as *ewri*.[79] The legislators determined the position of the Justiciar: *Nádor*,[80] and the jursidiction of the county-judge: *iudex in parochia sua*.[81] Terms such as *ewri; decurion[e]s*, and *civitates* may have denoted royal fortifications; officials and members of the garrisons of these fortifications evidently came under special royal jurisdiction. The similarity between the provisions called for by the legislature to protect the interests of the king's itinerant justices, and the provisions called for by the legislature of the English king, Henry II (1154-89), are striking indeed.[82] It may be said that the Hungarian legislators established the jurisdiction of common law in the county courts of the realm.[83] The royal county judges, all of whom were royal appointees, administered the king's law, not unlike the itinerant justices [in the eyre] of the English monarch, Henry II.[84] The domestic situation in Hungary was, must have been, still far from being settled, however; the legislators called, for instance, for the punishment of false judges, or judges who delayed to take action on the case assigned to them. All proceedings were to be conducted in writing. The defendant of a case was invited by writ, issued by the itinerant justice, to attend court.[86] If the defendant was found guilty of the charge brought against him, he could appeal his sentence. The judges were instructed to be knowledgeable about the law, and conscientious in their handling of legal matters and court cases.[87] In some instances, such as unsheathing the sword in public; breaking into somebody's home, etc., the judge could enter the case only after a writ had been issued and the accused invited to appear before the court.[88] The court system may have been primitive in the 1080s, but, for the first time since the days of King Stephen, the state was required to bring legal matters in the realm up to date; to make the law work.

The legal reforms of Ladislas formed the background of the canonization procedures of the first Hungarian saints in 1083. The canonization took place only after law and order were restored in the realm, and was performed in the presence of the papal legate specially dispatched for the occasion.[89] It must have been a part of the legate's mission to survey the Hungarian domestic scene of the early 1080s. The *vitae* of King Stephen, of Bishop Gerard, and of Prince Emery were prepared to provide written evidence for the "translation" of the bodies of the three individuals to be canonized.[90] It is from the written material authorizing the "elevation" and "translation" of the remains of the body of King Stephen that, for example, the compiler of Stephen's *Vita maior* obtained information for his narrative report.

It is characteristic feature of these "lives," however, that their compiler-authors transposed the historical surveys of their own time: the turbulent and unsettled late 1070s and early 1080s, into the background discussion of the age of King Stephen and Bishop Gerard. The author of Stephen's *Vita maior* made, in fact, the statement that the people of King Stephen's times were children of darkness; the lost sheep of God, who believed in, and followed the insane notions of the sacriligious heathen.[91] One must examine the political-social background of the legislative acts of Ladislas in order to understand the background of the first Hungarian saints because the author-compilers of those "lives" reported, perhaps unintentinally, the conditions of their own times, the 1080s, in their reports on the national Hungarian leaders of the early eleventh century. For this reason alone, it may be unacceptable to say that Pope Gregory VII sought and obtained the political and spiritual alliance of Ladislas and that, consequently, Rome authorized the canonization of the first Hungarian saints; reading the sources, one may conclude a different argument. The sources create the impression that the canonization of the first Hungarian saints occured precisely because the Holy See intended to use the canonizations to improve the religious and political atmosphere in the realm of Ladislas so that the seed of Christianity planted in the early eleventh century may bring good fruit.[92]

It may have been the attitude of the Roman See toward Hungary that caused the German monarch, Henry IV, to invade Hungary in 1080.[93] Henry IV accomplished nothing by his campaign in the realm; and yet, he had in the same year defeated his opponent, Rudolph, whose death enabled Henry IV to take a firm stand toward Rome. Henry attacked the papacy. Although the Norman allies of Pope Gregory expelled the invading Germans from Rome, the furious Roman population forced the pointiff to flee Rome for his life; he died in exile in May, 1085.[94] The German court now sought an alliance with Ladislas in spite of the fact that Ladislas did not recognize the anti-pope, Clement III, created by Henry IV. Ladislas acknowledged only Pope Victor III, the former abbot of Montecassino, as the legitimate successor to Gregory VII; his delegates dispatched to attend the gathering of the German princes at Speyer in August, 1087, did in fact promise active military aid: 20,000 troops, for the cause of Victor III.[95]

A German chronicler who tells of the behavior of the Hungarian delegates at the assembly of Speyer, 1087, and uses expressions such as "legitimate pope," "schismatic," etc., in his statement that the Hungarian delegation in Speyer behaved with courage and dignity.[96] On the other hand, it seems to be more than likely that the preoccupation of Henry IV with papal matters enabled Ladislas to occupy Slavonia, which once formed a part of the German district of administration of Carinthia.[97] It is a strange coincidence, however, that the *Chronicon pictum* did not mention the occupation of Slovenia,[98] though its author-compiler did mention, early in the reign of Ladislas, the conquest of Dalmatia and Slavonia—in that order—by Ladislas. The omission may have been due to a problem of geography. Slovenia, located between the Drave and Save rivers, was on the left hand side of the Save; by conquering it at first, Ladislas established, in Slovenia, a direct border with Croatia.[99]

The report by the *Chronicon pictum* that Ladislas first captured Dalmatia and then only did he take Croatia, seems to be contradicted by the fact of geography that Ladislas had to occupy Croatia first. However, the reasoning of the chronicler that Zwoinimir was married to a daughter of Béla I of Hungary (and thus to a sister, or the sister of Ladislas), and died without a male heir; and that the widowed queen suffered a good deal of harrassment at the hands of her dead husband's enemies, is, as supported by various sources, acceptable.[100] Zwoinimir died in 1089 and directly after him the Tirpimer, Stephen II, occupied the throne of Croatia. The Tirpimer was the last scion of his family and had to be summoned from a monastery to accept the crown of the realm.[101] The Hungarian chronicler says only that Ladislas conquered Croatia and Dalmatia[102]—here, on the second mentioning of the double event the chronicler records a different and correct procedure,—and placed the conquered area under his administration.[103] Ladislas is reported to have acted out of compassion for his distressed sister; however, Ladislas was said to be the only heir to the throne of Croatia.[104]

There is no further evidence of any contact between Rome and the Hungarian court, perhaps on account of the difficult political and military situation of the papacy in the late 1080s.[105] However, it is evident from the tone and contents of the charter issued by Ladislas for the abbey of Somogyvár in 1091,[106] that he now began to emphasize his royal prerogative in ecclesiastical situations which he had established. In 1096 it was learned that the German monarch, Henry IV, planned to restore relations with Hungary. This decision was probably prompted by Ladislas' occupation of Croatia, which in Bálint Hóman's view caused a rift between Hungary and the Holy See.[108] The opinion of Vilmos Fraknói that Cardinal Teuzo, the papal legate who signed, among others, the charter of the Somogyvár abbey, had been dispatched by Rome to prevent the fulfillment of the negotiations between the two courts, cannot be proven on grounds of a lonely signature.[109] Only Berthold's *Chronicon* reports, anno 1092,[110] that Duke Welf [IV] of Bavaria prevented a Christmas meeting arranged for the German and Hungarian monarchs. Fraknói published the text of a letter of Ladislas addressed to Abbot Oderisios of Montecassino in which the King acknowledged his politicking against Rome: "quamvis peccator existam, quum cura terrene dignitatis absque grauissimis non potest promoveri criminibus" (Sinner I am because I find it not possible to promote the cause of earthly dignities [offices] without committing grave sins.)[111]

The Hungarian intervention in Croatia-Dalmatia disturbed the political interests of the Byzantine court in that the Byzantines considered the

area in their sphere of interest.[112] The *Chronicon pictum* reports that
the Cumans led by Krul, the son of Kapolcs, invaded Hungary exactly
at a time when Ladislas was preoccupied with the conquest of Slavonia.
Krul caused heavy destruction in Transylvania and in Bihar county;
crossed the Tisza river at Tokaj and continued to press westward with
his troops now divided into three corps. Two of the corps continued their
"fire and sword" policy west of the Tisza; one stayed behind in reserve.
Ladislas attacked the unsuspecting Cumans, who by that time were leaving
the realm with their rich booty of people and chattel, and defeated them.
He had the Cuman leaders executed, but spared the lives of the common
fighting men, whom he resettled in Hungary, in the area which they had
just devastated. In a follow-up second battle Ladislas also destroyed the
Cuman reserves led by Cuman prince Ákos.[113] Cumans were living in
Hungary from Tokaj in the east to Komárom in the west;[114] in Komárom,
two-thirds of the Cumans, or Cuman descendants, served as garrison troops
and lived with their families in the fortified areas. One-third of the Cumans
in Komárom were the personal retainers of the regional reeve.[115] These
Cumans, Anonymus says, may be identified with the descendants of the
Cumans who were captured and settled in Hungary by Ladislas in the
1080s, and with the Polovcians mentioned in the Russian Chronicle. The
Polovcians were constantly at war with their neighbors in the neighbor-
hood of Kiev.[116] Kiev was in the orbit of Byzantine influence. The Cumans led by Krut attacked Hungary under the direct command of the
Russian Kiev court, and Ladislas had no alternative but to invade Russian
territory. It has been said that the attackers came from the Byzantine
area south of the Carpathians and north of the Danube, under the guid-
ance of the Byzantine court.[117] Byzantium regarded Croatia as its shpere
of political interest, and took advantage of the involvement of Ladislas
in Slavonia at the time when the Cuman attack against Hungary occured;
the Byzantine court ordered the invasion by the Cumans of Hungarian
territory in order to prevent Ladislas from occupying Slavonia, seems
most likely. However, it is only an impression. The chronicler says that
when the "Russians" realized that Ladislas became serious about invading
Kiev, they, the Russians, decided not to fight Ladislas, but to make
peace with him instead.[118]

   The *Chronicon pictum* says that Ladislas had also invaded Poland,
laid siege to Cracow; defeated the Poles and took Cracow after its garrison

ran out of food supplies, at a time when the Hungarian besiegers, too, were short of food. Cracow surrendered, and Ladislas dictated the terms of the treaty.[119] From Poland, the king went to Bohemia, and soon left Bohemia with many Czech prisoners of war.[120] After three campaigns, Russian, Polish and Bohemian, he returned home and built a cathedral at Várad to give thanks to God for his victories.[122]

The Russian sources give no information about the "Russian" campaigns of Ladislas. The Russian chronicler mentions the siege by Coloman the Learned of Hungary (1095-1116) of Premysl, and reports that two bishops accompanied King Coloman on his expedition.[122] The Hungarian king lost the campaign, and one of his bishops, Koppány by name, died during the campaign.[123] The Polish annalist reports on the 1090 Hungarian-Polish relations differently.[124] Ladislas entered Polish territory only because of an invitation he received from Count Hermann Vladislas. The count asked the Hungarian monarch for aid in order to free his palatine Siecieh from captivity in Cracow.[125] The Polish monarch, Boleslav III, was angry with the archbishop of Cracow and had him beheaded. Fearing excommunication by the Church, Boleslav III fled to Hungary, where he behaved in a snobbish manner toward Ladislas who, nevertheless, treated him kindly. Ladislas also provided for the upbringing of Boleslav's children.[126] When Boleslav III died seemingly in exile, Count Hermann, who was Boleslav's younger brother, made sure that Miesko, Boleslav III's son and his, Hermann's, nephew, inherited the Polish crown; Count Hermann then married the widow of the Hungarian king Salomon.[127]

The Czech chronicler reports on the expedition of Ladislas to Bohemia that in 1086, Prince Wratislav of Bohemia obtained the royal title of King of Bohemia from the German court of Henry IV; whereupon the son of Wratislav, Bretislav by name, fled to the Hungarian court and stayed there for a year; then Bretislav returned to Bohemia.[128] The younger brother of King Wratislav was the bishop of Prague, who visited the court of Ladislas on his way to Rome. The bishop was going to the Holy See to complain about the manner by which Wratislav had separated the new bishopric of Olmütz out of the Prague diocese, without the approval of Rome and without consulting him, the bishop of Prague.[129] The bishop did not go to Rome, however; he died in Esztergom and was buried there.[130]

The reliability of the Hungarian chronicler is weakened by the fact that he placed the death of the "Roman Emperor" Henry IV in 1106, before the death of King Ladislas in 1095, by saying that the German princes and nobles had, upon the death of the Emperor, asked Ladislas of Hungary to be their next emperor.[131] Ladislas was very modest; he did not wish to increase the territory of his country and declined the offer.[132] János Horváth identified the unknown compiler of the *Gesta Ladislai regis* as the possible source of this particular passage in the *Chronicon pictum,* c. 140, without, however, identifying the compiler of the "gesta." Horváth insists that the Hungarian chronicler was not responsible for the errors that appear in the *Chronicon pictum;* the errors were made by a copyist or by persons who evidently attempted to interpret the material without really understanding its contents.[133]

The Hungarian chronicler reports that Ladislas celebrated Easter, 1095, at Bodrog, where he received ambassadors from the French, Spanish, English courts and from Brettany, who had asked him, through the interpretation of Prince William, the younger brother of the king of France, to be their leader to the Holy Land.[134] Ladislas agreed to their request, and asked Conrad of Bohemia to go with him on the crusade. However, Svatopluk, a relative of Conrad and of the bishop of Prague, had captured the city of Prague and made himself ruler of Bohemia. It was now Conrad who requested aid from Ladislas against Svatopluk.

Ladislas went to help Conrad and took his two nephews, Coloman, the future king, Coloman the Learned, and Álmos, on the campaign he did not finish. The Hungarian king fell ill on the Czech border and died.[135] He was buried at Várad, in the monastery [cathedral] he built, on July 29, 1095.[136]

2. The Synod of Szabolcs, 1092

In ciuitate Szabolch sancta synodus habita est, praesidente Christianissimo Vngarorum rege Ladislao.

Decretum I Ladislai regis

The national ecclesiastical synod of Szabolcs was held after Ladislas conquered Slavonia and had expelled the Cumans from the country. Encouraged by the reforms of popes Gregory VII and Urban II,[1] Ladislas's motives in summoning the synod were (1) to introduce church reforms in Hungary; (2) to settle legal aspects of ecclesiastical property claims and holdings in the realm; (3) to restore order in the outer and inner life of the Church and among the faithful; and (4) to define the order of liturgy and determine the number and identity of religious feasts to be observed in Hungary.[2]

The synod met on May 21, 1092,[3] with the possible approval and participation of the archbishop of Esztergom, whose name, however, is not mentioned in the record.[4] The participants of the synod comprised the entire hierarchy of bishops and abbots; the nobles and representatives of the lower clergy and the people, meeting under the presidency of King Ladislas.[5] This synod definitely differed in nature and composition from the assembly of "omnes nos regni Pannoniae optimates" (of all of us, the [best qualified] rulers of the realm of Pannonia [=Hungary]) gathered as a *conuentus* at Pannonhalma in 1078;[6] those assemblymen: *optimates,* might have included the nobility and upper clergy in their ranks and enacted legislation on ecclesiastical matters taken from the secular point of view.[7]

Archbishop Seraphim was appointed to the see of Esztergom only two or three years later.[8] The synod was not the annual field-day of the nobles, bishops and all free men of the realm. The monarch summoned it as a purely ecclesiastical gathering: "synodus sancta habita est" ([a] holy synod was held . . .); its decrees were agreed upon *canonice,* in a formal and canonical manner by all of its participants.[9]

The decrees of Szabolcs deal with the administrative and spiritual aspects of ecclesiastical life; as, for instance, the lives of the clergy and the faithful; with questions pertinent to the order and the liturgy of the Mass and other religions services; with personal conduct between Christians and non-Christians and with problems that may arise out of those relations. The synodal decrees warn the bishops of the need for the annual or semi-annual visitation of monasteries in their particular dioceses.[10] The synod rules that when a bishop, or the monarch himself, paid a visit to a monastery, the abbot and monks of the community were expected to await the visitor in front of the monastic church building and there to exchange the kiss of peace with their distinguished visitor.[11] The synod participants sought solutions to the ever presistent pagan cults of the witchcraft and witches in the Christian realm. Through the synod King Ladislas had completed the organization of the Church that had been established by King Saint Stephen.

Ladislas retained the administrative structure dating back to the days of the Church in Hungary under King St. Stephen, thus, if the inhabitants of a village community migrated elsewhere, the synodical decrees instructed the local ordinary to request aid from the county reeve to force those inhabitants to return to their former habitat.[12] The synod ordered the abbots to pay tithe to the bishop out of the income they received from the tenants of their monastic landholdings,[13] and it was decreed that any grant of land once made to the Church had to be handed over to ecclesiastical authorities. If the donor were to change his mind, the bishop was entitled to use legal force to remind the donor of his promise.[14]

Donations made to the Church or to a church were regarded as irrevocable, and if a priest had appropriated any church property, he had to repay it threefold.[15] The freemen stratum, an early form of the Third Estate in Hungary, too, had to pay tithe to the bishop, and the bishop in turn had to share income derived from this tithe with his clergy.[16] Church buildings destroyed in time of war, or by revolution, had to be rebuilt by the members of the parish, and the monarch during the reconstruction process was expected to donate a chalice and vestments to the parish church, while the bishop provided to the parish a priest and the necessary books for church services.[17] It was an additional duty for the bishop to rebuild or to renovate old churches.[18]

The development of the ecclesiastical administrative system in the realm must have reached its completion with the definition by the synod of the church calendar to be used in Hungary.[19] The calendar promulgated by the synod was identical with the one maintained by the universal Church, except that it included the feasts of the Hungarian saints.[20] The synodical articles decree that all faithful were to attend church service on Sundays and holidays of obligation. If the village was located too far from a church, the community was obliged to send one representative with a stick, three loaves of bread and a candle, to church.[21] The loaves of bread and the candle were offerings to be placed upon the altar;[22] this particular decree was identical in context with the ordinance of the 1078 Roman synod that says that every participant at Mass should bring with him to church some donation for Christ.[23] The stick mentioned served some specific purpose in the church services, if no more than that it was used to lean upon during church service after a long walk,[24] since benches or seats were not in use in Hun-garian churches during the 1090s. All business activity and manual work were forbidden on Sundays and holidays,[25] even to the exclusion of hunting.[26] Fasting and the keeping of ember days was encouraged;[27] lent began on Quinqugesima Sunday in late eleventh century Hungary.[28]

Paganism and the practice of pagan rites were strictly punished.[29] Individuals who failed to render a Christian burial to the dead were punished or taken to account because of their negligence; or, more than likely, because they may have secretly belonged to a group of pagan cults. The lord of the manor was obliged to provide a church funeral of any of his deceased servants or serfs; and the village elders had to assure a church funeral to the poor of the community and to migrants who lived in the community at the time of their death.[30]

Jews were not to be persecuted; however, the synod discouraged Christian-Jewish association. No Jew could marry a Christian; no Jew could keep a Christian slave or servant.[31] The synod would not allow the Jews to work on Sundays or holidays; and if a Jew breached the law, he had to surrender to the authorities the very tool he was working with.[32] On the other hand, the syond encouraged the Ismaelites to convert to Christianity,[33] with the understanding, however, that converts who dared to leave the Church would be forced by law to move out of the village community.[34] Visiting clergy were to be treated with suspicion by the diocesan bishop; a clergyman-in-transit was required to possess a letter of recommendation from his bishop or religious superior, though the bishop of the host diocese could still turn down such a letter of recommendation.[35] If the bishop, having decided to accept the letter of recommendation, welcomed the visiting cleric, the latter was not allowed to leave the host diocese without the permission of the ordinary.[36] The local ordinarius was held responsible for the behavior, education, and vocational training of his clergy; a visiting cleric was permitted to say Mass in a tent, if a tent were available. If not, he had to say Mass in a church.[37]

Clerical marriage was permitted if the priest were married for the first time; in this respect, the synod did not attempt to downgrade the directives of Rome concerning clerical marriages and celibacy.[38] Rather, it attempted to temper papal directives to specific Hungarian conditions. After decades of civil war there were very few priests available in the country; and yet, a priest married for a second time, or married to a widow for the first time, had to leave his wife or his church prebend, and to perform specific ecclesiastical penance.[39] The synod specially stated that priests in their first marriages were to remain married until Rome decided to the contrary.[40] If a priest married a slave girl, or took a maid or a slave girl for his mistress, he was to sell her and to give the money to the bishop.[41] The bishops were to enforce clerical discipline, and should they permit their clerics to live in scandalous marriages, the other bishops, or the monarch himself, was to intervene and punish the bishops in accordance with the canons of the Church.[42]

An individual who had found his wife guilty of adultery, could kill her, and marry again; however, if the relatives of the unfaithful and now murdered wife raised questions about the marriage, they could do so freely in front of a judge.[43] On the other hand, if an individual found his wife guilty of adultery and she admitted her guilt before a judge and promised to mend her manners, and to do penance in accordance with the canons of the Church, and yet her husband decided not to take her back, neither she could marry again.[44]

The bishop was held responsible for the persecution of witches and prostitutes;[45] he also presided over ordeals with witnesses present.[46] The synod would punish by death the rape of a maiden or of a woman.[47] If someone forced his way into another's home or drew his sword in public to injure or kill another for having entered his house, the synod

would punish him.[48] Evidently, forced entries into homes had still occurred because of women.[49] In 1092, the insult was not taken lightly,
and was punished accordingly.

Finally, the synod placed special emphasis upon the need for public
support of law courts. If an individual who was cited to appear before a
tribunal failed to do so, he was to be punished for disobedience of the
King's law.[50] Judged by the tone and provisions of the Synod of Szabolcs,
conditions in Hungary were far from satisfactory as yet in 1092. Through
the synod, Ladislas made every effort to improve those conditions toward
the end of his reign and in the interests of the commonwealth. It is evident
from the perviously-cited writ of Pope Urban II to Coloman the Learned,
nephew of Ladislas and his successor, that the new king, Coloman, was
prevailed upon by the Holy See to restore working relations with Rome.[51]
Coloman must have complied with the wish of the pontiff because in one
of his letters addressed to the abbot of Flavigny, Pope Paschalis II used
the kindest language to describe the reign and the memory of King
Ladislas.[52]

APPENDIX

AUTHORSHIP AND STATUS OF THE LAWS AND ADMONITIONS OF KING STEPHEN

Cum episcopis et primatibus Hungarie statutum a se manifestum decretum facit, in quo scilicet uniuscuiusque culpe contrarium dictavit antidotum.

Hartvic's *Vita s. Stephani regis*

St. L. Endlicher, a nineteenth century research scholar of the Hungarian Middle Ages (*Die Gesetze des hl. Stefan: ein Beitrag zur ungarischen Rechtsgeschichte* [Vienna, 1849]), made the remark that the first Hungarian monarch as a lawgiver was a true son of his age. Although aware of the meaning of hallowed traditional customs among the Magyars, King Stephen enacted law for his kingdom so as to unite, to fuse into one people the Magyars and the conquered non-Magyar social element, to form thereby a solid basis for historical development.

The Hungarian king did not stand alone in this respect; his contemporaries on the royal thrones of Europe were acting likewise. And yet, there was a real distinction between the legal actions of Stephen and those of Canute the Great of Denmark-England, Edward the Confessor, after the times of Stephen, or even a Henry I of France. These kings "legislated" on behalf of the Church in their particular kingdoms, but left the tradition of their peoples alone, while Stephen of Hungary made law (*nostrae statuimus genti*) for the Church in Hungary, in order to repay his political debts to the ecclesiastics, and to prevent the hierarchy's making Hungary, the infant kingdom, a Roman theocracy. Such an attitude is evident from both the text of the legal statutes and Hartvic's biography of King Stephen.

It is, therefore, a curious circumstance that Stephen's laws failed to survive *in toto*. The Admont MS 712, ff. 119-26, the mid-twelfth century codes that carries the laws, is the earliest version available to the student, while the second earliest variation of these laws is in the mid-fifteenth century Vienna MS 3662, ff. 98-105', now the Thuróczy-codex of the Széchenyi Library of the Hungarian National Museum, clme 407, ff. 75-79' a source which contained some additional material, six extra articles of the laws.

Of course, the problems which surrounded the survival of MSS in the Middle Ages must be considered. In Hungary in particular wars, especially the Tartar invasion of 1241-42, caused unspeakable damage to the monastic scriptoria and sacristies of the cathedral churches, not to mention the royal archives, while the late eleventh century burning of the papal depository where the correspondence with eastern European, including Hungarian, ruling courts were kept, added heavily to the painful damage.

On the other hand, it seems surprising that nothing remained of the correspondence between the Hungarian and western European royal courts, if not in Hungary proper, then at least in the West. Still, it was in the West, in the libraries of monastic houses mostly, that the MSS pertaining to the early Hungarian Middle Ages survived, though in part only, and form today a portion of the source material of Hungarian history of the Árpádian age, from the tenth through the thirteenth centuries.

The laws of Stephen also survived in a western religious house. There is no doubt that the Admont MS, or rather the few leaves that formed a part of the codex, is only a copy of an earlier work, and an incomplete transcript at that. Still, it is, to this day, the earliest source evidence of the legislative actions of the first Hungarian monarch. The chroniclers only referred to this legislative activity of the king. Thus, for instance, from Hartvic, c. 10, we know the approximate timing of the first royal legislation in Hungary. The annalists, however, provided no description of the contents of the legislation at the court.

The different editions of the text present further problems; for example, the first thirty-five articles in the Admont MS, reproduced in print by Henrik Marczali, correspond to only thirty-three articles in the Migne reprint, which is based on the *ASS* edition prepared by the learned Jesuit J. Stilting. There is art. 3 in Migne (*PL*, 151, col. 1246a) that

corresponds to art. I: 3 *and* 4 in the Admont MS; art. I:14 forms two
decrees, art. 16 and 13 (in that order) in Migne with the sentence, "si
alicuius servus servum alterius occiderit, reddatur servus pro servo aut
redimatur, et penitentiam, guod dictum est, agat," missing from the
Migne edition. Art. I:16 (Admont) is not in Migne, nor is art. I:21; L.
Erdelyi maintained that these decrees were left out of the Codex because
they carry information available in other decrees, which may be the case.
Thus, for example, the information covered by art. I:16 might be substituted by art. I:35 (Migne, c. 33), or by art. II:15 (Migne, c. 49), though
not in the Admont MS. Or, art. I:21 could be substituted by art. I:23
and 24 (cc. 21-22). Art. II:6 (Admont) breaks down into two decrees,
39 and 40 in Migne; articles II:14 through 19 (cc. 48-53) in the Thuroczy-
codex were omitted by the Admont scribe; therefore, art. II:13: *De
debilitatione membrorum* in the Admont MS is followed by a decree on
Adulatoribus, a decree numbered as art. II:20 in the Thuroczy MS, and
c. 54 in Migne.

The result is that in the study of Stephen's legislation, the historian
is confronted with a threefold problem. First, there is the lack of a complete text of the Stephanic laws. This is a problem because, judging by the
record, it is certain that Stephen did legislate, whether alone or together
with his Council, on several occasions during his reign. Second, it is difficult to distinguish the legislative role of the king from that of the already
mentioned *senatus regalis* or greater council. Finally, what is meant by
legislature or the enactment of legal statues in general is not easily determined. After all, the Middle Ages hardly knew of the enactment of laws in
the modern sense of the term, and as Dr. Fritz Kern has pointed out in his
masterful essay, "Recht und Verfassung im Mittelalter," *Historische
Zeitschrift,* 120 (1919), lff., not to mention the Hungarian Henrik Marczali,
"A kozepkori elmelet a kiralysagrol (Medieval theories about kingship),"
Budapesti Szemle, 65 (1891), 367ff., the medieval period knew only of
established customs, *consuetudines,* hallowed traditions in a people's
history. To quote Kern, "Recht ist alt und gut; das gute alte Recht is
ungesetzt und ungeschrieben," unwritten, oral tradition, whose "good-
ness" had been proven by constant usage through the centuries. Medieval
law, in short, was built on customs.

The twelfth century Hungarian chronicler, Anonymus, had proven that
the Hungarians, too, had and cultivated their traditional habits as legal

usages. Although there was what would be an equivalent to the codification of unwritten laws in the realm by the Hungarian court under the reign of the Angevins in the fourteenth, or by Matthias Corvinus in the fifteenth centuries, it was only in the 1500s that Istvan Werboczy succeeded in forming (in Latin) the first real Hungarian law code, *Tripartitum opus iuris incliti regni Hungariae.*

Ad primum: judging by the scant references of the record to the legislative undertaking of kings Stephen, Peter, Aba, and Andrew I, irregular legislation, always caused by some extraordinary event, took place in Hungary during the first six decades of the eleventh century. Of these legislative acts enacted at the meetings only meager remains survived, as, for instance, the skeleton of Andrew I's Ecclesiastical Ordinances of 1047, or the mere recorded fact that King Aba rescinded the previous legal acts of his predecessor, Peter Orseolo. "Habito sinodico concilio, cum communi epsicoporum et principum consilio omnia decreta rescindi statuit, quae Petrus iniuste secundum libitum suum disposuit." As for the code of laws by Stephen, as we have access to it today, only the outline remains; a sketch of the record of various legislative sessions held during the long reign of the first Hungarian king.

This assumption is significant for two reasons. First, since we have access to but one copy of the law collection, we are in no position to establish a critical text of the laws. Consequently, it cannot be determined whether it was the scribe at Admont, or the original compiler of the legal statutes, who was responsible for the Admont version. Second, the fact that the MS survived in an Admont codex means that strong contacts were maintained between the Hungarian court and the non-Hungarian religious community outside of Hungary. That is, the monks at Admont had to be in a good position to render an account, even if a scanty one, of the legal acts of King Stephen. I presume, of course, that the scribe copied his account from somewhere, perhaps from a MS brought by a member of the royal retinue visiting at Admont. (Keza, c. 61; the Chronicle, c. 126; the mother and wife of King Solomon [1063-1074] were both buried at Admont—cr. Chronicle, c. 136 [SSH, I, 181; 397; 411 respectively]; according to Heinrich von Mugeln's Chronicle, c. 47 [ibid., I, 105ff.], a fourteenth century author, King Solomon was by then considered a saint.)

Ad secundum: regardless of the fact that whether it was the Senate or the Council that assisted King Stephen in his activities, the fact remains that it was the king, who decided on legislation (cf. the Preface of the Laws). This circumstance alone shows why the Council (or the Great Council identified in the Laws as the *senatus totius*) strove so eagerly, upon the death of Stephen, to regain power in the realm. (Authority it had exercised in 997, when it approved of Stephen's succession to his father's rule [SSH, II, 407] ; however, Stephen's coronation was performed "presulibus cum clero, comitibus cum populo laudes adclamantibus" only [ibid., II, 414] ; as for the nomination of the Orseolo by Stephen as his successor, it did occure "accersitis episcopis et primis palatii de Christi nomine gloriantibus" [ibid., II, 431], in a flagrant violation of the principles laid down in articles IV and VII of the *Libellus* [ibid., II, 619ff.]).

Ad tertium ultimumque, concerning codification of his legal acts, Stephen may have had no legal expert to do the job for him. The theories of Balint Homan, *Magyar kozepkor* (The Hungarian Middle Ages) (Budapest, 1938), 206ff.; Imre Szentpetery, "Beitrage zur Geschichte des ungarischen Urkundenwesens," *Archiv fur Urkundenforschung,* 16 (1939), 157ff. (or *Regesta,* n. 2); F.L. Csoka, "Szent Istvan torvenyeinek es Intelmeinek szerzosege (The authorship of the laws and Admonitions of King Stephen)," *Vigilia,* 29 (1964), 391ff. (or his *op. cit.,* 58ff.), convincing as they are in this respect, lack hard core historical certainty. It is not known who the legal experts of the king were, if there were any. Stephen must have found someone who was capable of compiling on paper the acts of the legislative sessions. That this person did not codify the acts of every session seems to be evident from the scanty text. Obviously, he was called upon by the king to (a) either summarize, in full, the decrees enacted during his reign, or (b) to compile into a sensible work all of the acts enacted by Stephen and his council.

That the work lacks precision, normal sequence, clear terminology, grouping by subject matter, does not necessarily mean that Gerard of Csanad, the author of the somewhat disorganized *Deliberatio,* acted as the compiler of the laws; although the bishop admitted that he had no time for writing; although there are various parallels between the *Deliberatio* and the laws, there is no sufficient hard-core proof of his authorship of the laws. Likewise, the origins of the *Libellus* of royal instructions to Stephen's heir(s) on the Hungarian throne, create some problems. (Cf. K. Gouth "Egy forras ket tortenelemszemlet tukreben (One source in the light of two interpretations)," *Szazadok,* 76/1942/, 43ff.; A. Nagy Tasnadi, "A Thousand Years of Hungarian Constitution," *Hungarian Quarterly,* 5/1939/, 9ff.). Namely, the author spoke in this "Booklet" as the spiritual father to his spiritual—intellectual protege; such a circumstance may indicate a relationship that could have existed between Gerard and Prince Emery the Chaste, or Gerard, the cleric and native of Venice, and the Venetian born duke, Peter Orseolo, Stephen's actual successor on the throne, but it does not necessarily imply that Gerard was the author of it. The mere fact that he alone was mentioned in some detail by the chroniclers as the literator in the realm (cf. Hartvic, c. 14; Gerard's *Vita minor,* c. 4; *Vita maior,* c. 15; Karacsonyi, *Gellert,* 148ff.), is no sufficient proof on grounds that there were educated monks at Pannonhalma abbey; Maurus, the second bishop of Pecs, or Astric, Stephen's delegate abroad, were educated and well experienced individuals.

On the other hand, the identity of the addressee of the *Libellus* may require some explanation. As Hartvic explained, Prince Emery had been carefully prepared for his role as the country's future king; as a matter of fact, Stephen, feeling old and infirm, planned to withdraw from the care of earthly affairs and to make Emery regent while he, the old king was still alive, and to let Emery reign by himself. (This later statement is not from Hartvic, but from the Chronicle, c. 69). In other words, by 1031, Emery was a grown, mature young prince, ready to take over his father's political inheritance; his needs—religious, intellectual, and political—would have better been served by a more advanced royal "mirror," as, for example, the one by Hincmar of Reims, *De regis persona et de regio ministerio.* Peter Orseolo, though by 1038, he had spent thirteen years at the Hungarian court, still acted in a less trustworthy manner (Gerard's *Vita minor,* c. 5) as far as religion, public morals, and the military were concerned. The king knew of the weaknesses of his nephew, and did his best to correct them. This instance may explain the elementary nature and basic tone of the *Libellus.*

Finally, it must be remembered that even though Gerard of Csanad was not necessarily the author (or compiler) of the laws and the *Libellus,* he alone had the courage to fight King Peter on account of his public misdemeanor. Similarly, Gerard alone (at least on record) possessed the nerve to speak out against King Aba, accusing him to his face of the public murder of nobles, the country's opposition. In my opinion, only someone close to the person and memory of King Stephen, could have had such an insistence on his rights as acting mouthpiece of the public opposition representing the country's interests acting against royal tyranny.

Likewise, judged by the record, only Gerard could have organized a conspiracy agianst the non-Arpad kings because he knew that a non-Arpad had no chance to survive on the throne of Stephen (cf. *SSH*, II, 501; Chronciler, c. 81). Due to the insecure circumstances in 1038, Peter's actual succession merited only a temporary arrangement (no coronation). By 1046, however, when the German court openly interferred in Hungarian politics, no such compromise could be effective, and Peter, the compromised imperial appointee had to go. As Gerard of Csanad saw the problem, the king failed in his duties, and failed to listen to the Council of Elders for they alone spoke for the country's welfare (also, art. IV and VII of the *Libellus*). No king, no matter how omnipotent, was to act against the will of the Council and contrary to the interests of the nation. "Regale ornamentum scio esse maximum antecessores sequi reges et honestos imitari parentes;" cf. *Libellus,* art. VIII (*SSH,* 626); J. Deer, "A szentistvani Intelmek kerdesehez (Some remarks concerning King Stephen's Admonitions)," *Szazadok,* 76 (1942), 435ff.

NOTES

Notes to Introduction

1. The following *stemma* may help to clarify the first paragraph:

* The introduction appeared as a separate article in *Cithara: Essays in Judaeo-Christian Tradition*, 19-1 (1979), 40-49; published here with the permission of the President of St. Bonaventure University.

cf. B. Hóman-Gy. Szekfű, *Magyar Történet* (Hungarian history) (5 vols.; 6th ed.; Budapest, 1939), I, 19ff., although the stemma facing I, 80, is different. B. Hóman, *Geschichte des ungarischen Mittelalters* (2 vols.; Berlin, 1940-43), I, 27ff.; J. Szinnyei, "A magyarság eredete, nyelve és honfoglaláskori műveltsége (Hungarian beginnings; linguistic and cultural background)," *A finn-ugor őshaza nyomában* (In search of Finn-Ugrian country) (Budapest, 1973), 272ff.; J. Perényi, "A Keleten maradt magyarok problémája (Questions concerning the Magyars [Hungarians] who stayed behind in the east)," *Századok*, 109 (1975), 33ff.; A. Bartha, "Nyguat-Szibéria és a magyar őstörténet (Early Hungarians and western-Siberia)," *Archaeológiai Értesitő*, 102 (1975), 284ff.; idem, *Hungarian Society in the 9th and 10th Centuries* (Budapest, 1975), 47ff., and my review of the book in *American Historical Review*, 83 (1978), 1243f. P.

Váczy, *A középkor története* (The Middle Ages), vol. II of B. Hóman et al., *(ed), Egyetemes világtörténet* (Universal world history) (4 vols.; Budapest, 1936 etc.), 40ff., and 103ff.

2. In E. Szentpétery (ed), *Scriptores rerum Hungaricarum* (2 vols.; Budapest, 1937-38), hereafter SSH, I, 239ff.; Ch. Dawson's comments, "The Hungarian Middle Ages," in *Hungarian Quarterly,* 5 (1939), 585.; C.A. Macartney, *The Medieval Hungarian Historians* (Cambridge, 1953), 133ff.; J. Horváth, *Árpád-kori latinnyelvű irodalmunk stilusproblémái* (Stylistic questions concerning the Latin literature of the Arpadian age) (Budapest, 1954), 255ff.; C. Horváth, *A régi magyar irodalom története* (History of old Hungarian literature) (Budapest, 1899), 27, 32f.; J. Pintér, *Magyar irodalomtörténet* (History of Hungarian literature) (8 vols.; Budapest, 1930-41), I, 341ff.

3. See Iapetus, son of Gaia (=Earth), one of the Titans, according to Hesiod's Theogony, and grandfather of Deucalion, the Greek flood figure— cf. e.g., K. Prümm, *Religionsgeschichtliches Handbuch für den Raum der altchristlichen Umwelt* (Rome, 1954), 115f.; C. Kerényi, *The Gods of the Greeks* (London, 1951), 20ff., or the comments by H. Bengston, *Griechische Geschichte* (4th rev. ed.; Munich, 1969), 71. Iaphet, his Old Testament analogue, probably, was one of the sons of Noah and, according to legend, a very popular progenitor: he was father of Histion from whom descended the French, Italian, German, and British peoples—cf. "King Arthur and His Knights, the Mythical History of England," c. 2, in T. Bulfinch, *Mythology* (New York, 1970), 379.

4. SSH, I, 249, 8-20, even though the chronicler stated before (I, 248, 22-24) that "Hunor et Magor, patres Hungarorum, fuerunt filii Nemproth."

5. Ibid., I, 251, 11-21.

6. Ibid., I, 251, 12-17.

7. Cf. the "Clangentibus tubis" of Leviticus, 23:24.

8. That is: (that your posterity might learn) that I made the sons of Israel to dwell in tents . . .

9. See his *Historia scholastica* in Migne, PL, 198, col. 1214a.

10. Macartney, 89ff.; J. Horváth, 350ff.; Pintér, I, 275ff.; text in SSH, I, 141ff.

11. Ibid., I, 143f.: c. 4.

12. Ibid., c. 5; note that Keza called Bereka *Belar.*

13. Ibid., I, 33ff.; Macartney, 59ff.; J. Horváth, 196ff.; Pintér, I, 211ff.; L.J. Csóka, *A latin nyelvű történeti irodalom kialakulása Magyarországon a XI–XIV században* (Development of Latin historical literature in Hungary from the 11th to the 14th centuries) (Budapest, 1967), 427ff.

14. Cf. P. Váczy, "Anonymus és kora (Anonymus and his age)," Separatum: reprint from *Memoria saeculorum Hungariae,* vol. I (Budapest, 1974), and my review of this volume in *Austrian History Yearbook,* 12-13 (1976-77), 494ff.

15. SSH, I, 34 2-4; 34, 1.

16. Anonymus, c. 1; *Chronicon pictum,* c. 6; J. Deér, "Szkitia leirása a Gesta Hungarorumban (The description of Scythia in the Gesta Hungarorum)," *Magyar Könyvszemle,* 37 (1930), 243ff.

17. SSH, I, 35, 6-7: "Et primus rex Scithie fuit Magog, filius Iaphet et gens illa a Magog rege vocata est Moger."

18. Ibid., I, 35, 17-18.

19. Referred to as "Text T" by Macartney, 34ff.; J. Horváth, 270ff., named the author the "Historian of Stephen III."

20. G. Kristó, "Az Exordia Scythica, Regino és a magyar krónikák (Exordia Scythica; Regino and the Hungarian chronicles)," *Filológiai Közlöny,* 26 (1970), 106ff.; Macartney, 67; text by T. Mommsen, *Chronica minora,* II, 319ff.

21. G. Karsai, "Névtelenség, névrejtés és szerzőnév középkori krónikáinkban (Anonymity and authorship of medieval Hungarian chronicles)," *Századok,* 97 (1963), 666ff., argued that the author-compiler of the *Chronicon pictum* remained unknown; G. Kristó, "Anjou-kori krónikáink (Hungarian chronicles of the Angevin age)," ibid., 101 (1967), 457ff., reasoned that Canon Mark de Kalta and a Franciscan friar were the compilers.

22. His *Chronographia* in G.H. Pertz (ed), *Monumenta Germaniae historica, Scriptores* (30 vols. in 32; Berlin, 1826 etc.), hereafter MGHSS, VI, 301, 68, spoke of "genus Hunorum quod fuit primum inter paludes Meotidas." Regarded as the best medieval universal chronicler by A. Moliner, *Les sources de L'histoire de France* (6 vols.; Paris, 1902-06), II, 310, Sigebert was downgraded by W. Wattenbach, *Deutschlands Geschichtsquellen im Mittelalter* (2 vols.; 6th rev. ed.; Berlin, 1893-94), II, 161: "aber an Genauigkeit in der chronologischen Anordnung fehlt es

ihm mehr, als man erwarten sollte."

23. *Chronicon pictum,* c. 3; Comestor, c. 37 (Migne, PL, 198, cols. 1087f.); Anselmi Laudunensis *Glossa ordinaria,* in A. Borst, Der Turmbau von Babel: Geschichte der Meinungen über Ursprung und Vielfalt der Sprachen und Völker (2 vols.; Stuttgart, 1957-59), II-2, 624ff.; 724f.

24. "Prima die Septembris festum tubarum, vel clangores, pro liberatione Isaac, quod cereorum dicitur;" df. Migne, PL, 198, col. 1214a. "Septem festa Judaei habuerunt: Sabbatum, Neomeniam, Pentecosten, Pascha, et festum Tubarum, festum Propitiationis, Scenopegiam;" ibid., 198, col. 1214b. S. Kohn, "Héber kútforrások és adatok Magyarország történetéhez (Hebrew sources concerning Hungarian history)," *Történelmi Tár,* 1881, 12ff.

25. Cf. G. Moravcsik—R.J.H. Jenkins (ed), Constantine Porphyrogenitus: *De administrando imperio* (2nd ed.; Washington, DC., 1967), c. 38; G. Pauler—S. Szilágyi (ed), *A magyar honfoglalás kútfői* (Historical sources concerning the Hungarian conquest) (Budapest, 1900), 110ff.

26. See Regino Prumensis *Chronicon,* a. 889 (MGHSS, I, 599f.).

27. A.J. Toynbee, *Constantine Popphyrogenitus and his World* (London, 1973), 464ff.

28. Cf. Emperor Leo VI the Wise, *Tactica,* const. xviii: 39, 41, 44, 46, etc., in Migne, PG, 107, cols. 672ff.; also, Leo Grammaticus, *Chronographia,* ibid., 108, cols. 1099 and 1102.

29. Cf. Moravcsik-Jenkins, cc. 3, 13, 38; G. Moravcsik, Bizánci krónikák a honfoglalás előtti magyarságról (Byzantine chroniclers on the early Hungarians)," *Studia antiqua,* 4, (1957), 275ff.

30. His *Chronographiae libri VI,* vi:9 (Migne, PG, 109, col. 374); St. Katona, *Historia critica regum Hungariae stirpis Arpadianae* (13 vols.; Pest-Buda, 1779-90), I, 153ff.

31. P. Veress, "Outline of the Ethnic History of the Hungarian People," *Néprajzi Értesítő,* 54 (1972), 155ff.; structure and basic vocabulary of Hungarian are Finno-Ugrian. Vogul (Manshi) and Ostyak (Chanti) are closely related to it; cf. G. Székely, "La Hongire et Byzance aux Xe—XIIe siecles," *Acta historica,* 13 (1967), 291ff. On the meaning and usage of *Onogur,* see Moravcsik (above, n. 29).

32. See the Trier *Decretum,* a. 926 in E. Martene—U. Durand (ed), *Veterum scriptorum et monumentorum collectio* (9 vols.; repr. New York, 1968), I, 280ff., and cf. *Annales Sangallenses minores,* a. 892:

"Arnolfus contra Moravenses pergebat et Agarenos, ubi reclusi erant, dimisit" (MGHSS, I, 77); in 955, Otto the Great "cum Agarenis pugnabat" (ibid., I, 79).

33. Martene-Durand, I, 230ff., or Migne, PL, 131, cols. 963ff.; K.J. Heilig, "Der Brief des Remigius von Auxerre um 900 über die Ungarn," *A bécsi Magyar Történettudományi kutatóintézet évkönyve,* 3 (1933), 18ff.

34. K. Krumbacher, *Geschichte der byzantinischen Literatur* (2nd rev. ed.; Munich, 1897), 325ff.; also, G. Moravcsik, *A magyar történet bizánci forrásai* (Byzantine sources of Hungarian history) (Budapest, 1934), 68ff.

35. G. Moravcsik, "Byzantinische Mission im Kreise der Türkvölker an der Nordküste des Schwarzen Meeres," *Proceedings of the 13th International Congress of Byzantine Studies, Oxford, 1966* (London, 1967), 39ff.

36. Cf. L. Dindorf (ed), *Ioannis Malalae Chronographia* (Bonn, 1831), 431, 16-433, 2; or, Migne, PG, 97, cols. 636ab, 638b, 637b-638b, and 639a.

37. Dindorf, 431, 16-21: "ut res ibi Romanas Bosporumque custodiret."

38. Ibid., 432, 3-4.

39. Ibid., 432, 5-6.

40. Ibid., 432, 6-8; the Huns were "Idolorum cultores."

41. Ibid., 432, 10-12: "regem suum e medio tollunt; et in eius locum, Mougel, fratrem eius sufficiunt."

42. Ibid., 432, 12-13. It was not without justification that Mougel feared Byzantine reaction; cf. ibid., 432, 16-21, and 433, 1-2.

43. Cf. G. Németh, *A honfoglaló magyarság kalakulása* (Development of the Magyars as a People) (Budapest, 1930), 165ff.; G. Székely, "Törzsek alkonya—népek születése (Decline of tribal life—birth of a people)," *Századok,* 110 (1976), 415ff., dealt in depth with the research of G. Németh.

44. Malalas' *Chronographis* comes down to us in an eleventh century transcript; cf. Krumbacher, 331; however, Theophanes Confessor in the ninth century had in his *Chronographia* recorded lengthy details of the Malalas text, thereby preserving greater portions of it than were retained

FIVE HUNGARIAN KINGS

in the eleventh century transcript; cf. C. de Boor (ed), *Theophani Confessoris Chronographia* (2 vols.; Leipzig, 1883-85), I, 175, 24-176, 17 in reference to the Grod/Mougel affair. In the twelfth century, Gregorios Cedrenus had borrowed portions of the opus of the Confessor—cf. I. Bekker (ed), *G. Cedreni Ioannis Scylitzae opera* (2 vols.; Bonn, 1838-39), I, 644, 13—645, 6, concerning the Grod/Mougel event. C. de Boor, "Zu Theodorus Lektor," *Zeitschrift für Kirchengeschichte,* 6 (1883), 537ff.; Krumbacher, 326, raises the point that Malalas was a popular and provincial chronicler.

45. Moravcsik, *Byzantium,* 39.

46. W. Schubart, *Justinian und Theodora* (Munich, 1943), 174ff.

47. Cf. P. Krueger—T. Mommsen—R. Schoell (edd), *Corpus Iuris Civilis* (3 vols.; Berlin, 1895-99), vol. II: *Codex Iustinianus,* i:1, 8 and/or i:27, 1, 5.

48. See Justinian's writ to Pope John I (Migne, PL, 66, cols. 11ff., and 35ff.

49. Kruger-Mommsen-Schoell, vol. III: *Novellae,* 131: Justinian recognized the Roman primacy (Migne, PL, 66, col. 42c), and remained, in spite of his Monophysitic tendencies, an orthodox believer (ibid., 67, cols. 527ff.). Nevertheless, Rome remained on the defensive, as Pope Virgilius reports (ibid., 69, col. 22c); A. von Harnack, *Lehrbuch der Dogmengeschichte* (3 vols.; 4th rev. ed.; Tübingen, 1909-10), III, 251ff.

50. Cf. G. Moravcsik, "Muagerisz király (King Muageris)," *Magyar Nyelv,* 23 (1927), 258ff.; idem, "Zur Geschichte der Onoguren," *Ungarische Jahrbücher,* 10 (1930), 64f.

51. Kruger-Mommsen-Schoell, vol. III: *Novellae,* ii:2.

52. Hóman-Szekfű, I, 50ff.; I. Erdélyi, "Régészeti kutatások Baskiriában és a magyar űstörténet (Archaeological research in early Hungarian history)," *Archaeológiai Értesitő,* 99 (1972), 244ff.

53. E. Moór, "A Kaukázuson túli állitólagos 'szavard-magyarok' kérdéséhez (Essay on the so-called 'Savard Magyars' beyond the Caucasus)," *Századok,* 105 (1971), 961ff.

54. Cf. *Monologium Basilii Porphyrogeniti,* Migne, PG, 117, cols. 269ff.; according to tradition, the Apostle Andrew introduced Christianity to the Armenians—see Epiphanios, *Vita s. Andreae* (ibid., 120, cols. 241ff.).

55. E.W. Brooks (ed), *Historia ecclesiastica Zachariae rhetori vulgato*

adscripta (Lovanii, 1924), II, 134ff.; K. Ahren–G. Kruger, *Die sogenannte Kirchengeschichte des Zacharias Rhetor* (Leipzig, 1899), 254f.

56. A. v. Harnack, *Die Mission und Ausbreitung des Christentums in den ersten drei Jahrhunderten* (2 vols.; 4th rev. ed.; Leipzig, 1924), I, 108; II, 747ff.; P. de Lagarde, "Die Akten Gregors von Armenien," *Abhandlungen der Königlichen Gesellschaft der Wissenschaften zu Göttingen,* 35 (1888), 89ff., esp. 115f.

57. Cf. C. de Boor (ed), *Nicephori . . . opuscula historica* (Leipzig, 1888), 12.

58. See the *Acta sanctorum Bollandiana* (66 vols.; Antwerp, 1643 etc.), Nov. II, 386.

59. See his *Topographia* in Migne, PG, 88, col. 119b; on Indicopleustes, cf. Krumbacher, 412ff.

60. See H. Delehaye (ed), *Synaxarium ecclesiae Constantinopolitianae* in *Propylaeum ad acta sanctorum* (Brussels, 1902), 121.

61. *Acta sanctorum,* Iun. V, 190ff. ; Hóman-Szekű, I, 58ff.

62. Cf. de Boor, Theophani *Chronographia,* I, 373.

63. Preserved in the fourteenth century Bibliotheque Nationale MS 1555, ff. 23v–24r; cf. C. de Boor, "Nachträge zu den Notitiae Episcopatuum," *Zeitschrift für Kirchengeschichte,* 12 (1890), 519ff., esp. 531, and 533f.; on the date of the list, see H. Gelzer, "Die kirchliche Geographie Griechenlands vor dem Slaweneinbruch," *Zeitschrift für wissenschatfliche Theologie,* 35 (1892), 419ff.

64. Moravcsik, *Byzantium,* 42ff.; G. László, *A honfoglaló magyarság kialakulása* (Development of the conquering Magyars) (Budapest, 1967), 419ff. 65.

65. Cf. C. de Boor (ed), *Excerpta de legationibus* (Berlin, 1903), 586, 7-12, who also records the contact made by the Saragurs, Ogurs, and Onogurs with Byzantium in the year 463 (ibid., 212f., and 575ff.); H. Homeyer, *Attila der Hunnenkönig von seinem Zeitgenossen dargestellt* (Berlin, 1951), 36ff.

66. See G. Moravcsik, *Byzantinoturcica* (2 vols.; Budapest, 1942-43), II, 194ff.; Niketas Paphlagonesis, in Migne, PG, 105, col. 64.

67. G. László, "A kettős honfoglalásról (Some remarks about the two-fold conquest of the mid-Danube region)," *Archaeológiai Értesitő,* 97 (1970), 151ff.; Z. Gombocz, "Életföldrajz és a magyar őstörténet (Economic geography and ancient Hungarian history)," *Finn-ugor őshaza,* 308ff.

68. Cf. S.H. Cross–O.P. Sherbowitz-Wetzor (edd), *The Russian Primary Chronicle* (Cambridge, Mass., 1953), 55 and 62; St. Katona, *Historia pragmatica Hungariae* (3 vols.; Buda, 1782 etc.), I, 18ff.

69. Cf. Pauler-Szilágyi, 352ff.

70; Ibid., 354; P. Király, "A magyarok emlitése a Metód legendában (The Magyars mentioned by the Methodius legend)," *Magyar Nyelv,* 70 (1974), 269ff., and 496ff.

71. Pauler-Szilágyi, 354.

72. Ibid., 354; Katona, *Historia pragmatica,* I, 11ff.

Notes to Chapter I

1. Cf. Anonymus, cc. 1 ff., in SSH, I, 13ff.; Keza, cc. 1 ff., ibid., I, 129ff.; RHM, I, 1ff., and 83ff.; Macartney, 59ff.; B. Hóman, *Magyar középkor* (Hungarian Middle Ages) (Budapest, 1938), 63ff.; G. Györffy, *Krónikáink és a magyar őstörténet* (Early Hungarian history and the chroniclers) (Budapest, 1948), 11ff.; idem, *A magyarok elődeiről és a honfoglalásról* (Hungarian ancestors and the conquest– (Budapest, 1958), passim; idem, "Anonymus Gesta Hungarorumának kora és hitelessége (The reliability of Anonymus and his age)," *Irodalomtörténeti Közlemények,* 74 (1970), 1ff.; J. Györy, *Gesta regum–gesta nobilium* (Budapest, 1948), 96ff., says that Anonymus was a participant in the delegation sent by the Hungarian king to the court of Aragon. L. von Heinemann, "Zur Kritik ungarischer Geschichtsquellen," *Neues Archiv,* 13 (1887), 61ff., comments on Keza, as he has edited portions of Keza's text for the MGHSS, XXIX, 526ff. On the composition of the *Chronicon pictum* (SSH, I, 217ff.), see H. Marczali, *Ungarns Geschichtsquellen im Zeitalter der Árpáden* (Berlin, 1882), 50ff., and, more recently, L. Juhász, "A Képes Krónika szövegkritikájához (Textual criticism of the Chronicon pictum)," *Filológiai Közlöny,* 12 (1966), 23ff.

2. On the date of the conquest, see J. Deér, "A IX századi magyar történet időrendjéhez (On the dating of the late ninth century Hungarian events)," *Századok,* 79-80 (1945-46), 3ff.; G. Györffy, *István király és műve* (King Stephen and his work) (Budapest, 1977), 25ff., and his essay, "A besnyűk európai honfoglalásának a kérdéséhez (The appearance of the Cumans in Europe)," *Történelmi Szemle,* 14 (1971), 261ff.; Regino in MGHSS, I, 599f.

3. See Gy. László, *Hunor és Magyar nyomában* (In search of Hunor and Magor) (Budapest, 1967), 83, argued that the Hungarians were a part of the Hun establishment; E. Ivánka, "Görög szertartás és közép-kori magyarság Erdélyben (The Byzantine rite and the Hungarians in medieval Transylvania)," *Erdélyi Tudósitó,* 29 (1941), 100ff., stressed a similar argument. The Black-Ugrians mentioned by Nestor's Russian Chronicle (*ed. cit.,* 56 and 62, and 235, notes 10 and 28) were identified by Gy. Györffy, "Kurszán és Kurszán vára (Kurszán and his castle)," *Budapest Régiségei,* 16 (1955), 9ff., as the people of Árpád and Kurszán. On this, see also F. Dvornik, *Les slaves, Byzance et Rome* (Prague, 1933), 60ff.

4. Cf. *Relatio fratris Ricardi, O.P., de facto Ungariae Magnae invento tempore Domini Gregorii IX,* in SSH, II, 535ff., and RHM, I, 248ff.; Hóman, *Ungarisches Mittelalter,* I, 53ff. Selections from Byzantine sources may include Leo VI the Wise, *Tactica,* sect. xviii, cc. 44-75 (as, for instance, in Migne, *PG,* 107, cols. 672ff.), and Constantine VII Porphyrogenitus, *De administrando imperio (ed. cit.),* cc. 37-40; Moravcsik, *Byzantinoturcica,* I, 204ff.

5. On Hungarian defeats on German soil, see Widukind of Corbey, *Annalium libri tres,* i:38, and iii:44 (in MGHSS, III, 434, and 457f.); *Chronicon pictum,* cc. 60 etc.; G. Cedrenus (ed), *Compendium historiarum* (2 vols.; Bonn, 1838-39), II, 328, recorded Hungarian ventures on Byzantine territory; see also J. Hergenröther, *Photius* (3 vols.; Regensburg, 1867-69); repr. Darmstadt, 1966), III, 709.

6. Cf. J.F. Böhmer *et al* (edd), *Regesta imperii;* vol. II-1: *Die Regesten der Kaiserzeit, 918-973* (repr. Hildesheim, 1967), 247; Thietmar's *Chronicon, libri VIII,* ii:20 (30-31) (MGHSS, III, 753); M. Linzel, "Die Kaiserpolitik Ottos des Grossen," in his *Ausgewählte Schriften* (2 vols.; Berlin, 1961), II, 201ff. Bruno of Querfurt, *Vita s. Adalberti Praganensis,* c. 23 (MHHSS, IV, 607). Around 900, Archbishop Theotmar of Salzburg gave a discouraging report on Christian conditions in Hungarian territory (Mansi, *Concilia,* XVIII, col. 205ff.; Migne, *PL,* 131, col. 1179ff.). The Theotmar report is, however, *dubiae fidei;* cf. H. Fichtenau, Beiträge zur Meidävistik, vol. II: *Urkundenforschung* (Stuttgart, 1977), 157ff.

7. Stephen's succession in 997 was smooth: "post obitum vero patris Stephanus adhuc adolescens favore principum et plebis in patris solium laudabiliter provectus." Cf. Hartvic, *Vita s. Stephani regis,* c. 5 (SSH,

II, 407; Stephen's *Vita minor,* c. 2; ibid., II, 394). Anonymus spoke of Álmos as "primus dux Hungarie, a quo reges Hungarorum originem duxerunt" (ibid., I, 33), and "de cuius progenie Arpad descenderat" (ibid., I, 40); Álmos' descendants were to succeed "ad ultimam generationem" to Hungarian leadership: "dux Almus ipso vivente filium suum Arpadium ducem ac preceptorem constituit" (ibid., I, 52).

8. According to contemporaries, Géza was strict, "admodum crudelis et multos ob subitum furorem suum occidens," said Thietmar. viii: 3 (ix:4) MGHSS, III, 862; Aventinus, *Annales Boiorum,* emphasized that Géza was kind to his guests, "licet alienus a religione Christi esset, nostros tamen amavit, ab Ottone pacem impetravit; cf. F. Cisneros, *Avertini Annales,* (Basiliae, 1780), 393. Anonymus, c. 57, implied that it was Taksony, father to Álmos, who held the political initiative; "Thocsun vero dux cum omnibus primatibus Hungarie potenter et pacifice per omnes dies vite sue obtinuit omnia iura regni sui, et audita pietate ipsius multi hospites confluebant ad eum ex diversis nationibus" (SSH, I, 114). Otto I the Great was described as "dominus pene totius Europae" by Widukind, iii:46 (MGHSS, III, 459), meaning "western" Europe—see F. Dölger, "Europas Gestaltung im Spiegel der fränkisch–byzantinischen Auseinandersetzungen des 9 Jahrhunderts," in Th. Meyer (ed), *Der Vertrag von Verdun, 843* (Leipzig, 1943), 203ff.

9. "Itaque cum die barbarica gens Hungarorum errore infidelitatis sue teneretur et ritu gentilium vanas sacrilegiasque supertitiones sequeretur;" Stephen's *Vita minor,* c. 2; the derogatory remark concerning Géza, "qui cum christianus efficeretur, ad corroborandam hanc fidem contra reluctantes subditos sevit et antiquum facinus zelo Dei exestuans abluit," MGHSS, III, 862, proves Géza's change of policy. Bruno of Querfurt displayed a similar attitude toward Géza: "inmo uxor eius, quae totum regnum manu tenuit, virum et quae erant viri ipsa regebat." Cf. ibid., IV, 607; Hartvic, c. 5.

10. SSH, II, 394, 20-21; Herimannus Augiensis, *Chronicon,* a. 995, gave the reason why: "Gisela Stephano regi Ungariorum, cum se ad fidem Christi converteret, quasi vere iuxta nomen suum fidei obses in coniugium data." MGHSS, V, 117, and confirmed by *Auctarium Garstense,* a. 1009 (ibid., IX, 657), and Ekkehardi Uraugiensis *Chronicon,* a. 1001 (ibid., VI, 192); the German sources state that the conversion of Hungary was the work of Emperor Henry II. "Heinricus imperator sororam suam Giselam Stephano regi eorum matrimonio copulavit. Stephano rege

baptizato, universa Pannonia verbum vitae suscepit;" cf. *Vita s. Heinrici II imppratoris* by Adalbert of Babenberg, i:29-30 (ibid., IV, 810).

11. That Stephen relied heavily upon his *hospites* is evident from his Admonitions alias *Libellus de institutione morum*, a. VI (SSH, II, 625; Migne, *PL*, 151, col. 1240c); J. Deér, "Szent István politikai és egyházi orientációja (King Stephen's political and religious orientation)," *Katolikus Szemle*, 1 (Rome, 1949), 27ff.; on the *Libellus*, cf. M. Manitius, *Geschichte der lateinischen Literatur des Mittelalters* (3 vols.; Munich, 1911-31), II, 82f.

12. Chronicle, c. 64; Stephen's Vita minor, c. 3.

13. Hartvic, c. 6 (SSH, II, 408; MGHSS, XI, 232); evidently, this is why the *Vita minor*, c. 3, spoke of "quidam vero nobilium," who "iudicia regis contempserunt" (ibid., XI, 227; SSH, II, 395). The *iudicia regis* can be viewed through the opinion of others: "Stephanus rex Ungarorum sacramenta suscepit baptismatis et per eum omnis populis sibi subiectus," wrote Bonitho of Sutri, *Liber ad amicum* (Migne, *PL*, 150, col. 816); "eo tempore sanctus Stephanus Ungariam gubernabat eamque tunc primum ad fidem minis et blanditis convertebat," recorded Martinus Gallus, *Chronicon Polonorum*, i.; 8 (MGHSS, IX, 437). Pope Innocent III praised in his letter to Emory of Hungary, dated Sept. 15, 1204, the determined policy of Stephen; cf. Migne, *PL*, 215, col. 413.

14. Chronicle, c. 64 *and* cc. 38 etc.; K. Kniewald—F. Kühár, "A Pray kódex sanctoraléja," repr. from *Magyar Könyvszemle*, 1939; P. Radó, "Hazánk legrégibb liturgikus könyve: a Szelepcsényi kódex (Le plus ancien livre liturgique de la Hongrie: L'evangeliaire de l'archeveque Szelepcsényi)," repr. from ibid. 1939. L. Mezey, "Pannonia quae et Ungria," *Vigilia*, 35 (1970), 795ff., argued that the Frankish missionaries were actually Germans; on the other hand, J. Bóna, "Cunpald fecit: a petőházi kehely és a frank térités kezdetei a Dunántúlon ('Cunpald fecit:' the chalice of Petőháza and the origins of Frankish missionary work in Transdanubia)," *Soproni Szemle*, 18 (1964), 127ff., and 218ff., called attention to the early beginnings of the work of Frankish missionaries in western Hungary. According to Leo Marsicanus, *Chronica monasterii Casinensis*, ii:65 (MGHSS, VII, 674), and Hartvic, c. 7, the missionaries were effective.

15. Chronicle, cc. 40 and 41; A. Hauck, *Kirchengeschichte Deutschlands* (9th ed.; 5 vols in 6; Berlin, 1958), III, 271, mentioned that King

Stephen was in need of German help.

16. Cf. the writ of Pilgrim, dated 974 (?) to Rome in Marczali, *Enchiridion*, 57ff., to be used with caution;—cf. Fichtenau, 166ff.; A. Lhotsky, *Quellenkunde zur mittelalterlichen Geschichte Österreichs* (Graz-Cologne, 1963), 167ff.;—even though the claims of Pilgrim remained entrenched in German circles—see Magnus of Reichersberg, *Annales Reichersbergenses* (MGHSS, XVII, 481). Archbishop Theotmar of Salzburg reported on Christian conditions in Hungary, see Mansi, *Concilia*, XVIII, col 205, or Migne, *PL*, 131, col. 1179f., while Pope Benedict VI acknowledged that the imperial court may have had designs on Hungarian territory; cf. ibid., 135, col. 1081f.; Mansi, *Concilia*, XIX, col. 38ff.; Hauck, III, 163ff.

17. As, e.g., Adalbert of Prague—cf. Cosmas Pragensis *Chronica Bohemorum* (ibid., XVII, 712–; Th. v. Bogyay, "Adalbert von Prag und die Ungarn—ein Problem der Quellen-Interpretation," *Ungarn Jahrbuch*, 7 (1976), 9ff. Adalbert went to Rome, and from there to Hungary—see *Catalogus archiepiscoporum Gnesnensium* in A. Bielowski (ed), *Monumenta Poloniae historica* (6 vols.; Lvov-Cracow, 1864-93, repr. Warsaw, 1960-61), hereafter MPH, III, 391f. Aseric (Astric), a disciple of Adalbert, went to Hungary and became abbot of a monastery at Pécsvárad; cf. Canaparii *Vita s. Adalberti* (MGHSS, IV, 604), while another source (*De s. Adalberto*, c. 7; ibid., XV/2, 1180) implied that Adalbert and his disciples were active missionaries in Hungary; E. Szentpétery (ed), Regesta regum stirpis Arpadianae critico-diplomatica (2 vols.; Budapest, 1923-61), I, no. 6, cited the forged charter of the Pécsvárad abbey; B. Hamilton, "The Monastic Revival in Tenth Century Rome," *Studia monastica*, 4 (1962), 35ff.

18. Astric who became the archbishop of Esztergom (cf. *Chronicon Hungarorum mixtum et Polonorum;* MPH, I, 500 and 503), represented Hungary at the dedication of the Bamberg cathedral: "altare ante criptam consecravit Ashericus Ungarorum archiepiscopus;" cf. *Dediactio ecclesiae s. Petri Babenbergensis* in Ph. Jaffé (ed), *Bibliotheca rerum Germanicarum* (6 vols.; Berlin, 1865 etc., repr. Darmstadt, 1964), V, 481. The Bamberg bishopric was founded by Henry II, and authorized by Pope john XVIII, whose letter was presented to the German bishops at the Synod of Frankfurt, Nov. 7, 1007, attended by Astric; cf. *MGH. Dipl. reg. et imp. Germ.,*

III, 171–"Ungarorum archiepiscopus–; MGHSS, IV, 795f.; H. Zimmermann, "Gründung und Bedeutung des Bistums Bamberg für den Osten," *Südostdeutsches Archiv,* 10 (1967), 35ff. Astric-Anastasius (two names for the same person!) gave Stephen moral support vs. his opponents; cf. the Charter of Pannonhalma abbey, Szentpétery, *Regesta,* I, no. 2; text in L. Erdélyi (ed), *A pannonhalmi szent Benedek-Rend története* (History of the Benedictines of Pannonhalma) 12 vols.; Budapest, 1902-07), I, 589f., or Migne, *PL,* 151, col. 1253f. (condensed). On the activities of the Benedictines in Hungary, see Ph. Schmitz, *Die Geschichte des Benediktienerordens* (tr. L. Raebert; 2 vols.; Zurcih, 1947-78), I, 229ff., and, from a different angle, J. Stilting, "De sancto Stephano, primo Hungarorurm rege, commentarius praevius," ASS, Sept. I, 456ff.

19. Chronicle, c. 64; "die grosse Eigenthümlichkeit der Bilderkronik ist, dass sie den historischen Inhalt der anderen Chroniken in ganzem Umfange darbietet;" Marczali, *Geschichtsquellen,* 68.

20. According to Keza, c. 43, and the Chronicle, c. 65, the defeat of Koppány preceeded the trouble in Transylvania.

21. Hartvic, cc. 6-8; on Hartvic, cf. Gy. Rónay, "Szent István király legendái (The legends of King Stephen)," *Vigilia,* 36 (1971), 527ff.; Keza, c. 43.

22. MGHSS, III, 92; Chronicle, c. 65.

23. "Stephanus rex Pannoniorum, ex pagano christicola factus, verae fidei imitator erat Deogue devotus;" cf. *Fundatio ecclesiae s. Albani Namucensis* (MGHSS, XV/2, 964); W. Wattenbach, *Deutschlands Geschichtsquellen im Mittelalter* 2 vols.; 6th rev. ed.; Berlin, 1893-94), II, 209.

24. Chronicle, c. 66, events in Transylvania, "Hungarice Erdeelw; . . . sic dici solet: Erdeelui Zoltan."

25. *Vita maior s. Gerhardi episcopi,* c. 8 (SSH, II, 489ff.); Macartney, 157ff. Hóman, *Ungarisches Mittelalter,* I, 168f., placed the Chan (Kean)–Ajtony affair into the first decade of the eleventh century.

26. Chronicle, c. 65; Horváth, *Stilusproblémák,* 160f.

27. Hartvic, c. 12; Chronicle, c. 66.

28. Horváth, *Stilusproblémák,* 350ff.; Marczali, *Geschichtsquellen,* 42ff.

29. Keza, c. 43.

30. Stephen's *Vita minor,* c. 5.

31. Gerard's *Vita maior,* c. 8; Gy. Moravcsik, "Görögnyelvű monostorok Szent István korában (Byzantine monasteries in the days of King Stephen)," *Szent István Emlékkönyv* (ed. J. Serédi; 3 vols.; Budapest, 1938), hereafter SIE, I, 299ff.

32. SSH, I, 315.

33. Ibid., II, 492; Gerard's *Passio* alias *Vita minor,* c. 3 (ibid., II, 473), failed to mention the event; ASS, Sept. VI, 722ff.

34. Stephen's *Vita minor,* c. 2 (in MGHSS, XI, 226, c. 1) P. Váczy, "Magyarország kereszténysége a honfoglalás korában (Christianity in Hungary at the time of the Conquest)," SIE, I, 213ff.

35. ". . . apud se cepit meditari, ut si populum iam pridem baptismatis consecratione renatum absque disciplina dimitteret, facile post errorem vanitatis sue iterum converteretur;" SSH, II, 395; MGHSS, XI, 226.

36. Anonymus, C. 5, projected a picture of the role and constituency of the Council of Elders: "tunc ipsi VII principales personae communi et vero consilio intellexerunt, quod inceptum iter perficere non possent, nisi ducem ac preceptorem super se habeant. Ergo libera voluntate et communi consensu VII virorum elegerunt sibi ducem ac preceptorem in filios filiorum suorum usque ad ultimam generationem Ulmum filium Vgek et qui de eius generatione descenderet . . . . Isti enim VII principes persone erant viri nobiles genera et potentes in bello, fide stabiles." SSH, I, 40; compare with Constantine Porphyrogenitus, c. 38, *ed. cit.*

37. In 997, the election of Stephen as ruler occured "favore principum et plebis" (Hartvic, c. 5) on grounds that his father, Prince Géza "Hungarie primatibus et cum ordine sequenti, per communis consilium filium suum Stephanum post se regnaturum populo prefecit;" Hartvic, c. 4. (MGHSS, XI, 231, c. 5). Probably for this reason, the nobles were absent from the coronation of Stephen!—ibid., XI, 233, c. 9; SSH, II, 414, c. 10. In turn, King Stephen will name his successor, Peter Orseolo "accersitis episcopis et primis palatii de Christi nomine gloriantibus; cf. idem, c. 22.

38. Who upon the earliest opportunity had taken actions vs. the Orseolo in 1041; cf. Keza, c. 47; Chronicle, c. 72. Cf. my essay, "The 1046 Csanád Assembly and the Unforeseen Consequences of the Assassination of Gerard of Csanád," *Proceedings of the XIVth Hungarian Convention, 1974* (Cleveland, O., 1975), 150ff.

39. See the prefatory note of the 1222 Hungarian Golden Bull in Marczali, *Enchiridion,* 134ff.; my article, "De facultate resistendi: Two

Essential Characteristics of the Hungarian Golden Bull of 1222," *Studies in Medieval Culture,* 5 (1975), 97ff.

40. Cf. King Stephen's *Leges,* aa. I:14, 15, 10; II:2, which denoted the *senatus* as an advisory council; text in L. Závodszky (ed), *Szent István, Szent Lászáó és Kálmán korabeli törvények és zsinati határozatok forrásai* (De fontibus legum et decretorum synodaliumque temporibus sancti Stephani, sancti Ladislai et Colomanni oriundorum) (Budapest, 1904), 141ff.; Marczali, *Enchiridion,* 67ff.; Migne, *PL,* 151, col. 1243ff., cc. 13, 16, 14, 19 and 35; Stephen's Admonitions mentioned *consilium regum,* a. VII, ibid., 151, col. 1241a; SSH, II, 625; Hartvic, c. 19: "sine consilio nihil agere."

41. Cf. Szentpétery, *Regesta,* I, no. 2.

42. ". . . ad custodiam corporalis sue duos principes Hunt et Paznan constituit. Totius autem exercitus sui principem et ductorem Vencilinum hospitem Alamanum genere prefecit;" Chronicle, c. 64; Pannonhalma Charter, *loc. cit.*

43. ". . . dic tribuno plebis in ulterioribus moranti, ut se provideat, viros ad pugnam eligat;" Stephen's *Vita minor,* c. 5? on Csanád, see SSH, II, 492.

44. "Cum his dei servus, princeps Christianissimus, aliquando communiter cum omnibus, aliquando singillatim cum uno quoque eorum colloquium habens," (Stephen) did establish "per consensum et subscriptionem Romanae sedis apostolici ceterarum fore constituens;" Stephen's *Vita maior,* c. 8 (SSH, II, 383; MGHSS, XI, 232), the ecclesiastical organization of his country. In the process he made Astric/Anastasius archbishop of Kalocsa, "electione canonica Astricum prefecit," and dispatched him to negotiate in Rome; cf. Hartvic, c. 9.

45. Cf. the letter of Emperor Otto III to Pope Sylvester II, dated Jan. 18-23, 1001, in P. E. Schramm, *Kaiser, Rom und Renovatio* (2 vols.; 2nd ed.; Darmstadt, 1957), II, 66f., and the remarks of Schramm, ibid., I, 161ff.; C. Erdmann, "Das ottonische Reich als Imperium Romanum," *Deutsches Archiv,* 6 (1943), 421ff.; M. Ferdinándy, "Das Ende der heidnischen Kultur in Ungarn," *Ungarische Jarhbücher,* 16 (1936), 63ff.

46. Hartvic, c. 9; the remark by Thietmar, *Chronicon,* iv:38 (59) that Stephen "imperatori gratia et hortatu . . . coronam et benedictionem accepit" (MGHSS, III, 784) prompted German historians, as, e.g. Schramm,

I, 152f., to express different views; Th. v. Bogyay, *Stephanus Rex: Versuch einer Biographie* (Vienna-Munich, 1975), 23ff., accepted the view held by Thietmar.

47. "Quarto post patris obitum anno;" Hartvic, c. 9; *Annales Posonienses*, a. 1000 (SSH, I, 125); on the latter, cf. P. Radó, *Libri liturgici manu scripti bibliothecarum Hungariae* (Budapest, 1947), 40. The Pannonhalma Charter was issued in 1001, "indictione XV, anno Stephani regis secundo" (Erdélyi, *Rendtörténet*, I, 590), and since the fifteenth "indictio" lasted from September, 1001 through August, 1002,—see H. Grotefend, *Zeitrechnung des deutschen Mittelalters und der Neuzeit* (2 vols.; Hannover, 1891-92), I, 92ff.,—the Charter could have been issued during the second year of Stephen's reign. As for the coronation date; if Stephen's delegation went to Rome in the Fall of 1000, his coronation might have occured Christmas, 1001, assuming, of course, that the Christmas-style of time reckoning prevailed at the Hungarian court at the time. According to this reckoning system, Christmas was the first day of the new year—see ibid., I, 205f.; A. v. Brandt, *Werkzeug des Historikers* (2nd ed.; Stuttgart, 1960), 38ff.

48. "Presulibus cum clero, comitibus cum populo laudes congruas adclamantibus, dilectus deo Stephanus rex appellatur;" Hartvic, c. 10 (MGHSS, XI, 233, c. 9); L. Erdélyi, *Magyar történelem: művelődés és államtörténet* (Hungarian cultural and constitutional history) (2 vols.; Budapest, 1936-38), I, 45ff.; J. Szekfű, *Der Staat Ungarn: eine Geschichtsstudie* (Stuttgart, 1918), 28f.

49. Hence the warning of King Stephen to his successor: "sine consilio nihil agere" (Hartvic, c. 19; MGHSS, XI, 238, c. 16); Admonitions, art. VII, *loc. cit.*, and Hartvic, c. 22 (c. 18).

50. V. Fraknói, *Magyarország és a Szentszék* (Hungary and the Holy See) (3 vols.; Budapest, 1901-03), I, 5f.; Gy. Balanyi, "Szent István, mint a magyar kereszténység megalapitója és szervezője (King Stephen, founder and organizer of Christianity in Hungary)," SIE, I, 329ff.; idem, "Magyar szentek, szentéletű magyarok (Hungarian saints; saintly Hungarians)," *Katolikus Szemle*, 15 (Rome, 1963), 100ff.

51. At the Hungarian court, Rome was regarded as *caput mundi;* cf. Hartvic, c13.

52. Except for Heinrich von Mügeln, *Deutsche Ungarnchronik* c. 19 (SSH, II, 105ff., esp. 150); Lhotsky, 311; Macartney, 144ff.

53. Hartvic inserted an extra paragraph on Archbishop Sebastian (SSH, II, 416f.).

54. The unwillingness of the Council is evident from the fact that when Stephen decided to pass legislation, he increased its membership with Christian bishops, and, even then, he legislated by himself: "cum episcopis et primatibus Hungarie (note sequence!—bishops are mentioned first) statutum a se decretum manifestum facit." Cf. ibid., II, 415 (MGHSS XI, 234, c. 9); J. Balogh, "A magyar királyság megalapitásának világ-történelmi háttere (Politics and history as background for the establish-ment of the Hungarian kingdom:," *Századok,* 66 (1932), 152ff.

55. On the campaign, cf. *Fundatio ecclesiae s. Albani Namucensis* (*loc. cit.*).

56. Chronicle, cc. 81 etc.; Gerard's *Vita maior,* c. 15; King Andrew I's *Constitutiones ecclesiasticae,* ca. 1047; cf. Mansi, *Concilia,* XIX, col. 631f.; my essay, "The Negative Results of the Enforced Missionary Policy of King Stephen the Saint of Hungary: the Uprising of 1046," *Catholic Historical Review* 59 (1973), 569ff.

57. Cf. J. Deér, *Pogány magyarság, keresztény magyarság* (Pagan and Christian elements in Hungarian society) (Budapest, 1938), 94ff. As early as Febr. 964, the Roman Synod held under Pope John XII, did mention a missionary bishhop: "gentium episcopus," Zacheus by name, cf. MGHLL, sect. IV, Const. I, I, 533, of whom Liutprand of Cremona, *Liber de rebus gestis Ottonis magni imperatoris* (MGHSS, III, 340ff., c. 6) reported that he was sent to the Hungarians, was captured by them, and suffered martyrdom among them. F.L. Csóka, "A magyarok és a kereszténység Géza fejedelem korában (Hungarians and religion in the days of Prince Géza)," SIE, I, 267ff.

58. Stephen's Laws protected the lesser element of society entering the King's service; cf. art. II:19 and 16 (in Migne, cc. 43 and 50), on grounds "ut gens nostra monarchiae huius ab omni incursu et accusatione servorum et ancillarum remota et quieta maneat (a. I:20; c. 19); there-fore, "volumus ut firma pax et unanimitas sit inter maiores et minores, secundum apostolum: Omnes unanimes estote;" (a. I:35; c. 33). The scriptural quote is 1 Peter, 3:8, and Phil. 2:2. P. v. Váczy, *Die erste Epoche des ungarischen Königtums* (Pécs, 1935), 25ff.

59. Gerard's *Vita maior,* c 12; on the "age" of this *Vita,* see P. Váczy, "A korai magyar történet néhány kérdéséről (Some questions concerning

early Hungarian history)," *Századok*, 92 (1958), 265ff., esp. 276 and 312.

60. Keza, c. 53.

61. Gerard's *Vita maior*, c. 9.

62. Hartvic, c. 9; Stephen's *Vita maior*, c. 9, omitted the passage, the authenticity ot which is supported by Stephen's *Vita minor*, c. 2.

63. "Ut quicunque Ungarus, seu peregrinus in Ungaria . . . legem a divo rege Stephano traditam non reciperet, capite et bonis multaretur;" Eccl. Const., Migne, *PL*, 151, col. 1257a. M. Büdinger, *Ein Buch ungarischer Geschichte*, 1058-1100 (Leipzig, 1866), 89.

64. "Hunc secundum ecclesiasticam doctrinam instituens, iugum et legem disciplinae subpositis cervicibus adhibuit, omnesque inmunditias malorum prorsus destruxit;" SSH, II, 395; MGHSS, XI, 227, c. 1. Stephen followed his father's original policy—ibid., c. 1; SSH, II, 394, c. 2. Z. Tóth, "Tuhutum és Gelou: hagyomány és történelmi hitelesség Anonymus műveiben (Tradition and accuracy in the works of Anonymus)," *Századok*, 79-80 (L945-46), 21ff.

65. "Regina vero Kysla consilio iniquorum Petrum Venetum . . . regem fecit super Hungaros;"Keza, c. 45; by 1041, "principes et nobiles regni Hungarie episcoporum consilio in unum convenerunt contra Petrum." Cf. ibid., c. 47.

66. Ibid.

67. "Aba vero in regem consecrato;" ibid.

68. When Aba had a good number of his opponents murdered in cold blood (ibid., c. 49), Bishop Gerard of Csanád publicly censured the king for his misdeed; cf. Gerard's *Vita minor*, c. 5 (SSH, II, 476); the sermon by the fifteenth century Franciscan, Pelbartus of Temesvár, on Gerard in I. de Batthyány (ed), *Sancti Gerardi episcopi Chanadiensis acta et scripta hactenus inedita* (Alba-Caroliniae, 1790), 362ff.; C. Horváth, *A régi magyar irodalom története* (History of early Hungarian literature) (Budapest, 1899), 66ff. Evidently, the public rebuke of King Aba caused his downfall shortly afterwards—cf. Keza, c. 50.

69. Chronicle, c. 77.

70. Gerard's *Vita maior*, c. 15; Chronicle, c. 81.

Notes to Chapter II
Section 1

1. Cf. J.A. Endres, "Studien zur Geschichte der Frühscholastik: Gérard von Csanád," *Philosophisches Jahrbuch,* 26 (1913), 349ff.; Horváth, *Stilusproblémák,* 158ff.

2. The bibliography dealing with the reign of King Stephen I the Saint was adequately covered by D. Kosáry (ed), *Bevezetés a magyar történelem irodalmába* (Introduction to Hungarian historical literature) (3 vols.; Budapest, 1951-58), vol. III; recently, the revised edition of this work was prepared by Kosáry, *Bevezetés Magyarország történetének forrásaiba és irodalmába* (Introduction to the sources and literature of the history of Hungary) vol. I; Budapest, 1970), reviewed by J. Szentmihályi, *Magyar Könyvszemle,* 87 (1971), 255ff.; Hóman-Szekfű, I, 641ff.; A.F. Gombos, "Szent István király a középkori külföldi történetirásban (Medieval non-Hungarian literature dealing with King Stephen)," *SIE,* III, 279ff.; *idem,* "A Szent István korára és a korabeli keresztány magyar kapcsolatokra vonatkozó külföldi írók jegyzéke (A list of non-Hungarian writers dealing with the age of King Stephen and Hungaro-Christian relations)," ibid., III, 295ff.; R. Gragger (ed), *Bibliographia Hungariae* (2 vols.; Berlin, 1923-26), vol. I, listing non-Hungarian publications concerning Hungarian history, published between 1861 and 1921; Eckhart, 19ff.; recently, a fifteenth century German translation of Hartvic's opus was discovered in Budapest. Cf. A. Vizkelety, "Eine deutsche Fassung der Stephanslegende aus dem Jahre 1471," *Magyar Könyvszemle,* 84 (1968), 129ff. The *Vitae minores* of King Stephen and Bishop Gerard might have been composed as documents for their canonization in 1083; see Hartvic, c. 24 (*SSH,* II, 432ff.; Balanyi in *Katolikus Szemle,* 1963; J. Félegyházy, "Történelmi irodalmunk kezdetei (The beginnings of Hungarian historical literature)," *Vigilia,* 34 (1969), 329ff. The canonization had been authorized by Pope Gregory VII—cf. Berthold of Constance, *Chronicon,* a . 1087 (*MGHSS,* V, 446); Hartvic, c. 26; Rónay, *Art. cit.;* Gy. Szekfű, "Szent István a magyar történet századaiban (The image of King Stephen in Hungarian historiography)," *SIE,* III, 1ff.

3. Chroncile, c. 65; Macartney, *Historians,* 123; Hóman, *Ungarisches Mittelalter,* I, 169. On visitors, cf. the remarks of Iotsald, *Vita s. Odilonis*

abbatis V Cluniacensis, i:6 (7) (*MGHSS,* XV/2, 813), and of Ademarus Cabannensis *Chronicon,* c. 65 (ibid., IV, 145); Rudolph Glaber, *Francorum historiae* libri IV, iii:1 (ibid., VII, 52).

4. Chronicle, cc. 64-65.

5. *SSH,* II, 395, c. 3.

6. Gerard's *Vita maior,* c. 8 (ibid., II, 489ff.).

7. Ibid., II, 492.

8. Cf. F.A. Gombos, "Szent István háborúja II Konrád császárral (The war of King Stephen vs. Conrad II)," *SIE,* II, 107ff.

9. Cf. Wipo, Life of Emperor Conrad II, c. 22 (*MGHSS,* XI, 267); W. Ohnsorge, "Die legation des Kaisers Basileios II an Heinrich II," *Historisches Jahrbuch,* 73 (1954) 61ff.

10. "Contra quem rex (i.e. Stephen) consultum habens episcoporum et principum, ad tuendam patriam armatos totius Ungariae contraxit." Stephen's *Vita maior,* c. 14 (*SSH,* II, 389; *MGHSS,* XI, 237, c. 15); Hartvic, 16. The emperor suffered defeat—cf. ibid., and Wipo, c. 26 (*MGHSS,* XI, 268).

11. *SSH,* II, 483ff., c. 3.

12. Glaber, *Historia,* iii:1 (*MGHSS,* VII, 62); Adalbert of Babenberg, Life of Emperor Henry II, i:29-30 (ibid., IV, 810); Ekkehardus Uraugiensis *Chronicon,* a. 1038 (ibid., VI, 195).

13. *SSH,* II, 472, c. 2.

14. Cf. Iotsald (*loc. cit.*); ". . . clam dimissis itineris sui (i.e. Gerard) comitibus hunc solum invitum custodiamque adhibuit" (*SSH,* II, 472). "Ihersolimam ire noli, neque enim te permittam." Ibid., II, 488, c. 5.

15. As, for example, Bishop Bruno, the brother of Emperor Henry II, in 1004 and in 1006; cf. Thietmar, *Chronicon,* vi:2-3 (*MGHSS,* III, 805), and the letter of Bruno of Querfurt to Henry II (*MPH,* I, 224). About 1000, John Smera Polovecius, the court physician of Wladimir of Kiev, visited Hungary; cf. his writ to the prince in Migne, *PL,* 151, col. 1407f. Count Arnulf de Cham et Vochburg was visiting at the Hungarian court during the first decade of the eleventh century; cf. *MGHSS,* IV, 547. About 1026, six nobles from the west, bishops and abbots paid their visits to the court of King Stephen; cf. Ademar Cabannensis *Chronicon,* c. 65 (ibid., IV, 145f.). A year later, Archbishop Poppo of Trier, was a distinguished visitor at the court—according to Erchenfrid, *Vita s. Colomanni* (ibid., IV' 678).

16. *SSH,* II, 472, c. 2.

17. Ibid., II, 487f., c. 5.

18. F. Banfi, "Vita di s. Gerardo da Venezia nel codice 1622 della Biblioteka Universitaria di Padova," *Benedictina,* 2 (1948), 262ff.; Gy. Rónay, "Szent Gellert (Gerard of Csanád)," *Vigilia,* Budapest, 1946, 47ff.

19. This might have been the reason as to why Romuald and his companions were not welcomed in Hungary; see Peter Damian, *Vita s. Romualdi,* cc. 28-29 (*MGHSS,* IV, 853).

20. ". . . multa legi, multa cucurri. In spania fui doctus, in britannia eruditus, in scotia detritus, in hibernia studui, omnes liberales disciplinas commendaui memoriae, ideo nil lectionis me effugere potest." Cf. Gerard's *Deliberatio supra humnum trium puerorum,* preserved in a late eleventh century MS, No. 6211 of the Munich, Germany, Staatsbibliothek of 166 folios, f. 141', 17-21. Although Ignatius de Batthyány edited the Munich MS, and had it published in 1790—see below, ch. three—, this writer feels that, for the sake of accuracy, he had better turn to the MS itself, of which he obtained a microfilm. See further E. Mikkers, "Eremitical Life in Western Europe During the XIth and XIIth Centuries," *Citeaux: Commentarii Cistercienses,* 14 (1963), 44ff.

21. Abbot Rasina; cf. J. Karácsonyi, *Szent Gellért csanádi püspök élete és müvei* (Life and works of Gerard of Csanád) (Budapest, 1887), 48f.; Erdélyi, *Müvelődéstörténet,* I, 59, emphasized that Rasina was the abbot of Pannonhalma. Erdélyi might have based his assumption upon Gerard's *Vita maior,* c. 3 (*SSH,* II, 483f.), though the *Vita minor* offers no evidence on this.

22. Ademar Cabanensis *Chronicon,* c. 65; E. Sackur, *Richard, Abt von St. Vannes* (Breslau, 1886), 44f.; Endres, *art. cit.,* 351, n. 3.

23. *Annales Posonienses,* a. 1030: "Gerardus episcopus ordinatur" (*SSH,* I, 125), a work that had been described by Endlicher as "Chronicon Posoniense" (RHM, I, 55ff.), and Radó, 40, mentioned it as part of the Pray codex. Cf. L. Mezey, "A Pray kódex keletkezése (Origins of the Pray codex)," *Magyar Könyvszemle,* 87 (1971), 109ff.; P. Ratkos, "A Pray kódex keletkezése és funkciója (Origins and development of the Pray codex)," *Századok,* 102 (1968), 941ff.; Erdély, *Müvelődéstörténet,* I, 50. Yet, there is a piece of historical writing, "Cronica regni Hungariae" (ed. A. Domanovszky; *SSH,* II, 13ff.), known as the *Chronicon Posoniense*

(Macartney, *Medieval Historians*, 142f.), about which Marczali, *Geschichts-quellen*, 84, expressed a rather low opinion, "dass sie blos ein Abzug ist."
24. Karácsonyi, 42ff.; on Emery, cf. his *Vita* (*SSH*, II, 449ff.), and the remarks of A. Poncelet in *AASS*, Nov. II/1, 481ff.; Hóman, *Ungarishes Mittelalter*, I, 235f. According to Marczali, *Geschichtsquellen*, 21ff., Emery's Life had a "mystische Richtung."
25. In 995, Stephen received the hand of Gisela, the duaghter of Henry the Quarrelsome of Bavaria, in marriage; cf. Herimanni *Chronicon*, a. 995 (MGHSS, V, 117f.), and the marriage ceremony may have taken place in 996; cf. J. Karácsonyi, *Szent István király élete* (The life of King St. Stephen) (Budapest, 1904), 118, n. 4, and Prince Emery might have been born about 997.
26. *SSH*, II, 472, c. 2; the implication in his *Vita maior*, c. 5, may only contain later interpretation; cf. J. Horváth, Jr., "A Gellért legendák forrásértéke (The 'lives' of Gerard as historical source)," *A Magyar Tudományos Akadémia nyelv és irod.-tört. osztályának közleményei* (Proceedings of the Hungarian Academy of Science, section of language, literature and history) 13 (1958), 21ff.; Rónay, *art. cit.* (1946); J. Révay, *Árpádok virága, szent Imre herceg* (Flower of the Árpáds, Prince St. Emery) (Budapest 1929), 130ff.
27. ". . . secundum vite meritum episcopos et sacerdotes prefecit;" Stephen's *Vita minor*, c. 4 (*SSH*, II, 396); Hartvic, c. 14 (ibid., II, 422), in direct reference to Gerard of Csanád *(MGHSS*, XI, 236, c. 14). Karácsonyi, *Gellért*, 101ff.; idem, *Szent István*, 37ff.; Keza, c. 56.
28. See above, n. 20; Karácsonyi, *Gellért*, 125.
29. *Vita minor*, c. 1; *Vita maior*, cc. 1-2; Révay, 170ff.
30. "Pro nephas nostri uidentes non foris clamant, sed intus murmurant, atque sine iussv et interrogatu nil musitare audent, ne quidem aures offendant regales. Quomodo inquiunt displicentia loqui possumus regi? Ira succenditur, furore armatur, et nos insonabimus? Magis simulatum expetunt cachinum quam ualidum dei denunciunt uerbum. Hoc autem quidem ut eorum siue contigui, ab inditis non suspendatur officis, ipse uero ne priuentur paleis;" Munich MS, f. 15', 2-12. There is also a marginal annotation "de adulatoribus non audentes ueritatem predicare assimilantur ydolatris statuam adorantes nabuchodonosor." Or, to quote Gerard again, "hoc tempore omnes maledixerunt apud nos concitati zelo non solum diuinis ritibus et aecclesiae et sacerdotibus quin etiam ipsi dei filio ihesv christo domino nostro;" MS, f. 46', 1-4.

31. *Vita minor,* c. 6; *Vita maior,* cc. 9 and 11; "quia uero hora nos cogit ad horas immo praestolamur ad multa, ideo octaua istius modi operis schedula consuetum epilogum flagitat;" MS, f. 166', 6-8. "Scriptum reuerenter legimus, et in christi societate frequenter psallimus;" MS, f. 35', 19-20. Both passages seem to indicate that Gerard as a bishop conducted some kind of community life together with his clergy. It was he, who established the cathedral school at Csanád (*SSH,* II, 494f.), and placed its direction in the hands of his clerical household; cf. R. Békefi, *A káptalani iskolák története Magyarországon 1540-ig* (A history of the cathedral schools in Hungary until 1540) (Budapest, 1910), 70ff.

32. *Vita minor,* c. 2.

33. See the Vita Romualdi (full text in Migne, *PL,* 144, col. 953ff.), esp. cc. 13 and 49 etc.

34. Ibid.; or, *MGHSS,* IV, 853.

35. On this, cf. Peter Damian, Life of Rudolph and Loricatus,–the latter wore a coat of mail against the temptations of the devil!–in Migne, *PL,* 144, col. 1015, cc. 8 etc.

36. ". . . clam dimissis itineris sui. . .hunc solum. . .retinuit" (*SSH,* II, 472).

37. *Vita maior,* c. 5 (ibid., II, 487).

38. *Vita minor,* c. 2; D. Vargha (ed), *Szent Mór emlékkönyv* (Memorial volume to St. Maurus of Pécs) (Pécs, 1936), 363ff.; on Bél, cf. *SSH,* II, 475. It was located near Székesfehérvár, the royal headquarters; King Stephen I was buried at Székesfehérvár (Hartvic, c. 23; T. Bogyay, "Szent István koporsója (King Stephen's coffin)," *Katolikus Szemle,* 23 (1971), 209ff.; idem, "Über den Stuhlweissenburger Sarkophag des hl. Stefan," *Ungarn-Jahrbuch,* 4 (1972), 9ff.; Karácsonyi, *Szent István,* made the remark that King Stephen lived in a wooden palace–a hypothesis supported by Prince Emery's *Vita,* c. 3 (*SSH,* II, 453).

39. "Quamvis episcopalem dignitatem nimi providentia gubernaret, tamen heremum nusquam deseruit, verum iuxta urbes, ad quos (sic!) predicare veniebat, cellulam sibi silvarum secretiori loco construxerat;" (SSH, II, 475, c. 5). J. Deér, "Aachen und die Herrschersitze der Árpáden," *Mitteilungen des Institutes für österreichische Geschichtsforschung,* 79 (1971), 1ff.

40. *SSH,* II, 488, c. 5.

41. Stephen's Code of Laws, art. I:2 (*loc. cit.*).

42. "Videns autem rex regnum suum pacis tranquillitatem adeptum, servum Domini ab eremo convocat pontificaliqque infula decoratum populo suo predicare destinavit." (*SSH*, II, 473, c. 3).

43. "Sancta Dei ecclesia in pace collocata et ex Romana auctoritate iusse ordinata;" *Vita minor*, c. 5; "per consensum et subscriptionem Romanae sedis apostolici ceterarum fore constituens;" *Vita maior*, c. 8 (ibid., II, 383; *MGHSS*, XI, 233, c. 8).

44. "Cum his dei servus, princeps Chrsitianissimus . . . ;" Ibid.; Váczy, 50ff.; W. Neuss, *Das Problem des Mittelalters* (Komar in Elsass, n.d.), 51ff.

45. Cf. *MGHSS*, XI, 233, n. 35, in reference to a text in Migne, *PL*, 139, col. 274ff.; the papal record (*SSH*, II, 414, 9-11), cf. H.P. Lattin (ed), *Letters of Gerbert* (New York, 1961), 374, n. 34, failed to survive; the document registeres as such turned out to be a seventeenth century forgery. Cf. also J.F. Böhmer (ed), *Regesta imperii: Papstregesten, 911-1024* (rev. repr. Vienna-Graz, 1969), 374, no. +973, and the tendentious interpretation of Schramm, I, 152ff. (Schramm:s reaction to Hungarian criticism is recorded in the 3rd edition of his work, one vol., Bad Bomburg, 1962, 351). It is ironic that, in his collection of medieval sources, O.J. Thatcher (ed), *A Source Book for Medieval History* (New York, 1905), 121, included this piece of literature.

46. Hartvic, c. 10; *Vita maior*, c. 9: "benedictionis apostolice litteris allatis" (*SSH*, II, 384; *MGHSS*, XI, 233); Váczy, 93ff.

47. Stephen's Code of Laws, art. I:1-2; Admonitions, art. II-III (both *loc. cit.*).

48. Ibid., art. III; Laws, art. I:2.

49. But someone, who had divine support for his holding office of the king, "quoniam unaqueque gens propriis regitur legibus, idcirco nos quoque Dei natu nostram gubernando monarchiam . . . ;" preface to Stephen's Laws, *loc. cit.*

50. "Girardus de Venetia . . . , qui constitutione superna pontifex electus;" Hartvic, c. 14.

51. *SSH*, II, 473, c. 3.

52. "Cui superna pietas tantam gratiam contulit, ut eum omnes homines loci illius invicem (sic!) amarent et ut patrem colerent;" ibid.

53. "Factum est autem, postquam venisset ad regem et sua negotia feliciter peregisset, cum quidam nobilis gravi scelere apud regem accusatus fuissed et multitudo nobilium ei veniam impetrare nullatenus potuisset,

iste solus obtinuit." Gerard's *Vita maior,* c. 12 (ibid., II, 489).

54. "In libello autem quem ad andream presbiterum diuinae germanitatis uirum de diuino patrimonio expressimus, qui nunc apud abbatem richardum inconaminatum christi famulum diuinitus eruditum est . . .;" MS, f. 165', 21-25.

55. "Exterarum etiam monasteria provinciarum munificentie regie donis innumeris per nuncios suos sepe visitavit." *Cf. Vita maior,* c. 15 (*SSH,* II, 392; *MGHSS,* XI 238, c. 16); Hartvic, c. 19. Contacts were maintained with Odilo of Cluny—see *MGHSS,* IV 634.

56. Cf. Migne, *PL,* 141, col. 189f.; Bonipert was the first bishop of Pécs (cf. Szentpétery, *Regesta,* I, no. 5), who died around 1042; cf. *Annales Posonienses,* a. 1042 (*SSH,* I, 125); Wattenbach in *MGHSS,* XI, 238, n. 45.

57. *SIE,* 459, n. 1.

58. King Stephen did enact legislation dealing with church affairs in Hungary all by himself, as the first thirteen articles (the first twelve in Migne!) bear witness to this. It is true, of course, that some of the first thirteen articles (I:1—13) had been taken over from previous ecclesiastical legislation passed by church councils in the west, as, for example, art. I:1-2 were reproductions of art. 6 and 7 of the 847 Council of Mainz (Mansi, *Concilia,* XIV, col. 905), or art. I:4 (it is being the second half of c. 3 in the Migne reproduction) from c. 12 of the 888 Council of Mainz (Mansi, *Concilia* XVIIIA, col. 67f.). Cf. Závodszky, 13ff., or the recent essay by K. Eszláry, "Ansegise apát és Lévita Benedek 'Kapituláréinak' és Szent István törvényeinek hasonlatosságai (Similarities between the capitularies of Abbot Ansegis and Benedict Levita and the Laws of King Stephen)," *Proceedings of the Ninth Hungarian Convention* (ed. F. Somogyi; Cleveland, Ohio, 1970), 28ff. It might be of some significance that King Stephen did, in person, supervise the construction of a church building—see Chronicle, c. 67.

59. Accroding to Stephen's *Vita maior,* c. 11, and the report of Hartvic, c. 13 (*SSH,* II, 419; *MGHSS,* XI, 235, c. 12), King Stephen had homes-for-pilgrims established at Jerusalem, Rome ("in capite quoque mundi Roma"), and Constantinople ("urbs regia"),—evidently to maintain close (diplomatic) contacts with the outside world; Wattenbach noted (ibid., XI, 235, n. 39) that King Stephen, "consilio Gerardi episcopi," had a house established also at Ravenna. The Chronicle reported about a

visit of King Stephen to Rome (*SSH,* I, 317, 7), and in the fifteenth century Bishop Ranzano, Neopolitan ambassador at the court of Matthias Corvinus, recorded in his *Epitomae Ungaricarum* that King Stephen was about 33 years old when undertaking that journey to Rome; cf. Schwandt-ner, *Scriptores,* I, 322ff., esp. 593.

60. Wattenbach, II, 290, agrees, while Manitius, II, 82, disagrees with with point of view.

Notes to Chapter II
Section 2

1. Cf. Chronicle, cc. 64 etc. (*SSH,* I, 312ff.); Györffy, *Krónikáink,* 147ff.; P. Váczy, "A korai magyar történet néhány kérdéséről (Some remarks about early Hungarian historiography)," *Századok,* 92 (1958), 265ff.; Deér, *art. cit.* (1971); F. Pelsőczy, "Szent István, pap és király (King Stephen, priest and monarch)," *Vigilia,* 36 (1971), 513ff.; B. Hóman, *Történetírás és forráskritika* (Hungarian historiography) (Budapest, 1938), 261ff.; idem, *Tudományos történetírásunk megalapítása a XVIII század-ban* (The origins of learned Hungarian historiography in the eighteenth century) (Budapest, 1920), 69f. On the circumstances of Emery's death, see *Annales Hildesheimenses,* a. 1031 (*MGHSS,* III, 98); according to a Polish source, the accident took place in Poland since Emery was married to a Polish princess. Cf. Hungarian-Polish Chronicle, c. 9 (*MPH,* I, 508f., n. 43; *SSH,* II, 314f.); *Annales s. Crucis Poloniae (MGHSS,* XIX, 678); Rocznik Swietorkrzyski (*MPH,* III, 61); Hartvic, c. 19. William II Rufus of England died on a "hunting accident:" "dum in nova foresta... venatu esset occupatus, ... sagitta incaute directa percussus, vitam finivit;" Roger of Hoveden, *Chronica* (R.S. No. 51, 3 vols.; London, 1868), I, 155f.

King Stephen died in 1038; cf. *Vita maior,* c. 18 (*MGHSS,* XI, 239; the text in *SSH,* II, 392, ends much earlier, so that it makes no mention of Stephen's death). In the Szentpétery edition only Stephen's *Vita minor,* c. 8, and Hartvic, c. 23, report the death of the King, and the date rendered by Hartvic is 1033 (*SSH,* II, 431), in spite of the fact that the Vienna MS 3662, f. 92a, carries the entry "octavo." In the Szent-pétery edition of the *Vita minor* the Roman numeral VIII is carried in paranthesis, though the Lilienfeld MS 60, f. 167 a, has the number written *1038*. The Szentpétery edition of the *Vita minor* made the date appear as of September 1, though Wattenbach (*MGHSS*, XI, 229, n. 25) did point out that the date should read 18 Kal. Sept., as it was reported by the *Annales Altahenses*, a. 1038 (ibid., XX, 793), or by Wipo's Life of Conrad II, c. 38 (ibid., XI, 273). We ought to realize that the monkish chroniclers made it a habit of assigning to a more important feast the day of the earthly departure of an important personage; so, King Stephen died on the feast of The Assumption (Aug. 15). The reasoning of Domanovszky (*SSH*, I, 321, n. 7), based upon an earlier study by Hóman, *Gesta*, 26, that the scribe(s) of the codices committed many errors in recording dates, is not convincing. For instance, the *Annales Hildesheimenses*, a. 1038 (*MGHSS*, III, 101f.), made no mention of the death of King Stephen despite the fact that, supposedly, strong ties were maintained between the contemporary "intellectual" in Hungary and the abbey of Hildesheim; cf. L.J. Csóka, "Szent István Intelmeinek és törvényeinek szerzűsége (Essay on the authorship of the Laws and Admonitions of King Stephen)," *Vigilia*, 29 (1964), 453ff.; L. Mezey, "Litteratura, grammatica et musica," *Irodalomtörténeti Közlemények*, 74 (1970), 653ff.

On the other hand, the Chronicle did have outside, "foreign" contacts (Csóka, 344ff.), while the *Annales Altahenses* had access to Hungarian sources of information,—identified as the surroundings of King Solomon (of Hungary) and his mother; cf. Gy. Kristó, "Legitimitás és idoneitás (Legitimity and aptness)," *Századok*, 108 (1974), 585ff. Kristó thus repeated and confirmed the correctness of assertions made by B. Homan (in 1925), and P. Váczy (in 1941); cf. ibid., 589, nn. 22 and 23. By the same token, Hermann Contractus, who was described by Manitius, I, 63, as the greatest scholar of his age, must be regarded as a well informed and objective historian; cf. R. Buchner, "Geschichstbild und Reichsbegriff Hermann von Reichenau," *Archiv für Kulturgeschichte*, 42(1960), 37ff. On the chronicle (Gesta) of Simon de Keza, see Györffy, *Krónikáink*, 126ff., esp. 148ff., and J. Gerics, "Adalékok a Kézai krónika problémáinak megoldásához (Some remarks on solving certain problems of the Keza chronicle:," *Annales Universitatis scientiarum de Rolando Eötvös nominate*, sectio hist., 1 (1957), 106ff.; Csóka, 599ff., described the social outlook represented by Keza, explained in more detail by J. Szűcs, "Társadalomszem-

lélet, politika teória és történetszemlélet Kézai Simon Gesta Hungarorumában (Social outlook political ideas and the historical views presented
by Keza in his Gesta Hungarorum)," *Századok*, 107 (1973), 569ff.,
and 823ff.

2. Gy. Györffy, "Zu den Anfängen des ungarischen Kirchenwesens
auf Grund neuerer geschichtskritischer Ergebnisse," *Archivum Historiae
Politicae*, 7 (1969), 79ff.; Z. Tóth, *A Hartvik legenda kritikájához* (Essay
on the historical value of Hartvic's Life of King Stephen) (Budapest, 1942),
100ff., identified Hartvic as the abbot of Hirschfeld, and was harshly
criticised for doing so by J. Deér, *A magyar királyság kialakulása* (The
formation of the Hungarian kingdom) (Budapest, 1942), 5, n. 1. Yet,
according to Hartvic's preface (*SSH*, II, 401), he, Hartvic, might have
been a bishop in the personal service of King Coloman the Learned of
Hungary (1095-1116), himself a former bishop; Hartvic was born and
educated abroad, and composed his opus upon special royal command,
"incepturus opus, domine mi rex inclite, quod michi vestro regali pre-
cepto de vita beati regis Stephani potentialiter iniunxisti" (ibid.; Pintér,
I, 205),—a circumstance that may imply that he had access to the oral
tradition of the Árpád family. See further Gy. Pauler, "A Hartvik legen-
dáról (Some comments on the work of Hartvic),"*Századok*, 16 (1892),
286ff.; Wattenbach in *MGHSS*, XI, 222ff.; Horváth, *Irodalmi műveltség*,
28ff.; *Stílusproblémák*, 149ff. E. Bartoniek maintained that Hartvic
simply *rescribit* the information of the *vitae minor* and *maior* (*SSH*, II,
367), thus repeating the statement of Wattenbach, *Geschichtsquellen*, II,
210f., though it had been pointed out earlier that the reapplication of
selections taken from previous texts was a standard medieval procedure;
cf. K. Hampe, *Das Hochmittelalter* (5th ed.; Cologne-Graz, 1963), 221ff.;
F. Heer, *The Medieval World* (tr. J. Sondheimer; Cleveland-New York,
1962), 227ff.; Erdélyi, *Művelődéstörténet*, I, 46f., maintained that Stephen's *Vita minor* was composed about 1100. Compare with Horváth,
Stílusproblémák, 143f.

3. Cf. *MGHSS*, IV, 756; according to Wattenbach (ibid., XI, 233, n,
33), Anastasius and Asheric were the same person—a view presented by
Györffy, *art, cit. (Archivum hist. politicae, M.T.A. II oszt. közl.*, 1969)
as Fraknói, I, 358, n. 24, made the point, Astric (Asheric) attended the
dedication ceremony of the Bamberg cathedral as the Primate of Hungary;
Annales Altahenses, a. 1012 (*MGHSS*, III, 94); Thietmar, a. 1012 (ibid.,
III, 823); the Reichersberg Annals (ibid., XVII, 636).

4. On the wars of King Stephen, cf. his *Vita minor,* c. 5, and Hartvic, c. 14; *Fundatio ecclesiae s. Albani Namucensis,* 1047 (*MGHSS,* XV-2, 963) in reference to the victory of King Stephen and his human treatment of the Bulgarian POW's; Chronicle, c. 67 (*SSH,* I, 317). The marriage of Stephen is recorded by his *Vita minor,* c. 2, as an event that took place before his coronation. Also, A. Brackmann, "Die Anfänge der abendländischen Kulturbewegung in Osteuropa und deren Träger," *Jahrbücher für Geschichte Osteuropas,* 3 (1938), 185ff.

5. Cf. Stephen's *Vita maior,* c. 16; Hartvic, c. 22. In making his choice, Stephen relied upon the bishops, whom he had the right to nominate (SSH, II, 397), and only worthy persons did he select to the episcopal office: "secundum vitae meritum episcopos et sacredotes prefecit" (ibid., II, 396); Váczy, 59f.

6. On Suger, see Heer, 229; on Gerard being the Suger-type, see his own record (*SSH,* II, 499, 30-37). "Pro dolor, uero nunc multi pollutant in aecclesia, immo iam totum occupant orbem, et nemo est qui talium ineptiis contradicat. O quantos sentio diaboli filios, quibus loqui non patior;" MS, f. 46, 22-26. "Uae autem nobis qui contra istiusmodi imperium incitare non formidamus. Nullos tam caros nostra pannonia consueuit habere ut tales . . . ;" MS, f. 33', 2-5. In the point of view held by A. Lhotsky, *Europäisches Mittelalter* (Vienna, 1970), 336, Gerard of Csanád "war ein gebürtiger Franzose." May I respectfully note that the learned Austrian scholar tended to be somewhat less accurate in his handling east-European events; cf. my review of his *Das Haus Habsburg* (Vienna, 1971), in *Austrian History Yearbook,* 8 (1972), 276ff.

7. *SSH,* II, 497, 24-27; II, 498f.

8. "Quare hoc? Nimirum dixi quia filii diaboli qui potestates sunt tenebrarum ubique regnant et dominantur. Italia non consueuit hereses nutrire, ad presens in quibusdam partibus heresium fomentis habundare auditur. Gallia uero felix quae his munda perhibetur. Gretia infelix sine quibus numquam uiuere uoluit. Uerona urbium italiae nobilissima his grauida redditur. Illustris reuenna et beata uenetia quae numquam inimicos dei passae sunt ferre. Infelices et miserrimi qui dei et aecclesiae suae aduersarios questu lucri attollunt;" MS, f. 46', 24-26; f. 47, 1-10. "In spania fui doctus, in britania eruditus, in scotia detritus, in hibernia studui, omnes liberales disciplinas comendaui memorie, ideo nil lectionis mae effugere potest;" MS, f. 141', 19-22.

9. This is why he spoke so bitterly about the persecutions in 1046: "Prohibemur iam loqui, et episcopi nominamur, constituti etiam sub tributo humano, quibus totus comittitur diuino imperio mundus. Nam quorumdam nisi fallor intentio est quo ecclesiastica uirtus suffragantibus methodianistis atque indignitas apud nos circa hereticorum libitum tota quandoque infirmetur;" MS, f. 46', 17-23.

10. Judged again by his remarks, this time quoting from Ez. 22:24-29; MS, f. 64', 5-12. "Si prophetae falsi nihilominus sunt in terra non plura quanquam sepissime plura et inmunda, illi narrare possunt qui uix psalmis auditis in scola cathedras arripierunt episcopales. De cetero germania narret et pannonia non sileat;" MS, f. 65, 2-7.

11. Karácsonyi, *Szent Gellért*, 101ff.

12. Gerard's *Vita maior*, c. 9.

13. *SSH*, II, 473, 2-7; 476, 15-30.

14. Gerard's own observation (ibid., II, 499, 21-37); on the diocese being a part of the secular administration, see Neuss, 46ff.; Váczy, 51, remarked that the king "als der *grösste* Grundherr des Landes, behandelte seine Eigenkirche ganz wie ein Teil seines Besitzes."

15. Gerard's *Vita minor*, c. 3; Hartvic, c. 14 (*SSH*, II, 422, 11-19; MGHSS, XI, 236, c. 14); Békefi, 70ff.

16. Gerard's *Vita maior*, c. 9; Hóman-Szekfű, I, 197ff.; Gy. Volf, "Első keresztény térítőink (The first Christian missionaries active in Hungary)," *Budapesti Szemle*, 85 (1896), 177ff., and 363ff.; Csóka, *art. cit.* (*Vigilia*, 1972).

17. After quoting from Ier. 1:5-8 (and Luc. 21:15), Gerard continued: "Ista quippe sapientia imbutos sacer sermo consueuit uocare doctos et rutilantissimos quod potius est splendore, id est istar firmamentum splendoris aeternaliter lucere ob diuinissimam eruditionem...;" MS, 146, 3-7. C. Juhász, "Gerhard der Heilige, Bischof von Marosburg," *Studien und Mitteilungen zur Geschichte des Benediktiner-Ordens*, 48 (1930), 1ff.; G. Stadtmüller, "Das Abendland und die Welt der östlichen Christenheit," *Historishces Jahrbuch*, 74 (1955), 164ff. On the background, cf. A. Alföldi, "A kereszténység nyomai Pannóniában a népvándorlás korában (Christian remains in Pannonia at the time of the barbarian invasions)," *SIE*, I, 149ff.; R. Békefi, "Árpádkori közoktatásügy (Public schooling in Árpádian Hungary)," *Századok*, 30 (1896), 207ff.; Pintér, I, 124ff.

18. "Ad imperium regis" (*SSH*, II, 493); Gerard's own remarks: "Talis terra diuortium generat inter lucem et splendorem cui spera celi non lucet," and ends with a quote from Ps. 67:10; MS, f. 65, 7-11. J. Horváth, Jr., "A Gellért legendák forrásértéke (The source value of the 'lives' of Gerard)," *M.T.A. nyelv és irod. utd. oszt. közleményei,* 13 (1958), 21ff.; Horváth, *Irodalmi műveltség,* 35ff.; F. Kühár, "Szent Gellért Bakonybélben (The whereabouts of Gerard at Bakonybél)," *Pannonhalmi Szemle,* 2 (1927), 305ff.; Stilting, *loc. cit.*

19. *SSH,* II, 477.

20. Ibid., II, 500, 31-34.

21. Erdélyi, *Rendtörténet,* I, 590.

22. On Maurus, cf. Gerard's *Vita minor,* c. 2; Vargha, *passim;* Maurus did succeed the learned Bonipert—see Bonipert's writ to Fulbert of Chartres in Migne, *PL,* 141, 189f.—, as the second bishop of Pécs; cf. *Annales Posonienses,* 1036 (*SSH,* I, 125); Maurus also did author various works, as, for example, *Legenda ss. Zoerardi et Benedicti* (ibid., II, 347ff.); Horváth, *Stilusproblémák,* 123ff.; Pintér, I, 159ff. E. Petrovich, "Szent Mór pécsi püspök (St. Maurus, bishop of Pécs)," *Vigilia,* 36 (1971), 85ff. Horváth, *Stilusproblémák,* 181, made the remark that the passage in Gerard's *Vita minor* did carry the term: microcosmus; now it is possible that the scribe of the text knew, through cultural exchange, of the work of Bernard Sylvestris, *De universitate mundi,* the second book which is entitled *Microcosmus, . . . id est minor mundus;* cf. C.S. Barach *et al* (ed), *Bernardi Sylvestris De mundi universitate libri duo sive Megacosmus et Microcosmus* (Innsbruck, 1876), vi: 34-34.

23. *SSH,* II, 499, 30-32; therefore, the leaders of the Church should be setting an example by dying for their faith, if necessary. See further the admonitions of Gerard directed to his fellow bishops on the eve of his martyrdom (ibid., II, 477, 21-25), and compare with the Chronicle, c. 86 (ibid., I, 343f.).

24. Cf. King Andrew's *Constitutiones ecclesiasticae* (Mansi, *Concilia,* XIX, col. 631f.; Migne, *PL,* 151, col. 1257f.), art. 1-4.

25. See his *op. cit.,* I, 358, nn. 16-17. Gy. Moravcsik, "Görögnyelvű monostorok szent István korában (Byzantine monasteries in Hungary during the reign of King Stephen)," *SIE,* I, 299ff.

26. Cf. Hartvic, c. 13; F. Luttor, "Szent István egyházi kapcsolatai Rómával, Montecassinóval, Ravennával, Velencével és Bizánccal (The

ecclesiastical contacts of King Stephen with Rome, Montecassino, Ravenna, Venice and Byzantium)," *SIE*, I, 423ff.; Németh, *art. cit.*

27. See his *op. cit.*, 215ff.

28. Fraknói, I, 401f.

29. Hartvic, c. 13; Roma was "caput mundi;" cf. Stephen's *Vita maior*, c. 11 (*SSH*, II, 386).

30. Cf. Gerard's *Vita maior*, cc. 14-15, Hungarian political background in the *Annales Altahenses* (*MGHSS*, XX 794ff.); Chronicle, c. 71; on the circumstance of Gerard's death, see Chronicle, c. 86, and/or Gerard's *Vita minor*, c. 6; Keza, cc. 47 etc.

31. Gerard's *Vita maior*, c. 15.

32. Gerard's *Vita maior*, c. 6; *Vita minor*, c. 2.

33. *SSH*, II, 422, 11-19; Kühár, *art. cit.*

34. Gerard might have had his reasons, though. "Christi autem nonulli (sic) sacerdotum quomodo uicticent, solius uenationes et lites et rapinae, et oppressiones et scurrae, insolentiae uero ac cupiditates, transgressiones quoque diuini iuris, et concubinarum turmae narrare sufficiunt;" MS, f. 64', 23-26; f. 65, 1. "Prodolor (sic) uero nunc multi pulluant in ecclesia, immo iam totum occupant orbem, et nemo est, qui talium ineptis contradicat. O quantos sentio diaboli filios, quibus loqui non patior;" MS, f. 46, 22-26.

35. See confrontation with a driver (of horses) in *SSH*, II 497.

36. Ibid., II, 497, 24-27; 498.

37. Christianization remained an enforced affair; cf. ibid., II, 494, 2-9. Gerard's own remarks confirm this: ". . . dicant non insanie uigilias plenas habere in nocte morum ethnicorum prandia celebrantes, et usque auroram mensas predentes inlecebrossimas. Ut de his autem sic de ceteris quibus nulla in mundo est;" MS, f. 79, 6-11, not to mention the fact that Gerard himself preached through an interpreter. Cf. *SSH*, II, 477. Gerard's remarks referred to the behavior of baptized Hungarians; "Non aestimes frater carissime minorem persecvtionem et heresem antiquioribus hanc esse. In fide et ueritate fateor quod ui compellabantur intolerabilia mendatia in dei expendere sacerdotes. . .;" MS, f. 46', 7-11. For comparison, see J.F. Strayer, "The Two Levels of Feudalism," in *Life and Thought in the Early Middle Ages* (ed. R.S. Hoyt; Minneapolis, Minn., 1967), 51ff.

38. Gerard was an outspoken critic: *Sacerdotum vitia enumerat* (marginal entry by different hand; MS, f. 64', 6): "animam deuorauerunt; inopis (sic) et pretium acceperunt. Viduas eius multiplicauerunt in medio illius." Gerard now quotes from Ezechiel, 22;26, 27: "Sacerdotes eius contempserunt legem meam, et polluerunt sanctuaria mea. Inter sanctum et prophanum non habuerunt distantiam, et inter pollutum et mundum non intellexerunt;" MS, f. 64', 3-9.

39. "Dicant se non insanire qui cottidie scurrarum debachationibus insistunt. . . . Talia siquidem (sic) facientes insensatissimae bestiae sunt. De istius modi quippe optime uidetur dictum. Dixi in corde meo de filiis hominum, ut probaret eos deus, et ostenderet mihi similes esse bestiis;" MS, f. 79, 5-15, with quote from Eccl. 3:18.

40. Karácsonyi, *Szent Gellért,* 101ff.; he liked the Hungarians and looked upon Hungary (Pannonia) as his country. "Uae autem nobis qui contra istiusmodi imperium incitare non formidamus. Nullos tam caros nostra pannonia consuerit habere ut tales. . . ;" MS, f. 33', 2-5.

41. "Vbi itaque diuinae intellegentiae spiritus non est et notionis omnia transcendentis scientia, ibi asinorum procul dubio spiritus regnat. Uani sunt homines ait in quibus non est scientia dei, et de his quae uidebantur bona non potuerunt intellegere eum qui est. . . ;" MS, f. 77', 16-21.

42. "Pro nephas nostri uidentes non foris clamant, sed intus murmurant, atque sine iussv et interrogatu nil musitare audent, ne quidem aures offendant regales. Quomodo inquiunt displicentia loqui possumus regi? Ira succendtiru, furore armatur, et nos insonabimus?" MS, f. 15', 2-8.

43. "Tamen dicunt Umgari, quod ipse rex Stephanus sua praedicatione Ungaros convertit;" cf. Albericus Trium fontium (*MGHSS,* XXIII, 779); the process of conversion was an enforced affair—see Gerard's *Vita maior* (SSH, II, 493f.), while Gerard himself expressed doubts about its effectiveness: "scindetur Ungaria et solvetur a iugo Christianitatis, a sacerdotibus usque ad laicos laborque meus et praedicatio mea despicitur, et verbum Dei non recipietur" (ibid., II, 499). See also n. 37 above.

44. *SSH,* II, 475f.; "non sum propheta, non sum filius prophetae sed armentarius ego sum uellicans sicomoros;" MS, f. 15, 16-18.

45. "Hoc autem quidem ut eorum siue contigui, ab inditis non suspendantur officis, ipsi uero ne priuentur paleis. Dum offendere uero

minem propter hominem et ea quae sunt in usu hominum atque ob hoc placere gestit huic qui hodie est, et mane uestigium illius non inuenitur super terram . . .;" MS, f. 15', 10-16.

46. *SSH,* II, 395.

47. Cf. F. Barlow, "Edward the Confessor's Early Life, Character, and Attitudes," *English Historical Review,* 80 (1965), 225ff.; *idem, The English Church 1000-1066* (Hamden, 1963), passim; F. Dvornik, *The Making of Central and Eastern Europe* (London, 1949), 136ff.

Notes to Chapter II
Section 3

1. Cf. Hartvic, c. 14, SSH, II, 422, 11-16; *Annales Posonienses,* a. 1030, ibid., I, 125; Gy. Györffy, *Az Árpád-kori Magyarország történeti földrajza* (Geographica historica Hungariae tempore stirpis Arpadianae) (Budapest, 1963), 835ff., and 852.; idem, *István király,* 316ff.

2. It was the Byzantine monks who established a monastery at Marosvár first; cf. SSH, II, 492; Gy. Györffy, "A magyar nemzetségtől a vérmegyéig, a törzstől az országig (Clan and county; tribe and country)," *Századok,* 92 (1958), 12ff.; 565ff., esp. 587f. Also, F. Dölger, "Ungarn in der byzantinischen Reichspolitik," *Archivum Europae centro-orientalis,* 8 (1942), 315ff.

3. See G. Denzler, "Das sogenannte morgenländische Schisma in Jahre 1054," *Münchener Theologische Zeitschrift,* 17 (1966), 24ff.; the letter of Pope Leo IX to the Latin bishop of Trani, Migne, *PL,* 120, cols. 836ff., and the comments made by A. Michel, "Bestand eine Trennung der griechischen und römischen Kirchen schon vor Kerullarios?" *Historisches Jahrbuch,* 42 (1922), 1 ff.; M. Jugie, *Le schisme byzantine* (Paris, 1941), 205ff.

4. Györffy, *Egyházszervezés, loc. cit.;* Moravcsik, Byzantium and the Magyars, 61ff.; K. Bosl *et al, Eastern and Western Europe in the Middle Ages* (London, 1970), 43ff.

5. Gerard's *Vita minor,* c. 3; Hartvic, cc. 8 and 14.

6. As early as the 960s, the Byzantine Patriarch had attempted to create a missionary province in what can be called the Marosvár region;

cf. G. Cedrenus, *Compendium historiarum* (2 vols.; Bonn, 1838-39), II, 328, or Migne, *PG*, 122, col. 62.

7. " . . . clam dimissis itineris sui comitibus hunc solum invitum retinuit custodiamque adhibuit;" Gerard's *Vita minor*, c. 2; "Iherosolimam ire noli, neque enim te permittam;" *Vita maior*, c. 5; Karácsonyi, *Gellért*, 101f.

8. On the Hungarian "marches," see Stephen's *Vita minor*, c. 5, and the account of the *Annales Altahenses*, a. 1041; L. Novák, "Szent Gellért csanádi püspök," *Magyar Sion*, 3 (1868), 481ff. For comparison, cf. D.J. Geanakoplos, *Byzantine East and Latin West: Two Worlds of Christendom* (New York, 1966), 55ff.

9. SSH, II, 411f.; Váczy, 59f.

10. Hartvic, c. 8; SSH, II, 383, n. 3; Váczy, 61; Hóman, *Ungarisches Mittelalter*, I, 194f.; Gy. Volf, "Első keresztény térítőink (The first Christian missionaries in Hungary)," *Budapesti Szemle*, 85 (1896), 177ff.; and 363ff. The remark made by K. Hampe, *Das Hochmittelalter* (5th ed.; Cologne-Graz, 1963), 57, that "allein Rom untergeordnete, nicht von Deutschland abhängige Kirche," was really the Polish Gnesen, could also be applied to Hungary; and yet, as A. Dempf, *Sacrum imperium: Geschichts- und Staatsphilosophie des Mittelalters und* "Magyar emlekek Bécsben (Hungarian memorials in Vienna)," *Bécsi Magyar Évkönyv*, 1958 (Vienna, 1958), 67ff.

11. Hampe, *Kaisergeschichte*, 5ff.; A. Brackmann, "Die Anfänge der abendländischen Kulturbewegung in Osteuropa und deren Träger," *Jahrbücher für Geschichte Osteuropas*, 3 (1928), 185ff.

12. Gerard's *Vita maior*, c. 8; the entry in *Annales Hildesheimenses*, a. 1030, that "Cunradus imperator cum exercitui fuit in Hungaria" (MGHSS, XX, 97), stands all by itself; however, the additional remark made by the *Annales Altahenses*, a. 1030 (ibid., XX, 791), that the Emperor spent a night in Altaich abbey may indicate detailed preparations for an attack—in which he suffered defeat: "rediit autem de Hungaria sine militia et in nullo proficiens, ideo quod exercitus fame periclitabatur, et Vienni ab Ungaris capiebatur;" that the term *Vienni* meant Vienna, Wien, is noted *procul dubio* by W. v. Giesebrecht (ibid., XX, 791, n. 23). The forthcoming Vienna Treaty between King Stephen and the German court was signed on the "Hohe Markt" in Vienna; cf. A. Leopold,

13. Wipo, cc. 22 and 26 (MGHSS, XI, 267); this may be the reason why Stephen kept the conquered territory—*Annales Hildesheimenses*, a. 1031 (ibid., III, 97).

14. J. Kirchberg, *Kaiseridee und Mission unter den Sachsenkönigen und den ersten Saliern von Otto I bis Henrich III* (Berlin, 1934), 85ff.

15. Hóman, *Ungarisches Mittelalter*, I, 247.; M. Perlbach, "Die Kriege Heinrichs III gegen Böhem, 1039-41," *Forschungen zur deutschen Geschichte* 19 (1870), 427ff.

16. "... imperatoris filius Heinricus rex et ipse dux Baioariae, et Stephanus rex Ungaricus, cum iuramento invicem firmaverunt pacem;" MGHSS, III, 98, a. 1031.

17. SSH, II, 489ff.; C.A. Macartney, "Studies on the earliest Hungarian historical sources," *Archivum Europae centro-orientalis*, 4 (1938), 456ff., expressed some doubts as to the authenticity of the "Csanád narrative."

18. As Wipo remarked, "Ungaria . . . nec audire nos sustinuit;" MGHSS, XI, 257; on Wipo, see E. Erb, *Seschichte der deutschen Literatur bis zu 1160* (Berlin, 1965), 393f.; W. v. Giesebrecht, *Geschichte der deutschen Kaiserzeit* (ed. W. Schild; 6 vols.; Mersburg, 1929), I, 417ff., on the background, and, on the same, L. Bréhier, *Vie et mort de Byzance* (2nd ed; Paris, 1969), 226.

19. Gerard's *Vita maior*, c. 5.

20. J. Karácsonyi, "Mi köze a görög egyháznak a magyarok Megtéréséhez (How the Byzantine Church influenced the development of Hungarian Christianity)," *Katholikus Szemle,* 14 (1900), 306ff.: Gy. Pauler, "Mi köze a görög egyháznak a magyarok megtéréséhez," *Századok,* 34 (1900), 363f.

21. Gy. Németh, "A magyar kereszténység kezdetei (The Beginnings of Hungarian Christianity),"*Budapesti Szemle,* 256 (1940), 14ff.

22. Ajtony "accepit autem potestatem a Grecis et construxit in prefata urbe Morisena monasterium in honore beati Iohannis Baptiste, constituens in eodem abbatem cum monachiis Grecis, iuxta ordinem et ritum ipsorum. Serviebat namque eidem viro terra a fluvio Keres (Kőrös) usque ad partes Transylvanias et usque in Budin ac Zoren (Szörény; Turni-Sevrin), que omnia sub sua concluserat potestate. Unde procedebant in multitudine armatorum, regem autem minime reputabat;" SSH, II, 490.

23. Emperor Leo VI the Wise, *Tactica,* xviii:46 etc., in Marczali, *Enchiridion,* 12ff.; the Greek court had little trust in the Hungarians as military allies.

24. Chronicle, c. 83; *Annales Posonienses,* a. 1030.

25. Gerard's *Vita maior,* c. 8.

26. RHM, II, 310ff., aa. I;1-2; Admonitions, aa. 1-3 (SSH, II, 619ff); F. Heer,*Europäische Geistesgeschichte* (2nd ed.; Stuttgart, 1965), 80ff.; K. Morrison, *Tradition and Authority in the Western Church* (Princeton, 1969), 261ff.

27. RHM, II, 310ff., art. II:9 (in Migne, c. 43!), though the principle could be turned around– cf. ibid., a. II:8 (Migne, c. 42), or art. II:16 (not in the Admont MS; c. 50).

28. RHM, II, 310ff., a. I:2; according to the wording of art. I:20 (c. 19), "ut gens nostra monarchiae huius ab omni incursu et accusatione servorum et ancillarum remota et quieta maneat," and of art. I:35 (c. 33), "ut firma pax et unanimitas sit inter maiores et minores," the impression may be gained that the King had drawn some distinction between *maiores* and *minores,* the conqueror and conquered elements of society. (For a different view, cf. Váczy, *art. cit.* in SIE, I, 35ff.) Art. II:9 and 16 (cc. 43 and 50) may serve as proof of the twofold nature of that society–in that the King had to protect his low-born officials from the wrath of the nobles (of whom Gerard held a low opinion: "quorum deus uenter est, et gloria in confusione eorum qui terrena sapiunt. Dicant se non insanire qui cottidie scurrarum debachationibus insistunt;" MS, fol. 79, 3-9).

29. R. Békefi, "Árpádkori közoktatásügy (Public schools in the Árpádian age)," *Századok,* 30 (1896), 207ff.; Pintér, I, 124ff.

30. SSH, II, 494f., and compare with the remarks made by Gerard: "itaque melius est mitti in fornacem quam ad uocem talium statuam adorare. . . . Iste est caminus, quem sancti sibi eligunt inprimis (sic), quam fauea(n)t iussis nabuchodonosor, id est operibus diaboli," those who "societatem in christi regno non possident;" MS, fol. 3', 15-16; f. 4, 17-23.

31. Gerard's *Vita maior,* c. 10; R. Békefi, *A káptalani iskolák története Magyarországon 1540-ig* (History of the cathedral schools in Hungary until 1540) (Budapest, 1910), 15f.

32. Stephen's Laws, art. I:35.

33. F. Prinz, "Zur geistigen Kultur des Mönchtums im spätantiken Gallien und in der Merowingerzeit," *Zeitschrift für bayerische Landeskunde,* 26 (1963), 29ff.

34. Gerard's *Vita maior,* c. 14.

35. SSH, II, 496ff.

36. B. Hóman, *Magyar városok az Árpádok korában* (Hungarian towns in the Árpádian age) (Budapest, 1908), 39f.; L.J. Csóka, "Hol született szent Márton? (The questioned place of birth of St. Martin of Tours)," *Vigilia,* 43 (1969), 379ff.

37. SSH, II, 489, 27-28; G. Inczefi, "A földrajzi nevek értekelésének néhány kérdése (The importance of geographical names," *Magyar Nyelv,* 60 (1961), 80ff.

38. Chronicle, c. 95; E. Mályusz, "A magyar mediévalisztika forrás-kérdései (The source material of medieval Hungarian history)," *Levéltári Közlemények,* 38 (1967), 3ff.

39. Cf. W. Stubbs (ed), *Select Charters of English Consitutitonal History* (8th ed.; Oxford, 1900), 68f., and 103, on charter by Henry I for the holding of the hundred court. The English resolution, "exsurgat placitum de divisione terrarum (i.e. comitatus mei et hundreda), si est inter barones meos dominicos tractetur placitum in curia mea" (ibid., 104), may compare with Andrew's decree: "misit etiam rex clementis-simus per totam Hungariam precones, ut de singulis villis vocarentur duo seniores facundiam habentes ad regis consilium" (SSH, I, 359).

40. Ibid., I, 359, 1-15.

41. Stephen's Laws, art. I:32, 34, 35; II:3 and 5 (cc. 30, 32, 33, 37 and 41); A. Huber, "Beiträge zur älteren Geschichte Österreichs: über die älteste ungarische Verfassung," *Mitteilungen des Institutes für öst-erreichische Geschichtsforschung,* 6 (1885), 385ff.

42. Z. Tóth, "Szent István kegrégibb életirata nyomán (Comments on the earliest Life of King Stephen)," *Századok,* 81 (1947), 23ff.

43. Hóman, *Magyar középkor,* 213ff.; R. Sprandel, "Struktur und Geschichte des merowingischen Adels," *Historische Zeitschrift,* 193 (1961), 33ff.

44. Chronicle, c. 69.

45. Stephen's *Vita minor,* c. 7; Hartvic, c. 21; *Annales Hildeshei-menses,* a. 1031; according to the Polish sources, the accident happened in Poland because Emery was engaged to a Polish princess; cf. Hungaro-Polish Chronicle, c. 9, MPH, I, 508f., n. 43; or, SSH, II, 314ff.; *Annales s. Crucis Poloniae,* MGHSS, XIX' 678. Emery's *Vita* made no mention of the circumstances of his death; cf. SSH, II, 456f.

46. Stephen's *Vita minor,* c. 7; Hartvic, c. 21; GY. Pauler, *A magyar nemzet története az árpádházi királyok alatt* (History of the Hungarian nation under the Árpáds) (2 vols.; Budapest, 1893-95), I, 66ff.

47. Karácsonyi, *Gellért,* 125; E. Ivánka, "Szent Gellért görög műveltségének problémája (Had Gerard known Greek?)," *Értekezések a nyelvtudományok köréből,* 26 (1942), no. 3. A. Bordor, "Szent Gellért Deliberatiójának forrásai (The sources used in Gerard's Deliberatio)," *Századok,* 77 (1943), 173ff.; K. Redl, "Problémák Gellért püspök Deliberatiójában (Questions concerning Gerard's Deliberatio)," ITK, 69 (1965), 211ff.

48. Karácsonyi, *Gellért,* 203f.; it seems that the King alone showed interest in the outside world. "Qui cum Bohemia, Polonorum infertissimis inimicis pacem et amicitiam retinebat," wrote the Polish Gallus (MPH, I, 414); Raplh Glaber, *Historia Francorum,* noted that foreigners visiting Hungary made contact (only) with the King; cf. MGHSS, VII, 62; Hartvic, c. 13.

49. Gerard stressed the need for good missionary work; cf. SSH, II, 499, 30-37, and only qualified men were given positions of responsibility—Stephen's *Vita minor,* c. 4, whose legal status had been recognized through legislation; Stephen's Laws, art. I:2.

50. Evidence is based upon Gerard's *Vita minor,* in SSH, II, 473, 2-12; or, his *Vita maior,* ibid., II, 496f.; M. Oberschall Bárány, *The Crown of Emperor Constantine IX Monomachos* (Budapest, 1937), 41ff., and 89ff.; Moravcsik, *Byzantium and the Magyars,* 61ff.

51. On the meaning of terms such as *nation* or *national* at this time, see the study of J. Szűcs, "A magyar szellemtörténet nemzet koncepciójának tripologiájához (The concept of the "nation" in Hungarian intellectual development)," *Történeti Szemle,* 9 (1966), 245ff.

52. Cf. Gy. Moravcsik, "The Holy Crown of Hungary," *Hungarian Quarterly,* 4 (1938), 656ff., whose interpretation had been modified by Josef Deér, *Die heilige Krone Ungarns* (Graz, 1966), 197ff.; F. Dölger, "Rom in der Gedankenwelt der Byzantiner," in his *Byzanz und die europäische Staatenwelt* (rev. ed.; Darmstadt, 1964), 70ff.

53. See the writ of Pope Gregory VII to Géza I of Hungary, dated April 14, 1075 (Jaffé, *Bibliotheca,* II, 192f.; Migne, *PL,* 148, col. 422).

54. Hartvic, c. 13.

55. Gerard by quoting from Amos, 7:15; Ephasians, 4:23-24; Luke, 12:35; Ephasians, 6:14-17, said: "Uade et propheta ad populaum meum Israel;" MS, f. 15, 19-20. "Renouamini spiritu mentis uestre, et induite nouum hominem qui secundum deum creatum est;" MS, f. 41, 23-25. "Sint lumbri (sic) uestri precincti et indutos lorica iustitie, et preparatos pedes in preparatione euangelii pacis, scutum tenete fidei, et galeam salutis assumere et gladium spiritus, quod est uerbum dei;" MS, f. 42, 7-11.

56. SSH, II, 492ff.

57. A. Alföldi, *Magyarország népei és a római birodalom* The peoples in Hungary and the Roman Empire) (Budapest, 1934, 13ff.).

58. Pelsőczy, *loc. cit.*

59. E. Patzelt, "Die Mission Cyrills und Methodius in verfassungs-rechtlicher Schau," *Studi medievali,* 5 (1964), 241ff.

60. R. Sullivan, "Khan Boris and the Conversion of Bulgaria," *Studies in Medieval and Renaissance History,* 3 (1966), 53ff.

61. SSH, II, 476f.; the wording of this passage is different from the one in Vienna Nationalbibliothek MS 3662, f. 100'b: "Cum autem amici regis liberalibus studiis eruditi, hec audientes mirarentur, voluntes epis-copum ab indignatione regis defendere, innuebant interpreti, ut taceret. Quibus interpres timore tactus consensit."

62. SSH, ii, 475f.; II, 497.; Horváth in *ITK* (1969).

Notes to Chapter II
Section 4

1. Cf. Marczali, *Geschichtsquellen,* 24ff.

2. Balanyi in *Katolikus Szemle* (1963); on the canonization, cf. *Bernoldi Chronicon,* a. 1083 (MGHSS, V, 438f.); Gerard's *Vita minor,* c. 7; Stephen's *Vita minor,* c. 8.

3. *Geschichtsquellen,* 25f.; Horváth, *Stilusproblémák,* 158f.

4. Macartney, 154ff.; Csóka, 603f.

5. *Geschichtsquellen,* 26ff., in ref. to Chronicle, cc. 81, 82 and 83; Gerard's *Vita maior,* c. 15; Csóka, 263ff.

6. Hartvic, cc. 3, 4, 7, 9; Bogyay in *Ungarn Jahrbuch* (1976); P. Hilsch, "Der Bischof von Prag und das Reich in sächsischer Zeit," *Deutsches Archiv,* 28 (1972), 1ff.

7. Györffy in *MTA* (1969); Bogyay, *Stephanus Rex,* 23ff.

8. Cf. Bruno of Querfurt's *Vita s. Adalberti,* cc. 16, 17, 23 (MGHSS, IV, 603; 607); Adalbert's *Passio* (Migne, *PL,* 138, cols. 859ff.) contained no direct references to his activities in Hungary.

9. As, e.g. Adadmi *Gesta Hamburgensis ecclesiae pontificum* (ed. G.H. Pertz in *SS. rerum Germanicarum in usum scholarum;* Hannover, 1846).

10. "In libello autem,... qui nunc apud abbatem richardum incontaminatum christi famulum, diuinitus eruditum est...;" MS, f. 165', 21-25. Visit mentioned by Ademar Cabannensis *Chronicon,* iii:65(MGHSS, IV, 145); E. Sackur, *Richard Abt von St. Vannes* (Breslau, 1886), 44f., and referred to by R.W. Southern, *The Making of the Middle Ages* (London, 1953), 52f.

11. See the *kalendarium* of the late twelfth century Pray codex, ff. 1'-7, Febr. 24; entered *manu posteriore,* about the *translatio s. Gerardi.* Cf. Radó, 37; L. Mezey, "A Pray kódex keletkezése (Origins of the Pray codex)," *ITK,* 75 (1971), 109ff.

12. SSH, II, 472, c. 2.

13. Ibid., II, 488, c. 5.

14. Cf. Emery's *Vita* (ibid., II, 449ff.); Gy. Németh, "a magyar keresztenyseg kezdetei (Origins of Christianity in Hungary)," *Budapesti Szemle,* 256 (1940), 14ff.

15. *Annales Hildesheimenses,* a. 1031 (MGHSS, III, 98); Hartvic, c. 19 (ibid., XI, 238, c. 16).

16. Macartney, 153.

17. Gerard's *Vita maior,* cc. 1-3 (SSH, II, 480-83).

18. "Dicat mihi qui uult quia multa legi, multa cucurri. In spania fui doctus, in britannia eruditus, in scotia detritus, in hibernia studui; omnes liberales disciplinas comendaui memoriae, ideo nil lectionis mae effugere potest;" Ms, f. 141', 19-22.

19. Endres, *loc. cit.;* Gordon Leff, *Medieval Thought* (Baltimore, 1958), 96.

20. SSH, II, 483, c. 3.

21. Ibid.; Gerard's *Vita minor,* c. 2.

22. "Iherosolimam ire noli, neque enim te permittam" (*Vita maior,* c. 5.)

23. Marczali, *Geschichtsquellen,* 28f.

24. SSH, II, 42; Hartvic, c. 12; Chronicle, c. 83; Keza, c. 56; Csóka, 603f.; Horváth, *Stilusproblémák*, 158f.

25. Györffy in *MTA* (1969).

26. SSH, II, 397f., c. 5.

27. Lilienfeld MS 60, f. 164'a (also in SSH, II, 383).

28. The Rein MS 69 is the major MS of Hartvic's opus; the Lilienfeld MS is one of the important MSS of Stephen's *Vita maior*.

29. Váczy, 92ff., on Stephen's being a "päpstlicher Legat;" Pelsőczy in *Teológia* (1970).

30. Cf. Szentpétery, *Regesta*, I, no. 12; Erdélyi, *Rendtörténet*, X, 487ff., or Marczali, *Enchiridion*, 81ff.; Horváth, *Stilusproblémák*, 30ff.; Csóka, 362f. Gy. Kristó, "A tihanyi alapitólevél és XI századi szóbeliségünk (The Tihany Charter and Hungarian vocabulary in the eleventh century)," *Magyar Nyelv*, 66 (1970), 208ff. Tihany had Slavic origins: *tichij hod* (quiet place); it is possible that Byzantine monks have lived here as late as the times of King Stephen—see A. Tautu, "Residui di rito bizantino nelle regioni balcano-danubiane nell'alto medioevo," *Orientalia Christiana*, 15 (1949), 41ff., esp. 51ff.

31. SSH, II, 476f.; Gy. Gábry, "Symphonia Ungarorum," *Történelmi Szemle*, 13 (1970), 428ff.; Gy. Székely, "Evolution de la structure et de la culture de la classe dominante laique dans la Hongrie des Árpád," *Acta historica*, 15 (1969), 223f. On Hungarian speaking missionaries, SSH, II, 493.

33. *Ibid.*, II, 452f.; I, 125, a. 1036.; E Petrovich, "Szent Mór pécsi püspök (St. Maurus, bishop of Pécs)," *Vigilia*, 36 (1971), 85ff. On the literary activities of Bishop Muarus see Horváth, *Stilusproblémák*, 132ff.; Csóka, 101ff.

33. Gerard's *Vita maior*, c. 10; L. Elekes, "István király (King Stephen)," *Társadalmi Szemle*, 25 (1970), 66ff.

34. Stephen's Laws, aa. I:1-2, II:1, 8, 9 (cc. 1-2, 34, 42, 43 in Migne); Gy. Bónis, "Istvan Király az államalakitó (King Stephen, founder of the Hungarian state)," *Magyar tudomány*, 15 (1970), 777ff.

35. Querfurt, Life of Adalbert, cc. 13etc. (MGHSS, IV, 596ff.; the mentality and behavior of the nobles, and social conditions may be determined from the various articles of Stephen's Laws, as, e.g. aa. I:18, 26, 29, 35 (cc. 17, 24, 27, 33 in Migne), as if to support the picture drawn by Gerard: "Dicant se scientiatos et idola non adorare quorum deus uenter est, et gloria in confusione eorum qui terrena sapiunt? Dicant se non

insanire qui cottidie scurrarum debachationibus insistunt...;" MS, f. 79, 3-7, underscored by Gerard's *Vita minor:* "Rex Peter successit. Cui cum omnes Pannonie principes ex eis de rege regalem cathedram iniuria non usurpavit. Quo regnante, sicut propheta ait, 'sanguis sanguinem tetigit,' peccato peccatum adauctum est;" SSH, II 476.

36. Cf. J. Mabillon (ed), *Annales ordinis s. Benedicti* (6 vols.; Paris, 1703-39), V, 110.

37. MS, f. 24, 16-17.

38. SSH, II, 471, c. 1.

39. MS, f. 34', 14; "quia uero nos hora preterire festinat, incrastino autem ad insidentia consurgere arbitramur;" *ibid.*, f. 51, 21-23.

40. Keza, c. 61.

41. Závodszky, 13ff.; P. Lehmann, *Erforschung des Mittelalters* (5 vols.; Stuttgart, 1959-62), III, 173ff.

42. Gerard.s *Vita maior,* c. 10.

43. SSH, II, 473; E. Mályusz, *Egyházi társadalom a középkori Magyarországon* (The society of ecclesiastics in medieval Hungary) (Budapest, 1971), 13ff.

44. Gerard's *Vita maior,* cc. 9-10.

45. "Isti sunt primi canonici . . . , quod non essent alienigene, sed patriote. . . ;" *ibid.*; Heer, *Geistesgeschichte,* 80ff.

46. He proved successful; *Vita maior,* c. 14.

47. At the time when Count Csanád "monasterium edificavit introducens illuc memoratos Grecos monachos. . .cum abbate;" SSH, II, 492, 26-29. Gy. Györffy, *Az Árpád-kori Magyarország történeti földrajza* (Geographia historica Hungariae tempore stirpis Arpadianae) Budapest, 1963), 835ff.; idem, "Honfoglalás előtti népek és események Anonymus Gesta Hungarorumában (Peoples and events prior to the conquest of Hungary as described by Anonymus' Gesta Hungarorum)," *Ethnographia,* 76 (1965), 411ff.

48. "Iumenta uero inbecilles, et rudes, et sine alterius eruditione nil spiritualium considerare potentes, a mistica remotos amministratione (sic!), quibus diuinus paulus lo quitur dicens. . . ," MS, f. 79, 22-26, with scriptural quotes from Ps. 35:7, and I. Cor. 3:1. SSH, II, 496ff., and 498. P. Váczy, "Karoling művészet Pannóniában: a Cunpald kehely (Carolingian art in Pannonia: the Cunpald chalice)," *Soproni Szemle,* 18 (1964), 127ff., and 218ff.. R. Kottje, "Einheit und Vielfalt des kirchlichen Lebens in der Karolingerzeit," *Zeitschrift für Kirchengeschichte,*

76 (1965), 323ff.

49. Hartvic, c. 17; Gerard's *Vita maior,* cc. 14 etc. On his deathbed, King Stephen offered his realm to the protection of Mary, the Mother of God; cf. Hartvic, c. 22. Religious contacts with the Byzantines are evident in Gerard's Mariology—SSH, II, 473.; F. Kühár, *Mária tiszteletünk a XI és XII század hazai liturgiájában* (Mariology in the eleventh and twelfth century Hungarian liturgy) (Budapest, 1939), passim.

50. Hampe, *Kaisergeschichte,* 20ff.

51. Cf. E. Renauld (ed.), Michael Psellus, *Chronographia* (2 vols.; Paris, 1926-28), I, 38; G. Ostrogorsky, *Geschichte des byzantinischen Staates* (3rd ed.; Munich, 1963), 273f.

52. P. Herde, "Das Pasttum und die griechische Kirche im Süditalien vom 11 bis zum 13 Jahrhundert," *Deutsches Archiv,* 26 (1970), 1 ff.; my essay, "Hungaro-German relations During the Mid-Eleventh Century Against the Background of the Rome-Byzantine Schism," *Proceedings of the XV Hungarian Convention, 1975* (Cleveland, Ohio., 1976), 229ff.

53. On Peter's selection, cf. Hartvic, c. 22; Gerard's *Vita minor,* c. 5, and Gerard's comments' "Si prophetae falsi nihilominus sunt in terra, non plura quanquam sepissime plura et inmunda, illi narrare possunt qui uix psalmis auditis in scola cathedras arripierunt episcopales. . . ;" MS, f. 65, 2-6. The German Henry III made Peter Orseolo his vassal, and "illus etiam petentibus (sic!) concessit rex scita Teutonica;" *Annales Altahenses,* a. 1044 (MGHSS, XX, 800); Keza, c. 51, went into no detail, while the Chronicle altered the text of the German chronicler, "concessitque—i.e. Henry III—, petentibus Ungaris Hungarica scita servare et consuetudinibus iudicari" (SSH, I, 333). This circumstance may explain why Andrew I was crowned so swifty in 1047—see Keza, c. 57; Chronicle, c. 86.

54. Gerard's comments: "Pro dolor, uero nunc multi pollutant in aecclesia, immo iam totum occupant orben, et nemo est qui talium ineptiis contradicat. O quantos sentio diaboli filios, quibus loqui non patior," MS, f, 46, 22-26. Mikkers, *loc. cit.*; K.F. Werner, "Das hochmittelalterliche Imperium im politischen Bewusstsein Frankreichs, 10-12 Jahrhundert," *Historische Zeitschrift,* 200 (1965), 1 ff. Gerard sensed, in fact, the growing hostility of the people toward the Church and warned his fellow missionaries of an immediate uprising: "scindetur Ungaria et solvetur a iugo Christianitatis, a sacerdotibus usque ad laicos laborque meus et predicatio mea despicietur;" SSH, II, 499. On the results of the uprising, see his own remarks: "Prohibemur iam loqui, et episcopi nominamur,

constituti diuino imperio mundus;" MS, f. 46', 17-19.

55. Gerard's *Vita maior,* c. 15.

56. Cf. Stephen's Admonitions, art. II and III (SSH, II, 621f.; Migne, PL, 151, col. 1237ff.). The same policy was carried out by Andrew I soon after his coronation: "pontifices et collegia sacerdotum pristino more observarentur;" his *Constituiones eccl.,* aa. 2-4 (*ibid.* 151, col. 1257f.; Mansi, *Concilia,* XIX, col. 631f.).

57. SSH, II, 499; *Annales Altahenses,* a. 1046 (MGHSS, XX, 803); Keza, c. 53.

Notes to Chapter III

1. Cf. S.R. Maitland, *The Dark Ages: Essays to Illustrate the State of Religion and Literature in the Ninth-Twelfth Centuries* (3rd ed.; London, 1853), 259ff.; I. Zoltvány, "A magyarországi bencés irodalom a tatárjárás előtt (Benedictine literature in Hungary prior to 1241), " Erdélyi, *Rendtörténet,* I, 337ff.; E. Ivánka, "Szent Gellért Deliberaltioja," *Századok,* 76 (1942), 479ff.

2. Gerard's remark: "de diaboli uero spiritibus parum superius dictum scimus;" MS, f. 164', 24-25, may imply that he was sending his work piecemeal to Isingrim.

3. Cf. Gy. Pauler in *Századok,* 26 (1888), 57f.

4. MS, f. 123', 4-7.

5. *Ibid.,* f. 69', 2-4; F. Ibrányi, "Szent Gellért teológiája (Gerard's theology), " SIE, I, 493ff.; Karácsonyi, *Gellért,* 132f.

6. Manitius, II, 79; Leff, 96, called Gerard "one of the earliest upholders of the soverignty of faith,"—on the "primacy" of faith, see E. Gilson, *Reason and Revelation in the Middle Ages* (New York, 1938), ch. I. Ueberweg-Geyer, *Grundriss der Geschichte der Philosophie,* vol. II (Berlin, 1928), 187, said that Gerard was the one who conceived of philosophy as being the handmaiden of theology. Gerard received some evil criticism; cf. E. Mátrai-Ompolyi, *A bőlcsézet története Magyarországon a skolasztika korában* (Scholastic philosophy in Hungary) (Budapest, 1878), 25ff.; or his article in *Figyelő,* 4 (1878), 209ff.; Pauler, I, 66ff., 119f.; II, 787, though as Ibrányi, *loc. cit.,* pointed out, neither Ompolyi, nor Pauler were qualified to judge Gerard's opus; also, L. Halics, *A római Katholikus egyház története Magyarországon* (History of the Roman Catholic Church in Hungary), vol. 1 (Budapest, 1885), 147ff.,

Horváth, *Stilusproblémák,* 110ff., and compare with R. Cruel, *Geschichte der deutschen Predigt im Mittelalter* (Detmold, 1879; repr. Hildesheim, 1966), 80ff.; Csóka, 133ff.

7. MS, f. 56, 14-16; Batthyány, *Opera,* viif.

8. ". . . disputans secundum mediocritatem mean in primo capitulo epistole pauli ad hebreos;" MS, f. 69', 2-3.

9. To be followed by a quote from Ioan., 3:9; *ibid.,* f. 111', 12-16.

10. *Ibid.,* f. 143, 1-2.

11. ". . . quem ad andream presbiterum diuine germanitatis uirum de diuino patrimonio expressimus, qui nunc apud abbatem richardum incontaminatum christi famulum, diuinitus eruditus est;" *ibid.,* f. 165', 21-25; Karásconyi, *Gellért,* 191ff., 259ff.

12. Cf. *Vita Richardi abbatis,* c. 17 (MGHSS, XI, 288); also recorded by Ademar Cabanensis *Chronicon,* iii:63 (*ibid.,* IV, 145), who incidentally mentioned that King Stephen graciously received all foreigners visiting or passing through his country.

13. ". . . unmittelbare Kenntniss der griechischen Urtextes;" cf. E. v. Ivánka, "Das 'Corpus Areopagiticum' bei Gerhard von Csanád," *Traditio,* 15 (1959), 205ff.; idem, "Szent Gellért gőrőg műveltségének problémája (Whether Gerard knew Greek)," *Értekezések a nyelvtudományok kőréből,* 26 (1942), No. 3, in spite of the fact that the writings of Pseudo-Dionysius were already known in the west because of the translation by John the Scot; cf. M.L.W. Laistner, *Thought and Letters in Western Europe, 500-900* (2nd ed.; London, 1957), 323ff.

14. Then he quoted from Ephes. 5:8, and continued: "Lux deus est, et tenebrae nullae in eo. Ergo qui in hac luce non manent, in umbria sunt;" MS, f. 128, 19-23. T. Kardos, *Kőzépkori kultúra, kőzépkori művészet: a magyar irodalom keletkezése* (Origins of Hungarian literature in medieval culture and poetry) (Budapest, 1941), 46ff.

15. SSH, II, 619, 3-17, in ref. to Prov. 1:8.

16. SSH, II, 474; MS, f. 141', 19-23, cited in chapter II, section 2, note mentioned Thangmar of Hildesheim, possibly a resident at the court of King Stephen.

17. A particular incident recorded in Gerard's *Vita maior,* c. 12 (SSH, II, 498, 19-31), shows his influence upon the King; see also Hartvic, c. 14, and Iotsald, i:6 (MGHSS, XV-2, 813).

18. K. Redl, "Problémák Gellért püspök Deliberatiojában (Some questions concerning Gerard's Deliberatio)," ITK, 69 (1965), 211ff.; T. Hajdú in Erdélyi, *Rendtörténet*, I, 381ff.

19. D.G. Morin, "Un théologien ignoré du XIe siecle: l'eveque martyr, Gerard de Csanád, O.S.B.," *Revue Bénédictine*, 27 (1910), 516ff.; Manitius, II, 74ff.; A.M. Zimmermann, *Kalendarium Benedictinum* (4 vols.; Vienna, 1933-38), III, 96ff.; J. Karácsonyi, "Szent Gellért püspök müncheni kódexe (The Munich codex of Gerard's work)," *Magyar Könyvszemle*, n.s. 2 (1894), 10ff.

20. Ibrányi, *loc. cit.*; A. Bodor, "Szent Gellért Deliberatio-jának főforrásai (The main sources of Gerard's Deliberatio)," *Századok*, 77 (1943), 173ff., a very important article. F. Toldy, *A magyar szentek legendai a carthausi névtelentől* (Legends of Hungarian saints by the Anonymous Carthusian) (Pest, 1859), 50ff.; idem, *Geschichte der ungarischen Litteratur im Mittelalter* (Pest, 1865), 41ff.; C. Horváth, 20ff. Pintér, I, 152ff., is still the best.

21. Manitius, II, 77f.; M. Zalán, "Árpádkori magyar vonatkosású káziratok az osztrák könyvtárak kézirattáraiban (MSS of the Arpadian age related to Hungarian history in the Austrian libraries)," *Pannonhalmi Szemle*, 1 (1926), 46ff.; A Strittmatter, "Liturgical manuscripts Preserved in Hungarian Libraries," *Traditio*, 19 (1963), 487ff. On the "intellectual background" of the Benedictines, see V. Strommer (ed.), *Szent Benedek Emlékkönyv, 529-1929* (Memorial volume to St. Benedict of Nursia) (Pannonhalma, 1929), 266ff.

22. Horváth, *Stilusproblémák*, 30ff.

23. "Ergo nubes sine aqua omnes qui contra aecclesiam sapiunt, et magis erudiuntur ad superbiam diaboli, quam ad humilitatem christi, ut heretici et seculariter literati;" MS, f. 96', 20-23; he was given missionary help *ad imperium regis (SSH, II, 493, 13), and the entire missionary effort remained an enforced affair (ibid.*, II, 493f.); Gerard did remain sceptical (*ibid.*, II, 499). E. Horváth, "Medieval Hungary," *South Eastern Affairs*, 1 (1931), 1ff.

24. "Hunc secundum ecclesiasticam doctrinam instituens, iugum et legem disciplinae subpositis cervicibus adhibuit, omnesque inmunditias malorum prorsus destruxit;" SSH, II, 395. F.X. Seppelt, *Geschichte der Päpste* (5 vols.; 2nd rev. ed.; Munich, 1954-59), II, 392ff.; King Stephen by accepting the articles of some western church synods (Závodszky,

13ff.), kept his government in the mainstream of the west; cf. V.C. Koller, *De originibus et usu perpetua potestatis legislatoriae circa sacra regum Ungariae libellus singularis* (Vienna, 1764), 30ff.

25. For text, see Schramm, II, 66f., with comments *ibid.*, I, 161ff.; idem, "Die Anerkennung Karls des Grossen also Kaiser," *Historische Zeitschrift*, 172 (1951), 449ff.; K. Hampe, "Kaiser Otto III und Rom," *ibid.*, 140 (1929), 513ff.

26. Schramm, II, 67; Hartvic, c. 13, and Stephen's *Vita maior*, c. 11, referred to Rome as "caput mundi;" H. Sproemberg, "Die karolingische Reichsidee," *Zeitschrift für Religion und Geistesgeschichte*, 18 (1966), 370ff.

27. Schramm, II, 67; M. Uhlirz, "Kaiser Otto III und das Papsttum," *Historische Zeitschrift*, 162 (1940), 258ff.

28. SSH, II, 419, c. 13.

29. Thietmar, ii:4 (MGHSS, III, 746).

30. J.F. Böhmer (ed.), *Regesta imperii*, vol. II (Hildesheim, 1967), 247; G. Hahn, *Die abendländische Kirche im Mittelalter* (2 vols.; Freiburg i. Br., 1942), I, 237ff.

31. Thietmar, ii:4, and iii:46; the bull of Sylvester II to Stephen of Hungary (Migne, *PL*, 139, col. 274ff.) turned out to be "eine gewöhnliche Falschung;" cf. S. Heinlein, "Neuere Forschungen zur Sylvesterbulle," *Ungarische Rundschau*, 2 (1913), 912ff.; Wattenbach in MGHSS, XI, 233, n. 35.

32. SSH, II, 412.

33. On grounds that Stephen "vero merito Christi apostolus, per quem tantum sibi populum Christus convertit;" *ibid.*, II, 414. The idea of the European body politic may date to Charlemagne; cf. Einhard's *Vita Caroli magni*, c. 28 (MGHSS, II, 443ff.; the *carmina* of Theodulph of Orleans— MGH *Poetae latini*, I, 524; H. Fichtenau, *Das karolingische Imperium* (Zurich, 1949), 79. Before and during the battle of Augsburg, Aug. 955, Otto I behaved as "dominus pene totius Europae;" MGHSS, II, 459 and 746; Hahn, I, 233ff.

34. SSH, II, 395, 1-7.

35. Hartvic might have inserted this information because of the political pressure put upon Coloman the Learned of Hungary (1095-1116) by Rome; King Coloman did surrender his ecclesiastical privileges to the Holy See; see his *Refutatio investiturae episcoporum in Hungaria* (Mansi,

Concilia, XX, col. 1211f.). Hartvic did have access to information at the royal court—SSH, II, 401f.

36. *Ibid.,* II, 394, c. 2, and note 6 (MGHSS, XI, c. 1 and n. 17).

37. The statement of Thietmer, iii: 38, that "imperatoris autem predicti gratia et hortatu gener Heinrici, ducis Bawaiorum, Waic, in regno suimet episcopales cathedras faciens, coronam et benedictionem accepit" (MGHSS, III, 784), was being argued by Hartvic, c. 9, who said that Stephen sent his delegate *ad limina apostolorum* to Rome (SSH, II, 412).

38. Gerard provided some guidelines for royal behavior: "Verum nullus rex dici potest in ueritate nisi seruus dei et ipse. Cor ait regis in manu dei (Prov. 21:1). Nimirum serui dei qui se regit ad uirtutes et non ad uitia, ad uitam aeternam, non ad infernum, ad laudem dei, non ad extollentiam seculi. Illi uero qui tantum ut nomen habeant, et populum deuorent, et tributa expectant seque magnificent, et cetera circa mundi appetitum in uanum rumorem expendant, non reges, sed subuersores sunt, de quibus loquitur rex regum et dominus dominantium. Regnauerunt, sed non ex me, principes fuerunt (sic! = exstiterunt?), sed non noui illos (Osee, 8:4);" MS, f. 146', 20-26; f. 147, I-5. Hartvic, c. 9, did emphasize, through, that Stephen was acting with the approval of Rome.

39. Chronicle, cc. 72 and 81; Gerard did, in fact, compare religious conditions in Hungary with those of Galatia in the New Testament, and cited St. Paul's Letter to the Galatians to this effect; cf. MS, f. 79, 3-26.

40. "Ego dabo uobis, ait, os et sapientiam (Ier. 1:5-8; Luc. 21:15). Ista quippe sapientia imbutos sacer sermo consueuit uocare doctos et rutilantissimos quod potius est splendore, id est istar firmamentum splendoris aeternaliter lucere ob diuinissimam eruditionem;" MS, f. 146, 3-7. "Vade danihel, quia clausi sunt signatique sermones usque at tempus praefinitum. Eligentur et dealbabuntur, et quasi ignis probabuntur multi. Et impii agent impie neque intellegent omnes impii," and a quote from Dan. 12:10. *Ibid.,* 145', 20-24. Toldy, *Geschichte,* 63ff.; G. Pilati, *Chisae e stato nei primi quinsici secoli* (Rome—New York, 1961), 120ff.; H. Marczali, "A középkori elmélet a királyságról (The medieval idea of kingship)," *Budapesti Szemle,* 65 (1891), 367ff.

41. "Itaque melius est mitti in fornacem quam ad uocem talium... qui societatem in christi regno non posident statuam adorare;" MS, f. 3', 15-16 and f. 4, 22-23. S. Eckhart, "I Endre francia zarándokai (French pilgrims at the court of Andrew I of Hungary), " *Magyar Nyelv,* 32 (1936),

38ff., in ref. to *Vita Lietberti Camaracensi* (MGHSS, XXX, 854, and ASS, June VI, 596); A. Kuhn, "Der Herrschaftsanspruch der Gesellschaft und die Kirche," *Historische Zeitschrift*, 201 (1965), 334ff.

42. Keza, c. 53; Gerard's *Vita maior*, c. 15. "Omnibus inaudita seculi hereses repetere helemosinas pro animabus defunctorum christianorum more expensas. Non aestimes, frater carissime, minorem persecutionem et heresem antiquioribus hanc esse. In fide et ueritate fateor, quod ui compellebantur intolerabilia mendatia in dei expendere sacerdotes." MS, f. 46', 4-15.

43. Chronicle, c. 72; *Annales Altahenses*, a. 1041.

44. Keza, c. 47; or, the compiler of the *Annales Altahenses*, a. 1041, put it, "rex idem, habito sinodico concilio, cum communi episcoporum et principum consilio omnia decreta rescindi statuit, quae Petrus iniuste secundum libitum suum disposuit, et episcopis duobus pontificis vi sublata reddere voluit, sed quia alii ordinati erant, hoc Romani praesulis iudicio reservadum censuit" (MGHSS, XX, 795).

45. Gerard wrote "de Ecclesia christi et eius uictoria et de penis impugnantium eam, et fit continuata per quinque folia" (marginal note by different hand; MS, f. 48), in that he said that "sicut enim solaris splendor inluminat mundum, sic sanctae predicationis sermo inradiat aecclesiam saluatoris inmaculatissiman sponsam. . . . Omnis enim qui malum fecit, odiit lucem, et non uult uenire ad lumen ne arguantur opera sua," MS, f. 48, 6-23. Under the marginal note: "Nota de his qui sacris canonibus contradicunt," Gerard wrote: "Infelices et miserrimini qui dei et aecclesiae suae aduersarios questu lucri attollunt. Hoc autem diximus, ut demonstraremus circa dictum contrarias multas uirtvtes diaboli esse licet de multis exemplicaremus perpauca. Illud autem dico quod omnes qui sacris institutis contradicunt, uentrem colunt pro deo, unitam sibi praesentem uendicant pro paradiso et cetera;" *ibid.*, f. 47, 8-16. E.R. Curtius, *Europäische Literatur und lateinisches Mittelalter* (7th ed., Bern-Munich, 1969), 78, noted that "die beratende Beredsamkeit is ursprünglich politische Rede in Volksversammlung oder Senat. Auch sie wird in der Kaiserzeit Schulübung und heisst nun auch *suasoria* oder *deliberativa*. Der Schuler versetzt sich in de Lage irgendeiner bekannten Persönlichkeit der Vergangenheit und überlegt, wie zu handeln sei." The warning by Gerard to King Aba: "excitabitur in te gladius ultionis, qui a te auferet regnum, pre te fraude acquisitum" (SSH, II, 500, 25-27), was practically commented on by F. Heer, *Aufgang Europas* (Vienna, 1949), 112.

46. *Annales Altahenses,* a. 1044 etc.; Keza, cc. 45 etc.; Chronicle, cc. 70 etc.

47. The Chronicle, c. 83, reported that the attack upon Gerard had taken place according to plan: "cumque ad predictum portum venissent, ecce viri impii, scilicet Vatha et conplices sui...irruerunt in episcopos" (SSH, I, 340, 29-33).

48. SSH, II, 475f.

Notes to Chapter IV
Section One

1. "Tractavit de substituendo pro se rege, Petro vidilicet sororis sue filio;" SSH, II, 392; Keza, c. 45, also spoke of "Petrum Venetum filium sororis sue," though the Chronicle, c. 60, confused the picture by saying that Peter was "frater regine" (*ibid.*, I, 322). A. Dandalo, *Chronicon Venetum,* in Muratori, *Scriptores,* XII, 233ff.; on Queen Gisela, see also MGHSS, IX, 657 and XIX, 698. According to Hóman, *Ungarisches Mittelalter,* I, 248, Peter "konnte weder sein aufbräsendes, rachsüchtiges, italienisches Temperament, noch die von den ungarischesn Grosseltern ererbte Neigung zur Gewalttätigkeit unterdrücken; Er verstand die Seele seiner Ungarn nicht." Pauler, *Magyar nemzet,* I, 114f.

2. MGHSS, XI, 229; SSH, II, 399; Hartvic, c. 23, gave the year 1033 as Stephen's year of death: "XL-o VI-o anno regni sui;" of the non-Hungarian sources, many dated it 1038, as, e.g. Herimann Auguensis *Chronicon,* a. 1038 (MGHSS, V, 123); Annalista Saxo (*ibid.*, VI, 682); Ekkehardus Uragiensis *Chronicon,* a. 1038 (*ibid.*, VI, 195); *Annales Fuldenses,* a. 1038 (*ibid.*, XIII, 212); *Annales Mellicenses,* a. 1038 (*ibid.*, IX, 498), etc. Lilienfeld MS 60, f. 167'a, carried the date 1038 in non-Roman numerals.

3. Cf. Andrew II's *Decretum,* a. 1231 (Marczali, *Enchiridion,* 134f.; RHM, II, 428ff.; Szentpétery, *Regesta,* I, no. 479); Th. Bogyay, A 750 éves Aranybulla (The 750th anniversary of the Golden Bull)," *Katolikus Szemle,* 24 (1972), 289ff.

4. SSH, I, 113ff., c. 57.

5. Keza, c. 45.

6. Idem, c. 44.

7. Hartvic, c. 21.

8. Keza, c. 47.

9. Chronicle, c. 122 (SSH, I, 392); Váczy, 92ff.

10. Cf. W. Stubbs, *Select Charters of English Constitutional History* (8th ed.; Oxford, 1900), 17 and 100ff.

11. *Loc. cit.*

12. In the Migne, *PL,* 151, col. 1239bc edition.

13. *Ibid.,* col. 1241a; SSH, II, 625.

14. *Ibid.,* II, 622, art. iii; Migne, *PL,* 151, col. 1238b.

15. *Ibid.,* col. 1239a.

16. *Ibid.,* col. 1245ab; RHM, II, 311f.

17. *Annales Altahenses,* a. 1044; Chronicle, cc. 72etc; for comparison, R.E. Sullivan, "The Carolingian Missionary and the Pagan," *Speculum,* 28 (1953), 705ff. The heated controversy between the German Brackmann and the Hungarian Váczy should be mentioned here on grounds that their dispute had taken place at the peak of the Nazi propaganda aimed at the incorporation of "eastern," i.e., Polish, Hungarian territory into the Hitlerite Reich. It began with A. Brackmann's lecture, "Kaiser Otto III und die staatliche Umgestaltung Polens and Ungarns," *Abhandlungen der Preussischesn Akademie,* 1939, No. 1, probably based upon Brackmann's earlier essay, "Die Ostpolitik Ottos des Grossen," *Historische Zeitschrift,* 134 (1926), 242ff. Brackmann argued that (a) Germany in the 1930's found itself in a position to realize the aims of medieval emperors, goals only partially realized by Henry III and Frederick I Barbarossa; (b) the *Ost* was to be, by cultural means, incorporated into the German continental body politic. P. Váczy answered Brackmann in a very pointed essay (cf. *Archivum Europae centro-orientalis,* 5 1939, 328ff.), making the remark that, earlier, Brackmann had taken a far less martial view of the situation, as, e.g. evidenced by Brackmann's own essay, "Die Ursachen der geistigen und politischen Wandlung Europas im 11 und 12 Jahrhundert," *Historische Zeitschrift,* 149 (1934), 229ff. Váczy's reply had some effect because Brackmann, in his answer to Váczy, "Zur Entstehung des ungarischen Staates," *Abh. der Preussischen Akademie,* 1940, No. 8, rendered a more humble, almost apologetic explanation of his views.

18. MGHSS, XX, 800, 13-17 (a. 1044).

19. *Ibid.,* XX, 804f.; Hauck, III, 580ff. "Bendikt IX übertraf an moralischer Minderwertigkeit selbst einen Johann XII," wrote Funk-Bihlmayer, II, 44, since he was a "willensloses Werkzeug des Kaisers;" cf. H. Kühner, *Neues Papstlexikon* (Zurich, 1956), entry "Bendikt IX."

20. Gerard did view the office of the monarch as an institution under God: "istiusmodi thesaurum non potuit habere darius rex, non xerses (sic!), non arthaxerses (sic!), . . . non alexander macedo;" MS, f. 44', 26–f. 45, 1-3, and compare to Gerard's sermon in which he accused King Aba of the murder in cold blood of his opposition, SSH, II, 500, 26-27; II, 476, 29-30.

21. Keza, c. 50; H. Marczali, *Magyarország története az Árpádok korában* (Hungarian history in the age of the Árpáds) (Budapest, 1896), 26f. Even the Germans disliked the Orseolo: "nam idem Petrus quamdiu regnavit, in multus praevaricator exstitit;" *Annales Sangallenses* (MGHSS, I, 84). On Hungarian contacts with the west, see Iotsald, *Vita Odilonis,* i:6 (*ibid.*, XV-2, 813), or, the writ of Odilo of Cluny to King Stephen in SIE, I, 459, n. 1; Bishop Bonipert of Pécs to Fulbert of Chartres, in Migne, *PL,* 141, col. 189f.

22. "Elegerunt de semetipsis quemdam comitem nomine Aba;" Chronicle, c. 72. "Interea vero Petrus rex primo et secundo regnavit annis V et dimidio;" Keza, c. 58, and added: "Aba autem regnavit annis tribus." Peter was deposed: "principes Hungarorum et milites consilio episcoporum convenerunt adversus Petrum regem;" Chronicle, c. 72.

23. Cf. W. Mohr, *Die karolingische Reichsidee: Aevum Christianum* (Munster, 1962), 50ff.; E. Patzelt, *Die karolongische Renaissance* (Vienna, 1924), 114ff.

24. "Vt de his nihilominus de omnibus qui audita cruce et aeuangelio et utriusque fide stabilitate in aecclesia gratulantur, *magis adherent stultorvm* (sic!) neniis philosophorum, dictisque gentilium, quam eloquiis prophetarum et aeuangelistarum, quibus totus mundus inradiatus est. . . . Multa autem dicta et quibusdam sorte incredibilia animaduertimus;" MS, f. 61', 2-12. On the politics of the queen, cf. *Annales Altahenses,* a. 1041.

25. "Pro nephas nostri uidentes non foris clamant, sed intus murmurant, atque sine issv et interrogatu nil musitare audent, ne quidem aures offendant regales. Quomodo inquiunt displicentia loqui possumus regi? MS, f. 15', 2-6, with additional remark on margin: "De adulatoribus non audentes ueritatem predicare assimilantur ydolatris statuam adorantes nabuchodonosor;" *ibid.*, 1-4.

26. On 'investiture' in Hungary, see the comments by Gerard: "Si prophetas falsi nihilominus sunt in terra non plura quanquam sepissima

plura et inmunda, illi narrare possunt qui uix psalmis auditis in scola cathedras arripierunt episopales. De cetero germania narret et pannonia non sileat;" *ibid.*, f. 65, 2-7. Or, again, "discretio autem mundorum et inmundorum in perfectissima et mundissima superreponitur libertate quam hirciliter uiuentes non ualent animaduertere." Then he quotes, indirectly, Rom. 1:21, and continues: "Ni insipientibus deo preponere diabolum, carnalia spiritualibus, et regium manibus ferre pilleum, et christi uerba uentilare pedibus. Pro nefas frequenter talia uidimus;" *ibid.*, f. 146', 4-12. See further the review by A. Haussling of O. Nussbaum, *Klöster, Priestermönch und Privatmensch* (Bonn, 1961), in *Zeitschrift für katholische Theologie*, 85 (1963), 75ff.

27. Chronicle, c. 81.

28. "Denique piscatores ex illis legimus potius quam litteratos. Ille autem qui accepit potestatem coeli et dominationem in omni seculo post eum potius ut ita dicam sapiebat instrumenta pisces capiendi quam legere;" MS, f. 43, 22-26; f. 43', 1. "Ut episcopi habeant potestatem res ecclesiasticas providere;" Stephen's Laws, art. I:2. Also, A.M. Haas, "Mittelalterliches Mönchtum," *Neue Zürcher Zeitung*, Aug. 14, 1965, 11.

29. "Nimirum dixi quia filii diaboli qui potestates sunt tenebrarum ubique regnant et dominantur;" MS, f. 46', 24-26. "Infelices et miserrimi qui dei et aecclesiae suae adversarios questu lucri attollunt;" *ibid.*, 47, 8-10, and the summary of what follows annotated on margin: "Nota de his qui sacris canonibus contradicunt; *ibid.*, f. 47, 13-15. Compare with SSH, I, 325f.; it seems that King Aba, too, refused cooperation with Gerard: "Iterum autem nec his debet ignosci. Si enim tantum potuerunt scire, ut potuissent aestimarae seculum quomodo huius dominum non facilius inuenerunt?" He quotes from Wisdom, 13:4-10, and continues: "Haec fuit uitae humanae deceptio, quoniam aut affectui aut regi secuientes homines, incommunicabile nomen lapidibus et lignis inposuerunt;" MS, f. 78, 11-19.

30. "Uae nobis qui quotiens magis principi obedimus quam deo, tociens statuam auream adoramus, et ad uocem tubae fistulae, et citharae, sambucae, et psalterii et simphoniae, et uniuersi generis musicorum nosmet prosternimus. Haec quidem omnia secundum hoc instrumenta diaboli sunt;" *ibid.*, f. 3', 7-12.

31. "Pro dolor, uero nunc multi pollutant in aecclesia, immo iam totum occupant orbem, et nemo est qui talium ineptiis contradicat. O

quantos sentio diaboli filios, quibus loqui non patior;" *ibid.*, f. 46, 22-26, and compare with his remarks in SSH, II, 499; on the date, *Annales Posonienses,* a. 1047 (*ibid.*, I, 125), known as the "Chronicon Posoniense" to Radó, 40; on the reckoning of the date, Grotefend, II, 107.

32. Otto of Freising, *Gesta Friderici,* i:30 (MGHSS, XX, 368); on Otto, see A. Lhotsky, *Europäisches Mittelalter* (Vienna, 1970), 64ff.; E.F. Otto, "Otto von Freising und Friedrich Barbarossa," in W. Lammers (ed.), *Geschichtsgedanken und Geschichtsbild im Mittelalter* (Darmstadt, 1961), 247ff.

33. Keza, c. 47.

34. Idem, c. 49; Chronicle, c. 76, as if to comply with the spirit of Stephen's Admonitions, art. I (SSH, II, 620ff.).

35. The remark of H. Hürten, "Gregor der Grosse und der mittelalterliche Eposkopat," *Zeitschrift für Kirchengeschichte,* 73 (1962), 16ff., "die Frage, wie ein Bischof Leben und Amt führen soll, scheint im Mittelalter selten gestellt worden zu sein," would be contradicted by Gerard: "Prohibemur iam loqui, et episcopi nominamur, constituti etiam sub tributo humano quibus totus committitur diuino imperio mundus;" MS, f. 46', 17-20. He must have disliked both kings: "Cor ait regis in manu dei (Prov. 21:1). Nimirum serui dei qui se regit ad uirtutes et non ad uitia;" *ibid.*, f. 146', 21-23. Interestingly, both Keza, c. 47, and the Chronicle, c. 72, emphasized that the coronation of Aba was free of outside interference.

36. MGHSS, XX, 800.

37. *Ibid.*; according to Keza, c. 51, the Emperor "Petro restituit regnum."

38. Chronicle, c. 77.

39. Idem, c. 78; MGHSS, XX, 801, a. 1045.

40. Dated March 13, 1075, in Jaffé, *Bibliotheca,* II, 127f.; Migne, *PL,* 148, col. 373; Jaffé, *Regesta,* no. 4944.

41. Deér, 197ff.; P. Wirth, "Das bislang erste literarische Zeugnis für die Stefanskrone aus der Zeit zwischen dem X und XIII Jahrhundert," *Byzantinische Zeitschrift,* 53 (1960), 79ff.

42. *Annales Altahenses,* a. 1047; Chronicle, c. 86.

43. On Vata, SSH, II, 502f.; Gerard's reactions: "Pro nefas, frequenter talia uidimus. . .rex timetur qui nil nisi uermis ac putredo dicendus post mortem. . . .O mendatium seculi, o dementia mundi potius faborare

hominem feudissimum cimicis flagellorem quam illum per quem reges regnant et recta discernunt;" MS, f. 146', 11-21.

44. Peter died like a king; cf. SSH, I, 343; MGHSS, XX, 804; the Germans did not recognize his successor—*ibid.*, V, 126, 6-9. Time reckoning is a problem: a. 1047 is usually accepted, though one is to remember that, according to Byzantine style, 1047 began on Sept. 1, 1046 (Grotefend, I, 88ff.); the synod of Szabolcs, Hungary, 1092, aa. 37-38, recorded the feast of Gerard on Sept. 24; his *translatio,* Sept. 24; cf. Radó, 37, 38; Mansi, *Concilia,* XX, col. 758ff.; RHM, II, 325ff.; ASS, Sept. VI, 713ff., so, Gerard died in 1046. The chronicler relied upon Byzantine style time-reckoning because the area of the diocese of Csanád came, at first, under the jurisdiction of the Byzantine Patriarch; cf. Cedrenus, II, 328.

45. At a time when the old King decided to withdraw from the cares of worldly affairs; cf. Chronicle, c. 69. On the conspiracy, see Stephen's *Vita minor,* c. 7; Hartvic, c. 21; Pauler, I, 66ff.; Emery's *Vita* (SSH, II, 456f.), gave no details, and Macartney, 171, explained why.

46. "Andreas et Catholicus est vocatus;" Chronicle, c. 88.

47. Idem, c. 86.

48. SSH, I, 338.

49. Keza, c. 53.

50. "Misit etiam rex clementissimus per totam Hungariam precones, ut de singulis villis vocarentur duo seniores facundiam habentes ad regis consilium;" Chronicle, c. 95. On towns, cf. SSH, II, 496ff.

51. Chronicle, c. 94, and, by comparison, Otto of Freising, *Gesta,* c. 31 (MGHSS, XX, 369).

52. Gerard's *Vita maior,* c. 12.

53. After he spoke *de cavenda societate malorum* (Marginal entry by a third hand, MS, f. 33, 17), Gerard continued: "uae autem nobis, qui contra istiusmodi imperium incitare non formidamus. Nullos tam caros nostra pannonia non conseruerit habere ut tales;" *ibid.*, f. 33', 2-5. Then he quotes Ezekiel 22:29, and adds: "si talia cottidie in terra cernimus tuo arbitrio deputetur. Haec adhuc iniquitas in toto orbe terrarum uspiamque non dormit;" *ibid.*, f. 64', 16-20. The remark made by J.A. Jungmann about Gerard's *Deliberatio:* "fällt in seiner Weitschweifigkeit aus dem Rahmen (der Theologie) heraus und nähert sich eher einer Predigt," in H. Jedin (ed.), *Handbuch der Kirchengeschichte,* vol. III-1 (Freiburg-Basel-Vienna, 1973), 383, is a positive comment on the writing of Gerard of Csanád.

54. SSH, II, 472f.

55. "...qui porciliter conuersantur et secundum hominum desideria uitam consumere festinant;" MS, f. 40, 9-11.

56. SSH, II, 476, 23.

57. "Ubi itaque diuinae intelligentie spiritus non est,...ibi asinorum procul dubio spiritus regnat;" MS, f. 77', 16-18. Igitur nulla umquam amicitia habenda cum his quorum uita non est nisi peccatum, quibus benedictio christi tollitur, suaque laus in eorum ore non habetur;" *ibid.*, f. 33', 13-16.

58. Chronicle, c. 82.

59. SSH, I, 338ff.

60. The process of conversion was an enforced affair—cf. *ibid.*, II, 493f., and Gerard had doubts about its effectiveness, cf. *ibid.*, II, 499.

61. "...contra istiusmodi imperium incitare non formidamus;" MS, f. 33', 2-3.

Notes to Chapter IV
Section Two

1. "Qui erant de genere sancti regis Stephani;" cf. Gerard's *Vita maior,* c. 15; Keza, c. 53, who revealed (c. 44) why Stephen decided to send the Princes into exile—supported by the Chronicle, c. 69: "ut sic sibi salutem et corporum suorum seruarent integritatem" (SSH, I, 321). The Hungarian sources described the Árpáds as the offspring of Ladislas Szár; cf. Keza, c. 44; Chronicle, c. 69 and Anonymus, c. 15, while the *Annales Altahenses,* a. 1041 referred to them as the sons of Vazul, if *fratris* may stand for *patruelis* (Keza spoke of Vazul as "filium sui patruelis"). On the Hungarian contacts of the compiler of Altaich, see Domanovszky in SSH, I, 335, or Manitius, II, 394ff.; Gy. Kristó, "Anonymus magyarországi irott forrássainak kérdéséhez (Remarks concerning the written Hungarian sources of Anonymus)," *Magyar Könyvszemle,* 88 (1972), 166ff., expressed different views. On the background, cf. Hóman-Szekfú, I, 203ff.; Hóman, *Ungarisches Mittelalter,* I, 198ff.; Elekes, 87ff. L.J. Csóka, *Szent Benedk fiainak világtörténete különös tekintettel Magyarországra* (History of the Benedictines with specific emphasis upon Hungary) (2 vols.; Budapest, 1971, I, 247ff., and the excellent review essay of the work by P. Zakar in *Katolikus Szemle,* 24 (Rome, 1972), 85ff.

2. Keza, c. 53; Gerard's *Vita maior,* c. 15.

3. "Interea rex Petrus Hungaros priori gravimine cepit molestare;" Keza, c. 53.

4. "Omnes in unum convenerunt consilioque habito," wrote Keza, c. 53, who, in discussing the events of 1041, had mentioned "principes et nobiles regni Hungarie episcoporum consilio in unum convenerunt;" c. 47. The Chronicle, c. 72, spoke of "nobiles Hungarie . . . in unum convenerunt consilioque habito," though, in referring to the events of 1041, its author too remarked that "principes Hungarorum et milites consilioque episcoporum convenerunt." Gerard's *Vita maior,* c. 15, and simply that "Ungari miserunt sollempnes nuntios post filios Wazul" (SSH, II, 501).

5. Keza, c. 54; it is noteworthy that the bishops were being mentioned at first; "ab omnibus episcopis, nobilibus omnique populo." Cf. Gerard's *Vita maior,* c. 15 (SSH, II, 502, 1-17).

6. Munich MS, fol. 64, 25-26.

7. Munich MS, fol. 15', 13-16.

8. SSH, II, 501, 27-30.

9. Munich MS, fol. 79, 6-11.

10. Chronicle, c. 82.

11. SSH, II, 501, 12-18.

12. As it is evident from the report of the Chronicle, c. 83 (*ibid.,* I, 339f.).

13. The report of Gerard's *Vita maior,* c. 15 (SSH, II, 502, 21-24) is insufficient; however, the Chronicle, c. 83, made it clear that the attack by Vata occurred according to a plan; cf. *ibid.,* I, 340, 29-33.

14. Munich MS, fol. 64', 16-19, and compare with the previous remark of Gerard: "uae autem nobis qui contra istiusmodi imperium incitare non formidamus. Nullos tam caros nostra pannonia consueuit habere ut tales;" *ibid.,* fol. 33', 2-5.

15. SSH, II, 520, 12-14; my article in *CHR* (1973).

16. *Ibid.;* Banfi, *art. cit.*

17. The "revolutionaries" had seemingly possessed the approval of Andrew; cf. SSH, II, 501, 20-26; Chronicle, c. 82.

18. "Endre autem dux interim supervenientes Benatam (sic) episcopum a m nibus eorum liberavit, et sic prophetia sancti Gerardi impleta est;" SSH, I, 342.

19. *Ibid.,* II, 503, 23-26.

20. *Annales Altahenses,* a. 1046; Chronicle, c. 86.

21. Chronicle, c. 88.

22. Cf. Mansi, *Concilia*, XIX, cols. 631f.; Migne, *PL*, 151, cols. 1257f., aa. 1 and 4. King Andrew may have wished to correct many of the abuses complained about by Gerard: Plene omni dolo et omnia fallacia—Gerard wrote—filii diaboli inimice omnis iusticie, non definis subuertere ius domini rectas;" Munich MS, fol. 15', 2—fol. 16, 1-2. Or, "quare hoc?— Gerard said—nimirum dixi quia filii diaboli qui potestates sunt tenebrarum ubique regnant et dominantur." Fol. 46', 24-25.

23. Keza, c. 54.

24. SSH, I, 344, 1-6.

Notes to Chapter V
Section One

1. "Illis etiam petentibus concessit rex scita Teutonica;" cf. *Annales Altahenses*, a. 1044 (MGHSS, XX, 800, 36). "Ungarios petentes lege Baioarica donavit;" Contractus, a. 1044 (*ibid.*, V, 125, 6), a statement the *Chronicon pictum* changed to "scita Hungarica;" (SSH, I, 333, 15). On the background, see Hóman-Szekfű, I, 158ff.

2. SSH, I, 325, 3; *ibid.*, I, 174, 19-20.

3. MGHSS, XX, 802, 9-10 (a. 1045); Contractus, a. 1045 (*ibid.*, V, 125, 21-24); the Hungarian chronicler said the same—cf. SSH, I, 334, 4-7.

4. *Annales Altahenses*, a. 1046 (MGHSS, XX, 803, 16-20); J. Gerics, "Domanovszky Sándor, az árpádkori krónikakutatás úttörője (Alexander Domanovszky, pioneer researcher of the Arpadian age)," *Századok*, 112 (1978), 235ff.; A. Lhotsky, *Quellenkunde*, 173, expressed a different opinion. In fact, the statement made in the last sentence is based upon the Hungarian chronicler (SSH, I, 336, 2-22) who had, on a different occasion, described the Árpáds as the only royalbily to the Hungarian throne—see *ibid.*, I, 392, 19-23; Váczy, *Epoche*, 92ff.

5. *Chronicon pictum*, c. 85.

6. *Chronicon pictum*, c. 82.

7. SSH, I, 340, 29-33; it is to be noted, however, that the chronicler did mention the activities of another Vata "Vatha nequam," in 1073, who formed a conspiracy vs. Géza, the future Géza I; cf. *ibid.*, I, 378, 18-19. He described, under an entry anno 1113, a (royal) steward: reeve,

named Vatha, accused of conspiracy together with Prince Álmos, vs. King Coloman the Learned—cf. *ibid.*, I, 430, 19-20. There is an entry made, anno 1187, in the late twelfth century Pray codex about the royal reeve named Vatha, blinded upon orders from King Béla III; Vatha did form a conspiracy vs. King Béla—cf. *ibid.*, I, 127, 19, and Radó, *Libri*, 40.

8. *Chron. pict.*, c. 85; the basilica was named after St. Peter the Apostle, King Peter's patron saint.

9. SSH, I, 344, 2-4.

10. *Ibid.*, I, 344, 5-6: "in omnibus secundum legem illam viverent, quam sanctus rex Stephanus eos docuerat."

11. Cf. Mansi, *Concilia,* XIX, cols. 631f.; Migne, *PL,* 151, cols. 1257f.

12. "...ut deposito ritu paganismo...ad veram Christi fidem reverterentur, ... quam sanctus... docuerat;" SSH, I, 344, 3-6.

13. See *Constitutio ecclesiastica*, aa. 1 and 4, *supra*, note 11.

14. "Rex albus Andreas et Catholicus est vocatus;" SSH, I, 344, 23-24. While meant matriarchial, female predominance; black, patriarchial, male rule.

15. Cf. *Constitutio ecclesiastica*, introduction.

16. SSH, I, 345, 7.

17. Cf. Ioannes Cinnamus, *Epitomae rerum ab Iohanne et Manuele Comnenis gestarum,* v:1 (Migne, *PG,* 133, col. 551—"lex enim est apud Hungaros, ut semper ad fratres superstites diadema transmittatur." On Cinnamus, see Krumbacher, 279ff.

18. "...habito consilio diviserunt regnum inter tres partes, quarum ...tertia pars in proprietatem ducis est collata;" SSH, I, 345, 11-16. Note that the division occurred at the meeting of the Great Council, *habito consilio.*

19. *Ibid.*, I, 345, 24-25.

20. *Ibid.*, I, 345, 17-19.

21. Cf. Gregory of Tours, *Historia Francorum,* ii:7 (*MGH SS rerum Merovingicarum,* vol. I); Pintér, I, 111, on the founding charter of Tihany; text in Marczali, *Enchiridion,* 81ff.

22. For the pedigree, see Cross-Sherbowitz-Wetzor, chart facing p. 298; also, Katona, *Historia pragmatica,* I, 319ff.

23. Keza, c. 58; *Chronicon pictum,* c. 88 (SSH, I, 354, 17-19), mentioned the establishment of Tihany abbey; however, the Slavic name of Tihany: *tichij-hod,* implies the existence of an earlier settlement; it may be

that until the times of King Stephen, Slav monks lived there—cf. J. Csemegi, "A tihanyi barlanglakások (Cave-dwellings in Tihany)," *Archaeológiai Értesitő*, 3 (1946-48), 396ff.; Moravcsik, *Byzantium*, 61f.

24. ". . . qui tunc temporis uicem procurabat notarii in curia regali;" cf. E. Jakubovich-D. Pais (ed.), *Ó-magyar olvasókönyv* (Old Hungarian reader) (Pécs, 1929), 25; SSH, I, 348, note 1, and Horváth, *Stilusproblémák*, 306f.

25. *Chron. pict.*, c. 89; for reasons explained by Contractus, anno 1051, the emperor disregarded the Hungarian peace-offer; cf. MGHSS, V, 130, 9-10.

26. *Ibid.*, XXIX, 541, 4-11; SSH, I, 346, 10-17.

27. Contractus, a. 1052 (MGHSS, V. 131, 37-41); *Chronc. pict.*, c. 90. J. Gerics, "A krónikakutatás és az oklevéltan határán (Between chronicle research and documents)," *Irodalomtörténeti Közlemények*, 78 (1974), 218ff., provided an analysis of the *Chron. pict.*, c. 90.

28. SSH, I, 347, 14-17.

29. *Ibid.*, I, 348, 3-21.

30. *Ibid.*, I, 349, 11-20.

31. Horváth, *Stilusproblémák*, 309, note 11.

32. SSH, 349f.; her name was Judith, not Sophia.

33. *Chron. pict.*, c. 91; Henry IV was still a minor at this time.

34. *Annales Alt.*, anno 1052 (MGHSS, XX, 806, 2-7); it seems that it was Andrew who approached the papal court—cf. Hildebert, *Vita Hugonis*, ii:7 (Migne, *PL*, 159, col. 864cd), or the remark by Contractus: "interim domnus Leo papa, ab Andrea accitus . . . ;" MGHSS, V, 131, 41-42.

35. Cf. L. Huillier, *Vie de s. Hugues* (Paris, 1888), 68f.

36. Contractus, anno 1052 (MGHSS, V, 131, 41-43); *Chronicon* s. Benigni Divonensis (*ibid.*, VII, 237) spoke of the pontiff's visit to "finibus Hungariae;" compare with Jaffé, *Regesta*, I, nr. 4279, third entry; Fraknói, *Szentszék*, I, 360, note 58.

37. *Annales Altahenses*, anno 1052; papal excommunication of Andrew recorded by Contractus, anno 1052 (MGHSS, V, 127, 23-28).

38. Wibert, ii:8 (Migne, *PL*, 143, col. 496bc): "ideo Romana respublica subiectionem regni Hungariae perdidit." Contractus in his entry anno 1047 did not name Andrew king; in fact, he attempted to depict Andrew as someone badly in need of help (MGHSS, V, 127, 23-28).

39. *Annales Alt.*, a. 1058 (*ibid.*, XX, 809, 20-24); *Chronicon pictum,* c. 91.

40. SSH, I, 355, 5-9, and compare with (*ibid.*) I, 352, 8-23.

41. "Sed dux pro timore hoc fecerat;" *ibid.*, I, 353f.; esp. 354, 15-21.

42. ". . . quod raro factum est;" *ibid.*, I, 355, 19-24.

43. ". . . tribus agminibus soceri sui munitus reversus est in Hungariam;" *ibid.*, I, 356, 15-16.

44. *Ibid.*, I, 356, 16-19; *Annales Alt.*, a. 1060.

45. SSH, I, 356, 21-24.

46. *Annales Altahenses,* anno 1060 (MGHSS, XX, 810).

47. *Ibid.*, XX, 809, 22-24; the chronicler placed the blame upon Béla for the failure of the German court to gain control over Hungary—*ibid.*, 811 (a. 1061).

48. SSH, I, 357, 4-6.

49. *Ibid.*, I, 357, 9-14; *Annales Alt.*, a . 1060; Lampert of Hersfeld insisted that Andrew had fallen from his horse and trampled to death; MGHSS, V, 161f., anno 1061.

50. SSH, I, 356f.

51. "Dux igitur Bela vocatus Benyn victor cum triumpho venit in civitatem Albam;" *Chron. pict.*, c. 94.

52. Cf. Marczali, *Enchiridion,* 81ff.; Katona, *Historia critica,* I, 333ff.

53. At the Várkony meeting, where Béla agreed to the coronation of Andrew's five year old son by saying: "habeat filius tuus coronam, qui unctus est, et da michi ducatum" (SSH, I, 355, 16-18), Béla made it clear to his brother that he had understood politics.

54. On the schism, cf. M. Jugie, *Le schisme byzantine* (Paris, 1924), passim; G. Denzler, "Das sogenannte Schisma im Jahre 1054," *Münchener Theologische Zeitschrift,* 17 (1966), 24ff.

55. See the correspondence of Pope Leo IX with the Patriarch in Cornelius Will (ed.), *Acta et scripta quae de controversiis graecae et latinae saeculo XIo composita extant* (Leipzig-Marburg, 1861), 85ff.; A. Michel, "Bestand eine Trennung der griechischen und römischen Kirche schon vor Kerullarios?" *Historisches Jahrbuch,* 42 (1922), 1ff.

56. Cf. the "Pseudo-synod" held by the Patriarch in 1054, Mansi, *Concilia,* XIX, cols. 811ff.

57. Moravcsik, *Byzantium,* 61f.; it may be noteworthy to say that Andrew did establish Tihany after he reached an agreement with Béla

concerning his son's coronation and royal succession; "eo tempore rex Andreas iuxta lacum Balatini construxit monasterium in honore sancti Aniani, in loco qui dicitur Tyhon;" SSH, I, 345, 17-19. The compiler of the *Chronicon pictum* did make the remark though that the creation of the *pars tertia* for the benefit of the heir to the throne "seminarium fuit discordie et guerrarum inter duces et reges Hungariae," *ibid.*, I, 345, 16-17.

58. The founding charter of Tihany, issued by King Andrew was drafted by Bishop Nicholas of Veszprém, "qui tunc temporis vicem procurabat notarii in curia regali;" cf. *supra*, note 24, the chronicler of contemporary events—see Horváth, *Stilusproblémák*, 258ff.; the fact that Andrew's queen was Anne of Kiev (SSH, I, 19-21), whose sister: Andrew's sister-in-law, was the Queen of France (Cross-Sherbowitz-Wetzor, insert facing p. 298), may explain why the (lesser) patron of Tihany was a French saint.

59. Cf. Haller, II, 278ff., who spoke of a *deutsches Papsttum* and said that the co-workers of the "German Pope," Leo IX, were Germans, too (*ibid.*, II, 289ff.); his successor was Gebhardt, bishop of Eichstädt, "der zweite Mann im Reich" (*ibid.*, II, 307)—also, A. Mercati, "The New List of the Popes," *Medieval Studies*, 9 (1947), 71ff.,—and Seppelt, III, 32ff. The successor of Victor II was Stephen IX, also a German: Fredrick, abbot of Monte Cassino, although the German court gave him only a token recognition (Haller, II, 310f.), just as the court did not recognize his successor, Benedict X (*ibid.*, II, 312f.). The Cardinals finally elected Gerard of Burgundy (Bishop of Florence); his election was approved by Empress Agnes, and he took the name of Nicholas II on December 6, 1058; between April, 1058, and December, 1058, the German Benedict X was pope—cf. Hans Kühner, *Neues Papstlexikon* (Zurich, 1956), 59f.

60. Cf. Libuin—Lietbuinus, chancellor to the Roman See in 1085 (Jaffé, *Regesta*, I, nr. 4391), in Migne, *PL*, 143, col. 526; Bresslau, *Urkundenlehre*, I, 197, note 984.

61. Wibert, archdeacon of Toul—see Wattenbach, *Geschichtsquellen*, II, 128-, *Vita s. Leonis IX*, Migne, *PL*, 143, cols. 465ff., or ASS, Apr. II, 648ff.; Giesebrecht, II, 567; J. Gay, *Les papes du XIe siecle et la chrétienté* (Paris, 1926), 107ff.

62. Katona, *Historica pragmatica*, I, 333ff.; F. Dölger, *Byzanz und die europäische Staatenwelt* (Ettal, 1953), 107ff.

63. "...ad veram Christi fidem reverterentur et in omnibus secundum legem illam viverent, quam sanctus rex Stephanus eos docuerat;" SSH, I, 344, 4-6, and compare with the Gerard of Csanád's *Vita maior,* c. 15 (*ibid.,* II, 503, 25-26).

Notes to Chapter V
Section Two

1. *MGHSS,* XX, 810, 20-22 (anno 1060).

2. *Ibid.,* XX, 813, 22-24 (anno 1065).

3. "...tunc sibi a tumulante milite impositum diadema non licuisse recusare;" *ibid.,* XX, 813, 24-25; the Hungarian chronicler mentions bishops only—*SSH,* I, 358, 4-6.

4. *Ibid.,* I, 358, 6-7.

5. *Ibid.,* I, 357, 4-18.

6. *Ibid.,* I, 345, 10-16; *Annales Altahenses,* anno 1063 (*MGHSS,* XX, 813, 25-28).

7. "...legati redeunt infecta pace," though the annalist says that Béla has not given up' "ipse autem, ingenita sibi calliditate pacem se cupere simulans, legatos subinde mittebat;" *ibid.,* XX, 813, 31-32.

8. "Quid plura? Adveniente igitur tempore opportuno rex ad fines Ungariae venit cum exercitu magno;" *ibid.,* XX, 813, 34-35.

9. "...urbem adeunt;" *ibid.,* XX, 813, 39-42.

10. "Bel autem cum filio non longe aberat.... Sed mox, ...spiritum exhalavit;" *ibid.,* XX, 813, 46-48; *Chronicon pictum,* c. 96; Lampert of Hersfeld, no friend of Henry IV—cf. Wattenbach, II, 105f.,—says that "Bel obiit;" *MGHSS,* III, 166.

11. *Ibid.,* XX, 813, 48; "...illa terra sine sanguine per regem Henricum regi Salomoni est restituta;" *ibid.,* XX, 813, 49. Hersfeld, *Annales,* a. 1063.

12. *Ibid.,* XX, 813f.

13. Keza, c. 59 (*SSH,* I, 358, 7-11; 20-24).

14. *Ibid.,* I, 358, 11-13; 24-25.

15. *Ibid.,* I, 358, 13-14.

16. *Ibid.,* I, 358, 16-20.

17. *Ibid.,* I, 359, 2-13.

18. "Misit etiam rex clementissimus per totam Hungariam precones, ut de singulis villis vocarentur duo seniores facundiam habentes ad regis consilium;" *ibid.,* I, 359, 20-22.

19. ". . . seniores facundiam habentes ad . . . consilium;" *ibid.*

20. *Ibid.*, I, 359, 27-33; it may be noteworthy though that "plebs autem constituit sibi prepositos;" *ibid.*, I, 359, 27.

21. As, for example, he handled the sudden emergence of the pagan revolt; "rex petivit inducias trium dierum ad deliberandum"—*ibid.*, I, 359f.

22. *Ibid.*, I, 180, 25-27; "tenuit autem regnum pacifice, sine molestatione hostium et quesivit bona genti sue;" *ibid.*, I, 358, 6-7. Albericus referred to Béla as "Banyn;" *MGHSS*, XXIII, 793, 795 and 798.

23. This is evident from the remark of the compiler of the *Annales Altahenses*, ibid., XX, 813, 37-42.

24. *Ibid.*, XX, 813, 40-41.

25. ". . . ad bellandum promptus inmensam multitudonorum collegerat;" *ibid.*, XX, 813, 46-47.

26. "Bel autem et cum filio non longe aberat;" *ibid.*, 813, 46.

27. *Chron. pict.*, c. 96.

28. ". . . sed mox, ut hos adversum se venientes cognovit, spiritum exhalavit;" *MGHSS*, XX, 813, 47-48.

29. That evidently caused paralysis of the body; "corruente solio confractus corpore irremediabiliter cepit egrotare." *SSH*, I, 360, 17-18.

30. *Ibid.*, I, 360, 20-21; Keza, c. 59.

31. "In Demes regali allodio;" *ibid.*, I, 360, 17.

32. "Duxeruntque eum seminecem ad rivulum Kynisua;" *ibid.*, I, 360, 18-19.

33. This seems to be evident from the first sentence of the *Chronicon pictum*, c. 97 (*SSH*, I, 361, 5-7), and from the observation made by the German chronicler, "filius autem, ne caperetur, vix fugiens evasit. Sicque Deus providentia gens et tota illa terra . . . regi Salomoni est restitutus;" *MGHSS*, XX, 813, 49-50; also, Hersfeldensis *Annales*, a. 1063.

34. *Chronicon pictum*, cc. 97-123; Horváth, *Stilusproblémák*, 315ff.

35. *Chron. pict.*, c. 97; *Annales Alt.*, a. 1063, ending portion.

36. *SSH*, I, 362, 1-3.

37. *Ibid.*, I, 362, 3-6; unlike the compiler of the *Annales Altahenses*, the Hungarian chronicler called Moson *castrum*.

38. *SSH*, I, 362, 6-19.

39. *Ibid.*, I, 362, 20-27.

40. *Ibid.*, I, 362, 22.

41. "...quia nichil mali ex utraque parte perniciosa fraude fuerat excogitatum, sed forte inopinatum evenerat incendium;" *ibid.*, I, 363, 24-28.

42. *Chron. pict.*, c. 85.

43. Szentpétery,*Regesta,* I, nr. 5; Fejer, *CD,* I, 291.

44. *SSH,* I, 364f.

45. The Hungarian chronicler says 13 years (c. 101).

46. *Chron. pict.*, c. 101.

47. "Kyrieleys," says the chronicler; *ibid.*, I, 367, 19.

48. "Rex autem Salomon acerrime animositas audacia fremebundus . . . ;" *ibid.*, I, 368, 2-3.

49. "Dux autem Geysa, sicut erat semper providus;" *ibid.*, I, 368, 5-6.

50. *Ibid.*, I, 368, 7-10.

51. *Chronicon pictum,* c. 104.

52. *Ibid.*, I, 369, 22-23.

53. "...per ingenia sufflabant ignes sulphureos in naves Hungarorum;" *ibid.*, I, 370, 8-9.

54. "Victi sunt ignivomi Greci ab Ungaris;" *ibid.*, I, 370, 10.

55. *Chronicon pictum,* c. 105.

56. "...priusquam rex et dux cum exercitu suo de ientaculis capita levassent;" *ibid.*, I, 371, 15-16.

57. *Chronicon pictum,* cc. 106-108.

58. *Ibid.*, c. 109.

59. *Ibid.*, I, 374, 18-21.

60. *Ibid.*, I, 375, 11-21.

61. *Ibid.*, I, 376, 4-9.

62. "...ad firmandam pacem et amicitiam;" *ibid.*, I, 376, 5.

63. *Ibid.*, I, 376, 18-19.

64. *Chronicon pictum,* c. 111.

Notes to Chapter V
Section Three

1. Cf. *SSH,* I, 377, 6-8.

2. Salomon asked both of them, "misit rex ad utrumque ducem;" *ibid.*, I, 337, 4-6.

3. *Ibid.*, I, 377, 9-12.

4. "Duces autem insidias regis percipientes sibi caute consuderunt;" *ibid.*, I, 377, 8-10.

5. *Ibid.*, I, 377f.; c. 112.

6. *Ibid.*, I, 378, 4-9.

7. It may be the sole meaning of the passage by the chronicler: "Post hec misit ad Geysam ducem rex Vyd Deo detestabilem et Ernei manusetum, quos Geysa fecit caute custodiri. Misit etiam dux ad regem episcopum Waradiensem et nequam Vatha, quos rex fecit similariter custodiri;" *ibid.*, I, 378, 12-20.

8. *Ibid.*, I, 379, 2-7; the chronicler reasoned (c. 113) that Géza was alone, receiving no aid from his brother or from his friends; on the other hand, Salomon was ready to attack him.

8a. *Chron. pict.*, c. 115.

9. *Ibid.*, I, 379, 8-9.

10. *Ibid.*, I, 379, 10-27.

11. *Ibid.*, I, 380, 10-19.

12. "Et cum. . .venerint, . . .contra nos stare non possint," *ibid.*, I, 380, 20-23.

13. "Et potestis facere, quia omnes consiliarii sui tibi fideles sunt;" *ibid.*, I, 380, 25-27.

14. *Ibid.*, I, 380, 27-29: ". . .et ducatum michi dabis, et ita confirmabis tuam."

15. *Ibid.*, I, 380, 2-4; also the remark, "rex autem hoc audito promisit (i.e. to Vid) se cogitaturum usque ad matutinas;" *ibid.*, I, 380, 29-31.

16. "Willermus Latinus;" *ibid.*, I, 381, 3-5, and note 1.

17. *Ibid.*, I, 381, 5-10.

18. *Ibid.*, I, 381, 10-21, and compare with the previous remark made by Vid to Salomon: "quia omnes consiliari sui tibi fideles sunt;" *ibid.*, I, 380, 26-27.

19. *Ibid.*, I, 382, 10-12.

20. "Regebat autem Uid (sic!) regem, sicut magister discipulum;" *ibid.*, I, 382, 31-33.

21. *Ibid.*, I, 382, 17-27.

22. At Kemei (Kemey), "apud ecclesiam filii Nog;" *ibid.*, I, 383, 7-29, and compare with the following statement: "omnibus autem militibus suis pereuntibus declinavit dux a bello . . . ;" *ibid.*, I, 384, 28-31.

23. *Ibid.*, I, 384.

24. *Ibid.*, I, 385, 26-27.

25. *Ibid.*, I, 386, 15-24.

26. Salomon had, in fact, accused Ernyei of treason—*ibid.*, I, 386f.

27. At *Racus:* Rákos meadow: *ibid.*, I, 387, 24-28.

28. ". . .descenderunt in allodio quod dicitur Zymgota;" *ibid.*, I, 388, 21-22, after Géza was told by Ladislas about a vision in which Géza appeared to be destined by heaven to be king. "Angelus Domini descendit de celo portans coronam auream in manu sua et impressit capiti tuo" (The Angel of the Lord descended from heaven carrying a golden crown and placed the crown upon your head.) *Ibid.*, I, 388, 11-12.

29. *Ibid.*, I, 388, 22-23.

30. *Ibid.*, I, 388, 12-20.

31. It occurred on early Friday morning, "in dilucolo autem sexte ferie," after Quinquagesima Sunday (*ibid.*, I, 388, 26-27, i.e., on March 14, 1074 (*ibid.*, I, 388, note 7), nine days after the battle of Kemej; the latter took place on Wednesday after Sexagesima Sunday, "quarta feria post dominicam qua cantatur Exurge;" *ibid.*, I, 385, 28.

32. *Ibid.*, I, 390f.; for the description of the battle, see the *Chronicon pictum*, c. 121.

33. ". . . sed maior pars militie regni Hungarie dicitur corruisse;" *ibid.*, I, 391, 7; Gy. Farkas, "A mogyoródi csata (The battle of Mogyoród)," *Vigilia*, 39 (1974), 249ff. Salomon lacked self-confidence: "iam enim cognoverat rex Salomon, quod non auxiliaretur ei Dominus in bello;" SSH, I, 393, 1-2; Lampert of Hresfeld, *Annales*, a. 1074, in MGHSS, V, 215f.

34. SSH, I, 394, 12-13.

35. ". . . confusus ad caesarem direxit gressus suos;" *ibid.*, I, 397, 23-24; Giesebrecht, III, 202ff.

36. *SSH*, I, 398, 8-15.

37. "Quapropter venies in Hungariam et tuam ulciscaris iniuriam super hostes tuos et regnum tibi vendices;" *ibid.*, I, 398, 18-21.

38. Eventually the German Henry IV withdrew his support from him— cf. *Chronicon pictum*, cc. 127-28; Lampert, *Annales*, aa. 1074, 1075 (*MGHSS*, V, 215f.; 227).

39. See Ph. Jaffé (ed), *Bibliotheca rerum Germanicarum* (6 vols.; Berlin, 1869-73; repr. 1964), II, 127f.; or, Migne, *PL*, 148, col. 373; Jaffé, *Regesta*, I, nr. 4886.

40. Cf. Jaffé, *Bibliotheca*, II, 77f.; Migne, *PL*, 148, cols. 335f., dated March 17, 1074; Jaffé, *Regesta*, I, nr. 4835. Second writ, dated March 23, 1075, *ibid.*, I, nr. 4944; Jaffé, *Bibliotheca*, II, 183f.; Migne, *PL*, 148, col. 414. Third writ, *ibid.*, 148, cols. 421f.; Jaffé, *Bibliotheca*, II, 192f., dated April 14, 1075—Jaffé, *Regesta*, I, nr. 4952. See further V. Fraknói, *Magyarország és a Szentszék* (Hungary and the Holy See) (3 vols.; Budapest, 1901-03—, I, 22ff.

41. "... qui debita fide et devotione apostolicae reverentiae vota concipiunt, nequaquam dubia ab eis praesidia et beneficia praestolantur. Unde etiam tuam monemus dilectionem, ut studia tua erga honorem apostolorum semper excrescant .... Tu autem si quid interdum aut de tuis causis, aut quod servitio apostolicae reverentiae pertineat, nostris auribus intimare cupias, habes egregium videlicet marchionem Azonem, ... per quem ea quae apostolicam audientiam referenda destinaveris, nobis aptissime indicari et commendari poterunt;" Migne, *PL*, 148, col. 335cd; Jaffé, *Bibliotheca*, II, 77.

42. Bearing in mind the fact that, in eleventh century time-reckoning, the year began on Christmasday; cf. Grotefend, I, 205f.; von Barndt, 36ff.

43. The chronicler did his best to defend the behavior of the hierarchy (*SSH*, I, I, 402, 22-25); after High Mass on Christmasday, it was Géza who prostrated himself, "cum lacrimis prostratus est archiepiscopo et aliis ecclesiasticis" (*ibid.*, I, 402f.), and confessed guilt, "quia regnum legittime coronati regis occupaverat;" *ibid.*, I, 403, 1-2. Archbishop Desiderius of Kalocsa was mentioned in a forged document dated 1093— cf. Fejér, *CD*, I, 480—, though the document was based upon an authentic one issued in 1091; cf. Szentpétery, *Regesta*, I, nr. 27. According to Pauler, *Magyar nemzet*, I, 127f., Géza had occupied the throne before March 17, 1074.

44. Promisit regnum redditurum Salomoni cum pace firma hoc modo, quod ipse coronam iure teneret, cum tertia tamen parte regni, que ducatui appropriata erat;" *SSH*, I, 403, 2-5.

45. Jaffé, *Bibliotheca*, II, 77f.; Migne, *PL*, 148, col. 335f.

46. *Ibid.*, 148, col. 335d.

47. This seems to be evident from the concluding sentence of the Pope's letter: "De caetero divina clementia et ab instantibus huius saeculi te adversitatibus protegat, et ad peragendum ea quae sibi beneplacita sunt invictas tibi vires et facultates tribuat;" *ibid.*, 148, col. 335d.

48. Cf. Lampert of Hersfeld, *Annales*, a. 1074 (*MHGSS*, V. 215f.)

49. *SSH,* I, 400, 7-15.

50. Migne, *PL,* 148, col. 375; dated October 28, 1074.

51. Fraknói, I, 23.

52. Migne, *PL,* 148, col. 375b.

53. "Regni insignia;" *ibid.,* col. 375c.

54. *Ibid.;* for a different point of view, see Deér, *Hl. Krone,* 197ff.

55. Migne, *PL,* 148, col. 375c.

56. *Ibid.,* col. 375d.

57. Hersfeld, *Annales,* a. 1075 (MGHSS, V, 227; 232).

58. Szentpétery, *Regesta,* I, nr. 20 (anno 1075).

59. "Ego Magnus, qui et Geisa in primis Hungarorum dux, postea vero gratia Dei rex consecratus;" Knauz, I, 53; Fejér, *CD,* I, 428.

60. *Ibid.;* "... et ex tempore vocatus est Magnus rex," SSH, I, 400, 24-25. Géza may have been born on Sept. 6, the feast of Magnus Confessor—cf. the Pray codex in Radó, *Libri liturgici,* 38—, consequently, named Magnus.

61. The letter is lost; the papal answer, however, is available—Migne, *PL,* 148, col. 414—, dated March 23, 1075; also, R. Schieffer, "Gregor VII—ein Versuch über die historische Grösse," *Historisches Jahrbuch,* 97-98 (1978), 86ff., esp. 95f.

62. Migne, *PL,* 148, col. 414d.

63. "... nisi sanctae et universali matri Romanae Ecclesiae;" *ibid.,* col. 414c.

64. "... sed ut filios suscipit universos;" *ibid.,* col. 414d.

65. "Cum vero res in manibus tuis sit, ... obedientiam legatis sanctae Romanae Ecclesiae, cum ad te venerint, exhibeas;" *ibid.,* col. 414d.

66. *Ibid.,* 148, col. 421f.; Jaffé, *Bibliothaeca,* II, 192f.; Jaffé, *Regesta,* nr. 4952.

67. Migne, *PL,* 148, col. 421c.

68. *Ibid.,* col. 421d.

69. SSH, I, 402, 23-25; the name appears in a document issued by Ladislas in 1093—cf. Fejér, *CD,* I, 480; Szentpétery, *Regesta,* I, nr. 27.

70. SSH, I, 402f.

71. *Ibid.,* I, 403, 6; it was the bishops' duty to render advice to the ruler—cf. King Stephen's *Admonitiones,* a. III (*ibid.,* II, 619ff.; Migne, *PL,* 151, cols. 1235ff., c. 3).

72. SSH, I, 403, 10-14.

73. Migne, *PL,* 148, cols. 481f.; Jaffé, *Bibliothaeca,* II, 279ff.; Jaffé, *Regesta,* I, nr. 5; Fejer, *CD,* I, 291.

74. Migne, *PL*, 148, col. 481d.

75. Cf. *Chronicon pictum*, c. 131.

76. Migne, *PL*, 148, cols. 481-482a; also, see P. Brezzi, "Ottone di Frisinga," *Bulletino dell' Instituto strico Italiano*, 54 (1939), 129ff.

77. Gy. Moravcsik, "The Holy Crown of Hungary," *Hungarian Quarterly*, 4 (1938), 656ff.; idem, *Byzantium*, 42f.

78. Deér, *Hl. Krone*, 72ff.

79. *Ibid.*

80. Cf. M. Gyóni, "A legkorábbi magyar–bizánci hazassági kapcsolatok kérdéséhez (Some remarks about the earliest Hungaro-Byzantine marriage contacts)," *Századok*, 81 (1947), 212ff.

Notes to Chapter VI
Section One

1. *SSH*, I, 403, 15; the chronicler called Géza *rex Magnus–ibid.*, I, 403, 14.

2. *Ibid.*, I, 403, 19-22.

3. *Ibid.*, I, 403, 25-27.

4. *Ibid.*, I, 403f.

5. *Ibid.*, I, 404, 1-2.

6. *Ibid.*, I, 403, 29-30, and compare with Marczali, *Enchiridion*, 215ff., esp. 216, the fifth through the third lines from the bottom of the page; the chronicler began to write the *Chronicon pictum* in 1358 (*SSH*, I, 239, 2-3).

7. *Ibid.*, I, 404, 1-2.

8. *Ibid.*, II, 433, 13-14.

9. On the other hand, it seems to be clear from the writ of Gregory VII to Nehemias of Esztergom that, as far as Rome had knowledge of the matter, the Hungarian hierarchy did participate in the election of Ladislas; "qui inter vos electus est cum aliis tuius confratribus et principibus terrae,"—cf. Jaffé, *Regesta*, I, nr. 5036; for text, Jaffé, *Bibliotheca*, II, 280f.,—and instructed Archbishop Nehemias to see to it that Ladislas would, in the future, establish contact with Rome. Cf. Migne, *PL*, 148, cols. 481d-482a.

10. *SSH*, I, 404, 4-14.

11. *Ibid.*, I, 404f.; see also *Vita s, Ladislai*, c. 4 (*ibid.*, II, 518, 3-6).

12. *Ibid.*, I, 405, 6-11.

13. "Divina dispensatione regni gubernacula suscepit;" *ibid.*, I, 405, 12-13.

14. "... sciebat, quod rex non tamen regat, quam regatur; ... adauxit enim rem publicam Hungariae;" *SSH,* I, 405, 18-406, 7. Ladislas provided good justice to his people, "quod rigore iustitiae lenitatem preferebat," said Bishop Benedict of Várad in his *Sermo I* about Ladislas; cf. P. Lukcsics, *Szent László ismeretlen legendája* (The unknown legend of St. Ladislas) (Budapest, 1939), 31.

15. Zwoinimir, king of Croatia since 1076 (*SSH,* I, 406, note 3), who had previously requested military aid against the Carantanians from Salomon of Hungary and Géza, his, Zwonimir's, brother-in-law,—see *Chronicon pictum,* cc. 99 (*ibid.,* I, 363f), and 132 (*ibid.,* I, 406), and compare with Thomas of Spaleto, *Historia Salonitanorum (MGHSS,* XXIX, 570ff.), c. 17.

16. *SSH,* I, 406 (c. 132).

17. *Ibid.,* I, 407, 5-7.

18. *Ibid.,* I, 407, 7-10.

19. *Ibid.,* I, 407, 10-13; 19-20.

20. "Porro Salomon erat in Poson;" *ibid.,* I, 407, 1.

21. *Ibid.,* I, 407, 22-23.

22. *Ibid.,* I, 408, 2-4.

23. Ladislas had previously promised Pope Gregory that he would enter the service of St. Peter and behave like an obedient son,—see the letter, dated March 19, 1079, of Pope Gregory VII addressed "Ladislao Hungarorum regi;" Migne, *PL,* 148, col. 534d; Jaffé, *Bibliotheca,* II, 361f.; Jaffé, *Regesta,* I, nr. 5120.

24. Cf. *MGHSS,* V, 311; Lamperti *Annales,* a. 1077 (*SS rerum Germanicarum,* 301, 17-32).

25. Cf. Pauler, *Magyar nemzet története,* I, 188.

26. *MGHSS,* V, 311.

27. Cf. Migne, *PL,* 148, cols. 534f.

28. *Ibid.,* 148, col. 481a.

29. Cf. Bernoldi Constantiensis *Chronicon,* anno 1083 (*MGHSS,* V, 438f.); "... a Sancta Romanae Ecclesiae synodo iniunctum est, ut sanctorum corpora summo honore afficerentur... Veniente etiam sedis Apostolicae legato ... sacrum corpus canonisatum est;" Fejér, *CD,* I, 460.

30. *SSH,* II, 434, 5-8.

31. *Ibid.,* II, 433, 16-18.

32. *Ibid.,* II, 433, 16-18.

33. J. Horváth, *Stilusproblémák,* 270ff.

34. Cf. Stubbs *Select Charters* 287

35. *Chronicon pictum* c, 134.

36. *SSH,* I, 409f. (c. 135).

37. *Ibid.,* I, 410f. (c. 136); Keza, c. 61, reported that Salomon appeared, once, in front of Ladislas begging for alms, and before Ladislas could recognize him, Salomon disappeared (*ibid.,* I, 181); Bűdinger, 74f., and 74, note 4.

38. *SSH,* I, 410f (c. 136); von Mugeln, c. 47.

39. Migne, *PL,* 148, col. 535ab; A. Dempf, *Sacrum imperium: Geschichts- und Staatsphilosophie des Mittelalters und der politischen Renaissance* (4th ed.; Munich-Vienna, 1973), 187f.

40. "Rex vicarius Christi est;" cf. *Ordo coronandi regem Romanorum* in G. Waitz, "Die Formeln der deutschen Königs- und der römischen Kaiserkrönung," *Abhandlungen der hist.-phil. Klasse der Gesellschaft der Wissenschaften zu Göttingen,* 18 (1873), 42, and F. Kern, *Gottesgnadentum und Widerstandsrecht* (Kiel, 1914), 200f., and 311.

41. ". . . nos regni Pannonici optimates . . . fecimus conuentus;" *RHM,* II, 334; Marczali, *Enchiridion,* 93.

42. ". . . culpa ultra precium gallinarum;" *ibid.,* art. 1.

43. "nisi ceciderit in ecclesiam;" *ibid.*

44. ". . . et quesumus qualiter malorum hominum impedirentur studia et gentis nostre expedirentur negocia;" *ibid.;* the legislators also decreed that students in minor clerical orders who had been accused and found guilty of lesser crimes, be beaten the first time they committed a crime.

45. *RHM,* II, 334ff., art. 1, and compare with the legislation of Henry I of England; cf. Stubbs, 97.

46. *RHM,* II, 334ff., art. 6.

47. *Ibid.,* II, 310ff., art. II:7 (and *loc. cit.*).

48. *Ibid.,* art. I:31.

49. *Ibid.,* II, 334ff., art. 12, and art. 10b.

50. *Ibid.,* II, 337, art. 10b.

51. *Ibid.,* art. 12.

52. *Ibid.,* II, 335, art. 5.

53. *Ibid.,* II, 336f., art. 9.

54. *Ibid.,* II, 338f., art. 14-15.

55. *Ibid.,* art. 16.

56. *Ibid.,* art. 3.

57. *Nuncii,* the King's itinerant justices (art. 5 and 6), and the *iudex, iudici,* regional (county) judges (art. 6ab).

58. *Ibid.*, art. 13-16.

59. "... si uero mercator fit contractus, fiat coram iudice et theloneario et testibus;" *ibid.*, art. 7.

60. *Ibid.*, art. 16.

61. *Ibid.*, art. 6ab.

62. *Ibid.*, art. 8 and 10a.

63. *Ibid.*, art. 10a.; St. Katona, *Historia pragmatica Hvngariae* (3 vols.; Buda, 1782 etc.), I, 450ff.

64. Hartvic, c. 24.

65. For text, see *RHM*, II, 340ff.; Marczali, *Enchiridion*, 96ff.; textual comments by Katona, *Historia pragmatica*, I, 452f.

66. Katona, *ibid.*, I, 452, provided an interesting reason for the legislation: "quod vitium licentia militum, tempora belli spoliis agendis affuetorum, iniuxerat."

67. *RHM*, II, 341, art. 1.

68. Were he seek refuge in a church, "si presbyter postea eum emancipauerit, et ipse uice eiusdem seruus sit ecclesiae;" were he to steal again, "tollantur ei oculi." Cf. *ibid.*, II, 343, art. 4.

69. *Ibid.*, II, 345f., art. 14.

70. *Ibid.*, II, 341ff., art. 1, 20, 23, 24 and 25-27; "ut nuncius regis per omnes ciuitates dirigatur, qui congreget centuriones et decuriones eorum qui ulogo Ewri uocantur, cum omnibus sibi commissis, et precipiat eis, ut si quem furti culpabilem sciant, ostendant" (art. 1); compare with Stubbs, 104ff., c. 29 (Henry I), and 140ff., Assize of Clarendon, aa. 1 and 12, etc.; G.O. Sayles, *The Medieval Foundations of England* (rev. ed.; London, 1964), 325ff.

71. *Ibid.*, art. 6-7, 9-10.

72. *Ibid.*, art. 18-20.

73. *Ibid.*, art. 13: *joccerydech* (=ioccedeth): "rerum furtiuarum collector."

74. "... ciuium uel uillarum, qui dicuntur Evvrek, uel serui detinentur illi qui dicuntur uulgo Wzbeg, cuiucunque personae adheserint. . . ;" *ibid.*, II, 342, art. 2.

75. *Ibid.*, art. 21, at the annual field day of the nobles and free men before the King—cf. Andrew II's *Decretum I,* anno 1222 (*ibid.*, II, 412ff.).

76. *Ibid.*, II, 341ff., art. 22.

77. *Ibid.*, art. 29-30.

78. *Ibid.*, art. 13 and 21.

79. *Ibid.*, art. 1, par. 2.

80. "Palatinus comes;" *ibid.*, art. 3.

81. *Ibid.*, art. 16; his position was protected by law—cf. *ibid.*, art. 24, 26 and 27, second par.

82. ". . . ut nuncius regis per omnes ciuitates dirigatur, qui congreget centuriones et decuriones eorum, qui uulgo Ewri uocantur, cum omnibus sibi commissis, et percipiat eis, ut si quem furti culpabilem sciant, ostendant;" *ibid.*, art. 1, and Stubbs, 143ff., art. 1.

83. See art. 23, 25 and 26 (*RHM*, II, 341ff.).

84. Stubbs, 143ff., art. 1.

85. *RHM*, II, 341ff., art, 24.

86. *Ibid.*, art. 26-27.

87. *Ibid.*, art. 23 and 26, part. 2.

88. ". . . possit iudex sigilum suum mittere super quoscunque, exceptis presbyteris et clericis, necnon comitibus;" *ibid.*, art. 26, first par.

89. Cf. Bernoldi *Chronicon*, anno 1083 (*MGHSS*, V, 483f.); Balanyi, *art. cit.;* also, *SSH*, II, 433, 5-11, and *Vita s. Ladislai (ibid.*, II, 520f.).

90. Hartvic, c. 24.

91. See Stephen's *Vita minor*, c. 2 (*ibid.*, II, 394).

92. *Ibid.*, II, 433, 8-11.

93. Statement based upon the assertion of the *Chronicon pictum* that, in the fourth year of his reign, Ladislas did conclude peace with Salomon (*ibid.*, I, 407, 6-7), in order to eliminate the case of continued German pressure upon the Hungarian court.

94. Giesebrecht, III, 459ff.; Haller, III, 16ff.

95. Cf. Bernoldi *Chronicon*, anno 1087 (*MGHSS*, V, 446); in fact, Ladislas persuaded Wratislav II of Bohemia to side with Pope Victor III—see F. Palacky, *Geschichte von Böhmen* (5 vols.; Prague, 1844 etc.), I, 298ff., supported by Cosmas of Prague, *Chronicae Bohemorum*, ii:37 (*MGHSS*, IX, 91f.).

96. Gebhardt, I, 250ff.; Giesebrecht, III, 406f.

97. ". . . venit et occupavit totam terram a Drauo fluvio usque ad Alpes, que dicuntur ferrae nullo obice resistente;" Spalatensis *Historia*, c. 17 (*MGHSS*, XXIX, 570ff); A. Lhotsky, "Die österreichischen Länder im Hochmittelalter," in his *Aufsätze und Vorträge*, vol I (Vienna, 1970), 245ff.

98. *SSH*, I, 406.

99. "Post haec transivit Alpes et cepit impugnare munitiones et castra, multaque proelia comitere cum gentibus Chroatiae;" Spalatensis *Historia*, c. 17.

100. *Ibid.*

101. Thomas of Spoleto argued that "iste Suonemerius ultimus fuit in regno Chroatiae;" *ibid.*, c. 16; F. Sisic, *Geschichte der Kroaten*, vol. I (Zagreb, 1917), 353f.; Ekkehardus Uraugiensis *Chronicon universale*, anno 1089 (*MGHSS*, VI, 199).

102. Dandalo, *Chronicon*, anno 1090 (Muratori, XII, 33ff., ix:8); Spalatensis *Historia*, c. 17.

103. "... integraliter sibi restituit;" *SSH*, I, 406, 13-14.

104. *Ibid.*, I, 406, 14-25.

105. *MGHSS*, VI, 364; Jaffé, *Bibliotheca*, II, 682; Haller, II, 415ff.; Seppelt, III, 92ff.

106. Cf. Szentpétery, *Regesta*, I, nr. 24; Marczali, *Enchiridion*, 101ff., to the effect that "sicut regales est monasterium, ita omnium bonorum consensu est prohibitio."

107. Cf. C. Erdmann (ed), Deutsches Mittelalter: die Briefe Heinrichs IV (Leipzig, 1937), 32ff.; K. Langosch (ed), *Die Briefe Kaiser Henrichs IV* (Munster-Cologne, 1954), 66ff. R. Bensen (ed), *Imperial Lives and Letters of the Eleventh Century* (New York, 1961), 170, note 105, and 171, rendered the wrong translation: Prince Álmos was the nephew and not the son of King Ladislas; "Ladislao autem migrato regnavit post eum filius Geichae regis, Kolomannus." Cf. Keza, c. 64 (*SSH*, I, 182).

108. Hóman-Szekfű, I, 358; Sisic, I, 257ff.

109. Franknói, I, 27.

110. *MGHSS*, V, 453; it is Christmas, 109*1* in our time reckoning; cf. v. Brandt, 39.

111. The King mentioned the delegates he dispatched to Rome: "capellaneos meos et Sorinem nostrum militem, quos V (=Urbano?) apostolico mitto;" Franknói, I, 404, dated it 1091.

112. Cf. Spalatensis *Historia*, c. 17.

113. *Chronicon pictum*, c. 137.

114. Váczy, *art. cit. (Mon. Hung. hist.*, vol. I).

115. Anonymus, c. 15.

116. Cross—Sherbowitz-Wetzor, 184.

117. *Chronicon pictum*, c. 138.

118. *SSH*, 1, 414f.

119. *Ibid.*, I, 414, 4-27.

120. *Ibid.*, I, 415, 27-32.

121. *Chronicon pictum*, c. 139.

122. Coloman was the nephew and successor of Ladislas; cf. *ibid.*, c. 140.

123. In the year 1097 or 1099—see Cross—Sherbowitz-Wetzor, 196, 198.

124. *Chron. pict.*, c. 145, and Martinus Gallus, *Chronicae Polonorum*, ii:4 (*MGHSS*, IX, 423ff).

125. *Ibid.*, 446f.

126. Gallus, *Chronicae*, ii:19.

127. The marriage must have taken place earlier, in 1088—cf. *ibid.*

128. Cosmas of Prague, *Chronicae*, ii:37 (*ibid.*, IX, 91f.).

129. See *ibid.*, IX, 91ff., for the text of the charter of the new bishopric; the visit of Bishop Gebhardt in Hungary, *ibid.*, IX, 95f., ii:41.

130. *Ibid.*, IX, 96, ii:41.

131. *SSH*, I, 416, 26-29.

132. *Ibid.*, I, 417, 4-11: "alienigenarum et ignotarum gentium regimen suscipere recusavit."

133. J. Horváth, *Stilusproblémák*, 331ff.

134. *SSH*, I, 417, 15-27.

135. *Chronicon pictum*, c. 140.

136. *Ibid.*, c. 141.

Notes to Chapter VI
Section Two

1. Cf. C. Mirbt (ed), *Die Publizistik im Zeitalter Gregors VII* (Leipzig, 1894), 266ff., and 326f.; the writ of Pope Gregory to the Archbishop of Mainz, dated March, 1074, in Jaffé, *Bibliotheca*, II, 523ff.; the report of Marianus Scotus, *Chronicon*, a. 1074, in MGHSS, V. 560ff.; Haller, II, 415ff.; Seppelt, III, 65ff.

2. For text, see RHM, II, 325ff.; Mansi, *Concilia*, XX, cols, 758ff.; selections in Marczali, *Enchiridion*, 87ff.; C.J. Hefele, *Conziliengeschichte* (2nd ed.; 6 vols.; Freibrug i. Br., 1873 etc.), V, 204ff. Text preserved in the fifteenth century Thuróczy codex, in the Széchenyi Library of the Hungarian National Museum, *Clme* 407, ff. 85r-88v, and in the sixteenth century Ilosvay codex, *Fol. lat.* 4023, ff. 20v-22r (codex copied "per manus Stephani de Iloswá, prepositi vicarii ecclesiae Agriensis," f. 138r.); my article, "Relations of the Hungarian Court With the Church at the Beginning of the Twelfth Century," *Proceedings of the XVIth Annual Hungarian Congress, 1976* (Cleveland, O., 1977), 227ff., esp. 234. Katona, *Historia critica*, II, 568, insisted that the synod was actually held at Buda, on grounds of a document issued at Buda on June 23, 1092—for the document, cf. Batthyány, *Leges*, I, 445; however, Katona failed to note

the fact that the document had to be a forgey because it described King Ladislas of Hungary as ruler of Austria, a title he never had—see *ibid.,* I, 442f., note *c*; also, Péterffy, *Concilia,* I, 13f.

3. ". . . anno incarnationis MXCII, XII Kalend. Iunii, in ciuitate Zabolcz . . . ; RHM, II, 326.

4. Péterffy, *Concilia,* I, 14, assumed that Seraphim was archbishop of Esztergom as early as 1092.

5. ". . . presidente christianissimo rege Ungarorum Ladislao, . . .cum testimonio tocius cleri et populi;" RHM, II, 326.

6. *Ibid.,* II, 334, art. 1.

7. ". . . in monte sancto fecimus conuentus, et quesumus qualiter malorum hominum impedirentur studia et gentis nostre expedirentur negocia;" *ibid.,* art. 1.

8. Cf. F. Knauz (ed), *Monumenta Ecclesiae Strigoniensis* (2 vols.; Esztergom, 1874), I, 68, noted that "archiepiscopatum tamen vivente adhuc Ladislao rege, adeoque vel 1094, aut certe 1095, obtinuit." P.B. Gams, *Series episcoporum Ecclesiae Catholicae* (Ratisbonae, 1873), 380, provided no answer.

9. ". . . in qua sancta synodo canonice et laudabiliter decreta hec inuenta sunt;" prologus, RHM, II, 326.

10. Cf. Szabolcs, art. 21, *ibid.,* II, 329.

11. *Ibid.,* 331, art. 36.

12. *Ibid.,* 329, art. 19; it must have meant that, at this time, there were many migrant villagers in the country, whose administration remained a problem.

13. RHM, II, 329, 330, art. 21 and 28.

14. *Ibid.,* II, 327, 330, art. 5 and 23.

15. *Ibid.,* art. 6, and compare with art. 8 of the 847 Synod of Mainz, in Mansi, *Concilia,* XIV, col. 906, and/or with art. 6 of the 888 Synod of Mainz, *ibid.,* XVIII, col. 66; the Hungarian law is more strict.

16. Cf. Szabolcs, art. 31 and 34, in RHM, II, 330, 331; art. 41 (*ibid.,* 332f.), defined in detail the manner of collection of the tithe.

17. *Ibid.,* II, 327, art. 7, and compare with King St. Stephen's *Leges,* art. II:1 (*ibid.,* II, 321).

18. *Ibid.,* II, 327, art. 8.

19. *Ibid.,* II, 332, art. 38 and 39.

20. ". . . et ab uniuersis collaudatum et canonisatum, ut uigilie celebrentur beati Stephani regis et Gerardi martyris. . . ;" *ibid.,* art. 38; Hefele, V, 206, listed it under art. 37 (!); art. 39 posted the feasts of King Stephen and of Bishop Gerard.

21. "... unus tamen ex eis nomine omnium ... ;" *ibid.*, II, 328, art. 11.

22. "... cum baculo ad ecclesiam ueniat, et tres panes et candelam ad altare afferat;" *ibid.*, art. 11, and compare with King Stephen's *Leges*, art. I:9 (*ibid.*, II, 313f.).

23. See the *Concilium Romanum*, anno 1078, in Mansi, *Concilia*, XX, col. 510.

24. Cf. Batthyány, *Leges*, I, 435, notes *d* and *e*.

25. RHM, II, 328f., art. 15 and 16.

26. *Ibid.*, art. 12.

27. *Ibid.*, art. 25.

28. *Ibid.*, II, 331, art. 32: it must have been a Hungarian custom: "se nostra consuetudini meliori."

29. *Ibid.*, art. 22.

30. *Ibid.*, art. 26, and compare with the resolutions, anno 895, of the *Concilium Triburiense*, in Mansi, *Concilia*, XVIII, col. 142.

31. RHM, II, 328, art. 10.

32. *Ibid.*, art. 27, and compare with universal Church law enacted in 845, art. 73, in Mansi, *Concilia*, XIV, col. 839. I. Hajnik, *Magyar alkotmány és jog az Árpádok alatt* (Hungarian constitutional and legal development in the reign of the Árpáds) (Pest, 1872), 179, says that close relations between the Church and the court of Ladislas led to hostility toward the non-Christian social element in thr realm; for a counterargument, see Gy. Bónis, *A jogtudó értelmiség a középkori Nyugat és Közép-Európában* (Position of the law-trained intelligentsia in medieval Western and Central Europe) (Budapest, 1971), 16ff.

33. RHM, II, 327f., art. 9.

34. *Ibid.*

35. *Ibid.*, art. 17, and compare with can. 73 of 845, in Mansi, *Concilia*, XIV, col. 839, and with can. 50, col. 830.

36. RHM, II, 329, art. 18.

37. *Ibid.*, art. 30, and compare with art. 9 of the 888 Synod of Mainz, Mansi, *Concilia*, XVIII, col. 67.

38. Cf. Marianus Scotus, *Chronicon*, a. 1074, in MGHSS, V, 560f., and Bertholdi *Annales*, a. 1078, *ibid.*, V. 308f.

39. RHM, II, 326, art. 1.

40. "... quousque nobis in hoc domini apostolici paternitas consilietur;" *ibid.*, art. 3, and compare with cc. 3 and 13 of the *Concilium Trullanum vel Quinesext.*, anno 692, in Mansi, *Concilia*, XI, cols. 942 and 947.

41. RHM, II, 327, art. 2.

42. *Ibid.*, art. 4, and the ordinances of Pope Urban II at the *Concilium Melfit*, a. 1090, can. 12, in Mansi, *Concilia*, XX, col. 724.

43. RHM, II, 328, art. 13.

44. *Ibid.*, art. 20.

45. *Ibid.*, art. 35, and compare with Stephen's *Leges*, art. I:33; G.L. Simmons, *The Witchcraft World* (London, 1974), 185ff., on the persecution of witches.

46. RHM, II, 330, art. 29.

47. *Ibid.*, art. 33.

48. See Stephen's *Leges*, art. I:16, 32 and 35; II:12.

49. RHM, II, 331, art. 20.

50. *Ibid.*, art. 42-43, and Ladislas *Decretum II*, art. 11 (*ibid.*, II, 338), and *Decretum III*, art. 15 (*ibid.*, 346).

51. Cf. Migne, *PL*, 151, col. 481b.

52. *Ibid.*, 163, col. 198; Jaffé, *Regesta*, I, nr. 6098.

The bibliography of the period is covered by D. Kosáry (ed), *Bevezetés a magyar történelem irodalmába* (Introduction to the literature of Hungarian history) (3 vols.; Budapest 1951-58), vol. III; *idem, Bevezetés Magyarország történelem irodalmába* (Introduction to the literature of Hun- reviewed by J. Szentmihályi in *Magyar Könyvszemle*, 87 (1971), 255ff., and–in an aggressive manner–by Gy. Ember in *Századok*, 107 (1973), 459ff.; T. Bogyay, "Ujabb szent István kutatások (Recent research dealing with King Stephen)," *Katolikus Szemle*, 23 (Rome, 1971), 289ff.; C.A. Macartney, *The Medieval Hungarian Historians* (Cambridge, 1953); A.F. Gombos (ed), *Catalogus fontium historiae Hungaricae* (3 vols.; Budapest, 1937-38); the valuable bibl. listings by Gombos and Cs. Csapodi in *Emlékkönyv szent István király halálának kilencszázadik évfordulóján* (Memorial volume to the 900th anniversay of King Stephen's death) (ed. J. Serédi; 3 vols.; Budapest, 1938), cited hereafter *SIE*, III, 279ff., and 295ff.; 647ff.; Bálint Hóman-Gyula Szekfó, *Magyar történet* (Hungarian history) (5 vols.; 6th ed.; Budapest, 1939), I, 641ff.; L.J. Csóka, *A latin nyelvű történeti irodalom kialakulása Magyarországon a XI-XIV században* (Development of Latin historical literature in Hungary during the eleventh -fourteenth centuries) (Budapest, 1967), is given a rather hostile though objective review by Gy. Kristó in *Századok*, 102 (1968), 610ff., and an unsympathetic reaction by Gy. Rónay in *Vigilia*, 36 (1971), 527ff.; J. Félegyházy, "Történelmi irodalmunk kezdetei (The beginnings of Hungarian historical literature)," *ibid.*, 34 (1969), 329ff.

The learned György Györffy made very important contributions to Hungarian historiography in the post-war period; his *Krónikáink és a magyar őstörténet* (Les chroniques hongroises et l'histoire primitive des Hongrois) (Budapest, 1948), is of basic importance, and so is "A magyar nemzetségtől a vármegyáig, a törzstől az országig (From Hungarian clans to the formation of the county; from tribal organization to that of a statehood)," *Századok*, 92 (1958), 12-87; 565-615; his *Az Árpád-kori Magyarország történeti földrajza* (Geographia historica Hungariae tempore stirpis Arpadianae) (vol. I; Budapest, 1963), 835ff., on the Csanád region; it was Györffy, who identified abbot Astric with Archbishop Athanasius in his "A magyar egyházszervezés kezdeteiről űjabb forráskritikai vizsgálatok alapján (About the beginnings of ecclesiastical organization in Hungary in the light of recent research)," *M.T.A. II oszt. Közleményei*, 18 (1969, 199ff., a very important contribution even if the idea itself is not new: Wattenbach mentioned it (*MGHSS*, XI, 233, n. 32); *Györffy* also pointed out that the mentioning by Regino's Chronicle of the Hungarians in 889 (*ibid.*, I, 599), may be a later entry, as it may refer to the events of the year 901; cf. his "A besnyők európai honfoglalásának kérdéséhez (Some questions concerning the European conquest and settlement of the Petzenegs)," *Történelmi Szemle*, 14 (1971), 281ff., or his new approach toward some questions on the Hungarian conquest of 896(?), "A honfoglalásról újabb történeti kutatások tükrében (About the Hungarian conquest in the light of recent research)," *Valóság*, 1973; Györffy's essay, "Anonymus Gesta Hungarorumának kora és hitelessége (Age and authenticity of Anonymus' *Gesta),*" *Irodalomtörténeti Közlemények*, 74 (1970), 1ff., is, together with Gy. Kristó's "Anonymus magyarországi írott forrásainak kérdéséhez (Les sources manuscrites du notaire Anonyme, auteur des Gesta Hungarorum)," *Magyar Könyvszemle*, 88 (1972), 166ff., and P. Váczy, "A korai magyar történet néhány kérdéséről (Some questions concerning the value of early Hungarian historical material)," *Századok*, 92 (1958), 265ff., very important in taking a new approach toward an old problem in Hungarian historiography.

The work by R. Gragger (ed), *Bibliographia Hungariae* (2 vols.; Berlin, 1923-26), vol. I, is, though out of date, useful in its listings of non-Hungarian publications on Hungarian history; E. Bartoniek's thin volume, *Magyar történeti forráskiadványok* (Published sources of Hungarian history) (Budapest, 1929) is worth mentioning, and so is the work of F. Eckhart, *Introduction a l'histoire hongroise* (Paris, 1928); H. Marczali, *Ungarns Geschichtsquellen im Zeitalter der Árpáden* (Berlin, 1882), is a classic and contains useful information; the bibliographical listings in the *Cambridge Medieval* History, IV-I, 977ff.; VI, 930ff.; VIII, 961ff., are helpful; for current literature, one should consult the annual listings of Hungarian historical literature in *Századok*.

On codex literature in Hungary, Polycarp Radó, *Index codicum manu scriptorum liturgicorum regni Hungariae* (Budapest, 1941); idem, *Beiträge zur Bibliographie der ungarischen Liturgiegeschichte* (Pannonhalma, 1942); idem, *Libri liturgici manu scripti bibliothaecarum Hungariae* (Budapest, 1947); A. de Ivánka rendered good listings in *Medieval and Renaissance Studies*, 4 (1958), 146ff., while the bibliographical essay of A. Strittmatter, "Liturgical manuscripts preserved in Hungarian libraries," *Traditio*, 19 (1963), 487ff., is a helpful summary.

The Hungarian sources of this period were carefully edited by fifteen contributors in E. Szentpétery (ed), *Scriptores rerum Hungaricarum*

(2 vols.; Budapest, 1937-38), cited *SSH;* see the comments of Christopher Dawson, "Hungarian Middle Ages," *Hungarian Quarterly,* 5 (Budapest-New York, 1939), 585ff.; there is another excellent collection of medieval Hungarian sources, including law collections and the acts of the first Hungarian parliaments in St. L. Endlicher (ed), *Rerum Hungaricarum monumenta Arpadiana* (2 vols.; Sangallen, 1849), referred to *RHM;* idem, *Die Gesetze des hl. Stefan: ein Beitrag zur ungarischen Rechtsgeschichte* (Vienna, 1849), including the legal collections of Stephen. The edition of Hungarian materials in the *Monumenta Germaniae historica, Scriptores* (as, e.g. Wattenbach's edition of King Stephen's *vitae,* vol. XI) is excellent, while the texts provided by the editors of the *Acta Sanctorum Bollandiana* (the *vitae* of Stephen and Gerard of Csanád; the laws and Admonitions of Stephen in vols. Sept. I, 456ff., and Sept. VI, 715ff.) are most useful, and so are the stimulating essays of the editor, J. Stilting; the Migne, *PL*, 151, col. 1203ff., version of the *vita, leges,* and *monita* of Stephen is a reprint from the *ASS*.

There are five other text editions of material which deserve consideration; C. Péterffy (ed), *Sacra concilia ecclesiae Romano-Catholicae in regno Hungariae celebrata* (2 vols.; Vienna, 1742), out of date, but useful; I. de Batthyány (ed), *Leges ecclesiasticae regni Hungariae et provinciarum adiacentium* (3 vols.; Alba-Carolinae, 1785; Claudipoli, 1824); G. Fejér (ed), *Codex diplomaticus Hungariae ecclesiasticus et civilis* (43 vols; Buda, 1829-44), a monumental work indexed by M. Czinár in 1866; G. Wenczel (ed), *Codex diplomaticus Arpadianus continuatus* (12 vols.; Pest, 1857 etc., in the *Monumenta Hungariae historica* series); D. Márkus (ed), *Corpus Iuris Hungarici: magyar törvénytár, 1000 - 1895* (20 vols.; Budapest, 1899 etc.), vol. I; L. Závodszky (ed), *A szent István, szent László és Kálmán korabeli törvények és zsinati határozatok forrásai* (De fontibus legum et decretorum synodalium e temporibus sancti Stephani, sancti Ladislai et Colomanni oriundorum) (Budapest, 1904), still the best edition of Stephen's laws, with the exception of the *Libellus* of Admonitions edited by I. Balogh for the *SSH*, II, 619ff. A very stimulating analysis of this material is provided by János Horváth, *Árpád-kori latinnyelvű irodalmunk stílusproblémái* (Some stylistic questions concerning the Latin literature of the Árpádian age) (Budapest, 1954).

Felix Schiller, "Das erste ungarische Gesetzbuch und das deutsche Recht," *Festschrift Heinrich Brunner* (Weimar, 1910), 379ff., is a basic work on the legislation of King Stephen; so is J. v. Sawicki's "Zur

Textkritik und Entsehungsgeschichte der Gesetze König Stefan des Heiligen," *Ungarische Jahrbücher*, 9(1929), 395ff.; the contribution of J. Balogh, "Szent István Intelmeinek forrásai (Sources used at the composition of Stephen's Admonitions)," and J. Madzsar, "Szent István törvényei és az úgy nevezett symachusi hamisítványok (The laws of Stephen and the so called Symachus forgeries)," *SIE*, II, 235ff., and 203ff., respectively, provide valuable information.

J. Balogh's essay, "The Political Testament of Saint Stephen," *Hungarian Quarterly*, 4 (1938), 389ff., is a good summary in English, while the article by A. Balogh, "Szent István kapcsolatai Cheh- Német- Franciaországgal és Belgiummal (Contacts between King Stephen's court and Bohemia, Germany, France and Belgium)," *SIE*, I, 449ff., is informative even though "Belgium" did not as yet exist on the map at the age of Stephen. The classic study by Gy. Pauler, *A magyar nemzet története az árpádházi királyok alatt* (History of the Hungarian nation in the age of the Árpáds) (2 vols.; 2nd ed.; Budapest, 1899) is a must; on the formation of the concept of *nation*, see the ideas of Jenő *Szűcs in Történelmi Szemle*, 9 (1966), 245ff.; his "Gentilizmus: a barbár etnikai tudat kérdése ('Gentilism:' some problems concerning the concept of the barbarian ethnic consciousness)," *ibid.*, 14 (1971), 188ff., and the summary of the "problem" by Gy. Granasztói, *Századok*, 107 (1973), 114ff.

The sources comprise the *vitae* of Stephen, and Hartvic's biography preserved in a twelfth century Rein MS (69) bearing the title *Vita s. Stephani regis Hungariae* (f. 27); the *Vita* and *Passio* of Gerard. The "shorter" lives of both Stephen and Gerard may have served as documentation pieces for their canonization—on whose background, cf. Hartvic, c. 25; Berthold of Constance, *Chronicon*, a. 1087 (*MGHSS*, V. 446), and Gy. Balanyi, "Magyar szentek, szentéletű magyarok (Hungarian saints; saintly Hungarians)," *Katolikus Szemle*, 15 (1963), 100ff., – as the proper of the Roman Missal for Stephen's feast summarized the reasons for his canonization: (a) defended the Church, "quem regnantem in terris propagatorem habuit; (b) made his people Christian, "familiam . . . de tenebris ad veram lucem convertit;" on the canonization, see also Gerard's *Passio (SSH*, II, 479). On the background and time of composition of Stephen's *vitae*, cf. E. Bartoniek's introduction in *SSH*, II, 365ff.

The *Vita* of Gerard is a fourteenth century piece, composed perhaps in the 1370's, when portions of Gerard's *reliquiae* were transferred from

Csanád to Venice; the *Vita* may have served as the authentication document of this transaction; see Gy. Rónay, "Szent Gellért," *Vigilia,* Dec., 1946, 47ff., and his review of D. Dercsényi's *Chronicon pictum: Képes Krónika* (2 vols.; Budapest, 1964) in *Vigilia,* 30 (1965), 44ff.; also F. Banfi, "Vita di s. Gerardo de Venezia nel codice 1622 della Bibliotheca universitarie de Padova," *Benedictina,* 2 (1948), 262ff., with the text following *ibid.*, 288ff.

Of the major historical sources of the period, the *Gesta Ungarorum* of Anonymus; the *Gesta* by Simon de Keza; the fourteenth century chronicles provide good information. In his outstanding study, Gy. Kristó, "Anjou-kori krónikáink (Hungarian chronicles of the Angevin age)," *Századok,* 101 (1967), 457ff., made the point that in the fourteenth century, Hungary had at least two important chroniclers: the Minorite friar of Buda, who served as the chronicler of Robert Charles, and Canon Mark de Kalta, the historian of the reign of Lewis the Great; Kristó disagreed with G. Karsai, "Névtelenség, névrejtés és szerzőnév a középkori krónikákban (Anonimity and authorship of medieval chronicles)," *Századok,* 97 (1963), 666ff., concerning the author of the *Chronicon pictum.*

Hungarian historiography—Hóman and his school—earlier held the point of view that the historical resources of the eleventh century were handled by a chronicler who worked during the reign of Ladislas I (1077-95)—cf. B. Hóman, *A szent László-kori Gesta Ungarorum és XII-XIII századi leszármazói* (The Hungarian *gesta* of the times of St. Ladislas, and its continuators in the 12th and 13th centuries) (Budapest, 1925), 79ff.,—and whom he called the "Chronicler of the age of Saint Ladislas." János Horváth, *op.cit.*, 315ff., attempted to identify this writer as the author, who did his work in the late eleventh-early twelfth century in the days of King Coloman the Learned (1096-1116), though certainly not before 1109 (*ibid.*, 330), and appropriately called him the "Chronicler of the age of the Learned Coloman."

The opus of this writer is lost, though the material covered by him survived incorporated in later chronicles, as, for instance, in paragraphs 25 through 139 of the fourteenth century Chronicle text (cf. *SSH,* I, 239ff., esp. 283-418); now *Horváth,* having compared and summarized the results of previous research, especially that by the learned Györffy (*Krónikáink, et al*), came to the conclusion that there had to be at least two Hungarian chroniclers who reported about eleventh century Hungary.

One of these chroniclers composed his piece during the reign of Andrew I (1046-60); he was Nicholas the royal chancellor ("qui tunc temporis vicem procurabat notarii in curia regali;" cf. Tihany charter, 1055, in H. Marczali (ed), *Enchiridion fontium historiae Hungarorum* [Budapest, 1901], 81ff., esp. 85), who with of his colleagues outlived the 1046 pagan uprising and crowned Andrew king (Chronicle, c. 86; *Annales Altahenses, (MGHSS,* XX, 803, a. 1046). Paragraph 35 of the fourteenth century text mentioned the existence of this source (*SSH,* I 292f.), and so did Anonymous, who spoke of "certa scripturarum explanatione et operta hystoriarum interpretatione" (*ibid.,* I, 34, 2-4), to distinguish it from unwritten tradition, "ut dicunt nostri ioculatores" (*ibid.,* I, 65, 9) of questionable value, "garguli cantibus ioculatorum et falsis fabulis rusticorum" (*ibid.,* I, 87, 9-10; Pintér, *op.cit.,* I, 211ff.).

The contribution of Nicholas consisted of information contained up to the first half of par. 91 in the fourteenth century text; from the second half of par. 91 on, the news were provided by the author of the age of Coloman, whose intelligence included the establishment of the Várad bishopric; this portion of the text, paragraphs 91 - 139, shows strong unity in contents, and reveals a unified approach in writing. Its author, however, remains unknown.

Horváth noted that a Bishop Koppány, who had been considered as the possible chronicler of the age of Coloman, could not have authored the text because it was composed in or after 1109, and Koppány died in the 1099 Russian campaign of King Coloman (*op.cit.,* 338f.); I must add here, merely for the sake of objectivity that in the Russian Primary Chronicle the death of *Koppány* was registered twice, under the year 1097 and 1099 (cf. S.H. Cross *et al.* (ed), *The Russian Primary Chronicle* [Cambridge, Mass., 1953], 196, 198).

Among the numerous essays dealing with early Hungarian history and historiography, I only mention R.F. Kaindl, "Studien zu den ungarischen Geschichtsquellen," *Archiv für österreichische Geschichte,* 91 (1902), 26ff.; H. Heinemann, "Zur Kritik der ungarischen Geschichtsquellen," *Neues Archiv,* 13 (1887), 61ff.; O. Rademacher, "Zur Kritik ungarischer Geschichtsquellen," *Forschungen zur deutschen Geschichte,* 25 (1885), 379ff.; E. Madzsar, "Die Lengende des hl. Gerhard," *Ungarische Revue,* 3 (1914), 288ff.; C.A. Macartney, "The Hungarian National Chronicle," *Medievalia et humanistica,* 16 (1964), 3ff.; L. Mezey (ed), *Codices latini medii aevi* (Budapest, 1961), is a convenient listing of source material;

István Fodor, "Őstörténetünk korai szakaszainak néhány fő vonása (Some features of early Hungarian history)," *Történelmi Szemle,* 15 (1972), 1ff.

Of the non-Hungarian sources, the *Annales Altahenses;* Hermann Contractus' *Chronicon;* the *vitae* of some contemporaries of King Stephen (all in the *MGHSS*) must be mentioned together with the comments made by an Otto of Freising (*ibid.,* XX) on twelfth century conditions in Hungary.

Of the works dealing with the life of King Stephen, see Gy. Györffy, *István király és műve* (King Stephen and his work) (Budapest, 1977); B. Hóman, *Szent István* (Budapest, 1938), available also in German and English translations; J. Serédi, "De sancto Stephano Hungariae protorege," *Archivum Europae centro-orientalis,* 4 (1938), 1ff.; Gy. Kornis, "Szent István a nemzetnevelő (King Stephen, 'praeceptor' of Hungary)," *SIE,* I, 19ff.; P. v. Váczy, *Die erste Epoche des ungarischen Königtums* (Pécs, 1935), a masterpiece of modern research and objective interpretation of this early stage of Hungarian history, and so is his "A királyság központi szervezete szent István korában (The centralized court of King Stephen)," *SIE,* II, 35ff.; M. Uhlirz, "Kaiser Otto III und das Papsttum," *HZ,* 162 (1940), 258ff., is worth citing; the essay of Gy. Szekfű, "Szent István a magyar történet századaiban (King Stephen's image through the centuries of Hungarian historiography)," *SIE,* III, 1ff., supplements his earlier work, *Ungarn, eine Geschictsstudie* (Stuttgart, 1918).

The Hungarian crown was given a detailed and scholarly treatment by J. Deér, *Die heilige Krone Ungarns* (Graz-Vienna-Cologne, 1966), the recently died, highly regarded Hungarian-medievalist (cf. Th. Bogyay about Deér in *Ungarn Jahrbuch,* 4/1972/), who may well be correct in his assumption that the present day Hungarian crown is a reproduction of the original Hungarian crown; unfortunately, J.D. Breckenridge in reviewing Deér's book failed to grasp the work's deeper meaning (Speculum 43/1968/,138ff.); also, P. Wirth, "Das bislang erste literarische Zeugnis für die Stefanskrone aus der Zeit zwischen dem X und XIII Jahrhundert," *Byzantinische Zeitschrift,* 53 (1960), 79ff. Of Deér's numerous works, his *A magyar királyság megalakulása* (The origins of the Hungarian kingdom) (Budapest, 1942), and *Pogány magyarság, keresztény magyarság* (Pagan and Christian elements in Hungarian Society) (Budapest, 1938), are very important, even if the latter is being attacked today by some Hungarian historians (cf. Granasztói, *art. cit.* in *Századok,*

107, (1973); Deér's essay, "A szentistváni Intelmek kérdéséhez (Some questions concerning Stephen's Admonitions)," *Századok*, 76 (1942), 435ff.

P.J. Kelleher, *The Holy Crown of Hungary* (Rome, 1951), dealt interestingly with the crown, though his limited knowledge of Hungarian and east European history proved to be a handicap; see Bogyay's review in *Byzantinische Zeitschrift*, 45 (1952), 419ff., while A. Boeckler in P.E. Schramm, *Herrschaftszeichen und Staatssymbolik*, vol. XIII-3 of the *Schriften der Monumenta Germaniae historica* (Stuttgart, 1956), wrote a somewhat tendentious essay on the subject. The writings of Gyula Moravcsik on the Hungarian crown (cf. *Cambridge Medieval History*, VI-1, 981f.), including his essay on the Greek inscriptions of the crown (*Egyetemes Philológiai Közlöny*, 59/1935/, 113ff.), and his opinion of the crown in the light in the then latest philological and historical research (*SIE*, III, 423ff., and the shortened English version, "The Holy Crown of Hungary," *Hungarian Quarterly*, 4/1938/, 656ff.), though excellent, are today somewhat out of date; speaking of the Hungarian crown, one should also cite the major study dealing with the remains of the so called Crown of Emperor Monomachos of Byzantium (1042-55), found in Hungary— see Magda Oberschall Bárány, *Konstantinos Monomachos császár koronája: The Crown of Constantinos Monomachos* (Budapest, 1937), a bilingual edition, 41ff., and 89ff.

The major opus, incomplete, of Gerard of Csanád, *Deliberatio supra hymnum trium puerorum*, was preserved in a late eleventh century MS (6211) of the Munich Staatsbibliothek; the material has been edited once by Ignatius de Batthyány (ed), *Sancti Gerardi episcopi Csanadiensis acta et scripta hactenus inedita* (Alba-Carolinae, 1790), 1-297; J. Karácsonyi, "Szent Gellért püspök müncheni kódexe (The Munich codex of Gerard)," *Magyar Könyvszemle*, 2 (1894), 10ff.; D.G. Morin, "Un théologien ignoré du XIe siecle: l'eveque martyr, Gérard de Csanád, O.S.B.," *Revue Bénedictine*, 27 (1910), 516ff. Gerard's monograph by J. Karácsonyi, *Szent Gellárt péspök élete és munkái* (Life and works of Bishop Gerard) (Budapest, 1887); Rónay's cited essay in *Vigilia*, 1946; M. Manitius, *Geschichte der lateinischen Literatur des Mittelalters* (3 vols.; Munich, 1911-33), II, 19, and 74ff., devoted a detailed study to Gerard's activities, and Gordon Leff, *Medieval Thought* (Baltimore, 1958), 87ff., paid respects to him; J.A. Endres, "Studien zur Geschichte der Frühscholasik: Gerhard von Csanád," *Philosophisches Jahrbuch*, 26 (1913), 349ff., wrote an original article on Gerard. Remig Békefi, "Szent István Intelmei (Stephen's Admonitions)," *Századok*, 35 (1901), 922ff., dealt with Gerard as a writer—the essay is 70 pages long,—while F. Ibrányi, "Szent Gellért teológiája (Gerard's theology)," *SIE,* I, 495ff., explained the theological development and position held by Gerard; A. Bodor, "Szent Gellért Deliberatiojának főforrásai (The major sources of Gerard's Deliberatio)," *Szásadok*, 77 (1943), 172ff.; Endre von Ivánka, "Das 'Corpus areopagiticum' bei Gerhard von Csanád," *Traditio,* 15 (1959), 205ff.; I. Zoltvány, "Magyarországi bencés irodalom a tatárjárás előtt (Benedictine literature in Hungary prior to the Tartar invasion in 1241-42)," in László Erdélyi (ed.), *A pannonhalmi Szent Benedekrend története* (History of the Benedictines of Pannonhalma) (12 vols.; Budapest, 1902-07), I, 337ff.; T. Hajdú, "Szent Gellért Deliberatio cimú múvének méltatása (Essay on Gerard's Deliberatio)," *ibid.,* I, 381ff., provided excellent information on the available material. May I add two of my essays dealing with this theme: "The Importance of Gerard of Csanád as the First Author in Hungary," *Traditio,* 25 (1969), 376ff.; "The Negative Reaction of the Enforced Missionary Policy of King St. Stephen of Hungary: the Uprising of 1046," *Catholic Historical Review,* 59 (1973), 569ff.

The general background is covered by B. Hóman and Gy. Szekfű, *Magyar történet* (Hungarian history) (5 vols.; 6th ed.; Budapest, 1939), vol. I; B. Hóman, *Geschichte des ungarischen Mittelalters* (2 vols.; Berlin, 1040-43), vol. I; L. Elekes *et al, Magyarország története 1526-ig* (vol. I of six volumes; Budapest, 1961), 39ff.; Gy. Moravcsik, *Byzantium and the Magyars* (Amsterdam-Budapest, 1970), 61ff.; F. Dvornik, *Byzantium and the Roman Primacy* (New York, 1966), 124ff.; Imre Timkó, "A honfoglaló magyarok és a bizánci kereszténység (The conquering Hungarians and Byzantine Christianity)," *Vigilia,* 35 (1970), 659ff.; Th. v. Bogyay, "Über den Stuhweissenburger Sarkophag des hl. Stephen," *Ungarn Jahrbuch,* 4 (Munich, 1972), 9ff.; idem, *Grundzüge der Geschichte Ungarns* (Marmstadt, 1967), a well written monograph on Hungarian history. B. Gebhardt, *Handbuch der deutschen Geschichte* (4 vols.; 8th ed.; Stuttgart, 1954-60), I, 224f.; 235ff., presents the German point of view, which as P.E. Schramm, *Kaiser, Rom und Renovatio* (3rd ed., Homburg, 1962), 350 acknowledges it, will seldom coincide with the Hungarian interpretation.

BIBLIOGRAPHY

A. Sources
1. *Manuscripts*
Széchenyi Library of the Hungarian National Museum, Budapest, Hungary
    Clmae 404, late XVth century
    Clmae 406, late XVth century
    Clmae 407, Xvth century
    Clmae 432, mid-XIIth century
    Clmae 17, late XIIth century
    Fol. lat. 4023, XVIth century
    Nyelvemlékek No. 1: Pray-codex, early XIIIth century.

Admont monastic library, Austria
    MS 712, XIIth century

Cistercian monastery at Heiligenkreuz, Austria
    Leg. mag. MS 13, fol. III, XIIth century

Cistercian monastery at Lilienfeld, Austria
    MS 60, XIIIth century

Cistercian monastery at Rein, Austria
    MS 69, late XIIth century

National Library, Vienna, Austria
    MS 832, XIVth century
    MS 3662, XVth century
    MS 1190, early IXth century
    MS 3471, XVth century
    MS 11677, XVth century
    MS 3455
    MS 8496

State Library, Munich, Germany
    MS 6211, late XIth century

2. *Printed Source Collections:*

Acta sanctorum Bollandiana (60 vols. to October XI; Paris-Rome, 1864-76)
    Leges sancti Stephani regis Hungariae
        vol. Sept. I
    Monita sancti Stephani regis ad filium
        vol. Sept. I
    Vita sancti Gerardi episcopi et martyris Csanadiensis
        vol. Sept. VI
    Vita sancti Ladislai I regis Hungariae
        vol. Junii VII
    Vita sancti Stephani regis Hungariae
        vol. Sept. I
Acta sanctorum Ungariae ex Bollandi et al . . . excerpta
    (2 vols.; Tyrnaviae, 1743-44).
Ignatius de Batthyány (ed.), *Leges ecclesiasticae regni Hungariae et provinciarum adiacentium*
    (3 vols.; Claudipoli, 1824).
    , *Sancti Gerardi episcopi Chanadiensis scripta et acta hactenus inedita* (Alba Carolinae, 1790).
Chronica Hungarorum impressa Budae, 1473, a facsimile edition of the original with an introduction by Vilmos Fraknói (Budapest, 1900).
D. Dercsényi (ed.), *Képes Krónika: Chronicon pictum* (in 2 vols.; vol. I: a fascimile edition of the XIVth century MS; vol. II: Hungarian translation of the Latin text, with explanation and notes; Budapest, 1964).
St. L. Endlicher (ed.), *Rerum Hungaricarum monumenta Arpadiana* (2 vols.; Sangalli, 1849; one volume reprint Leipzig, 1931).
    Decretum I Andreae II regis, anno 1222
    Decretum I sancti Ladislai regis, anno 1092
    De gestis Ungarorum liber Anonymi Belae regis notarii
    Gesta Ungarorum magistri Simonis de Keza
    Leges sancti Stephani regis.

Ph. Jaffé (ed.), *Bibliotheca rerum Germanicarum* (6 vols.; Berlin, 1865; repr. Darmstadt, 1964).

, *Regesta pontificum Romanorum* (2 vols.; Leipzig, 1885).

F. Knauz (ed.), *Monumenta ecclesiae Strigoniensis* (2 vols.; Strigonii, 1873-74), vol. I.

H. Marczali *et al* (ed.), *Enchiridion fontium historiae Hungarorum* (Budapest, 1901)

   ˘ Bulla auera, 1222

   Fundatio monasterii Tihanyensis, 1055

   Leges sancti Stephani regis

   Lex I sancti Ladislai regis

   Piligrini episcopi Pataviensis litterae ad Benedictum papam VI, anno 974

   Theotmari episcopi litterae ad Johannem papam IX, anno 900.

J.P. Migne (ed.), *Patrologiae cursus completus, series graeca* (166 vols.; Paris, 1854-57)

   Constantius VII Porphyrogenitos, De administrando imperio; vol. 113

   Leo Grammaticus, etiam Car, seu Asianus, Chronographia usque ad annum 948; vol. 108

   Leo VI imperator dictus Sapiens, Tactica vol. 107.

   , *Patrologiae cursus completus, series latina* (221 vols.; Paris, 1844-55)

   Andreae I regis Hungariae Constitutiones ecclesiasticae anno 1047; vol. 151

   Benedicti papae VI epistola ad Fredericum Salisburgiensem episcopum; vol. 135

   Gregorii papae VII epistola ad Geysam ducem Hungarorum, March 17, 1074; vol. 148

   , epistola ad Salomonem regem Hungarorum Oct. 28, 1074; vol. 148

   , epistola ad Geysam Hungariae ducem March 23, 1075; vol. 148

   , epistola ad Nehemiam archiepiscopum Strigoniensem, June 9, 1077; vol. 148

   , epistola ad Ladislaum Hungarorum regem March 21, 1079; vol. 148

   Innocentii papae III epistola ad regem Hungariae June 16, 1198; vol. 216

Innocentii papae III epistola ad virum nobilem A ducem June 15, 1198

, epistola ad archiepiscopos Strigoniensis et Colocanensis; Oct. 21, 1198

, epistola Johanni arc. Strigoniensi of June 15, 1209

, epistola capitulo Strigoniense, May 9, 1209

, *epistola* of Nov. 22, 1204; vol. 215

Leges sancti Stephani regis Hungariae vol. 151

Monita sancti Stephani egis ad filium vol. 151

Privilegium protoabbatiae sancti Martini concessum, anno 1001; vol. 151

Sylvester papa II Stephano Hungarorum duci; vol. 139

Urbani papae II epistola ad regem Hungariae Colomannum; vol. 151

Vita sancti Stephani regis Hungariae; vol. 151

Carl Mirbt (ed.), *Quellen zur Geschichte des Papsttums und des römischen Katholizismus* (6th ed. edited by Kurt Aland; 2 vols.; Tübingen, 1967 etc.), vol. I.

J.D. Mansi (ed.), *Sacrorum conciliorum nova et amplissima collectio* (31 vols.; Florence-Venice, 1759-98; rept. in 54 vols.; Osnabrück, 1968)

Synod of Szabolcs, 1092 vol. XX.

Monumenta Germaniae historica, Scriptores (ed. G.H. Pertz; 30 vols. in 32; Hannover, 1854 etc.)

Ademarus Cabannensis Chronicon Francorum vol. IV

Annales Altahenses vol. XX

Annales Hildesheimenses vol. III

Annalista Saxo, Chronicon regum Francorum vol. VI

Bertholdi Chronicon vol. V

Bruno Querfurtensi Vita s. Adalberti ep. et mart. vol. IV

Carmen miserabile M. Rogerio canonici Varadiensis vol. XXIX

Chronicon Venetum Iohanni Diaconi vol. VII

De gestis Ungarorum liber Anonymo Belae regis notarii vol. XXIX

Gesta Friderici I Imperatoris auctore Ottone ep. Fris. Vol. XX

Gesta Hungarorum M. Simonis de Keza vol. XXIX

Hroswithae Carmina de gestis Oddonis I Imperatoris vol. IV

Regino Prumensi Chronicon vol. I

Thietmari Merseburgensis Chronicon vol. III

Translatio sancti Epiphanii vol. IV

Vita s. Odilonis Cluniacensis vol. IV

Vita b. Richardi abbatis Virdunensis vol. XI

Vita minor s. Stephani regis Hungariae vol. XI

Vita maior s. Stephani regis Hungariae vol. XI

Widukindus Corbiensis, Rerum gestarum Saxonicarum vol. III

Wipo capellanus Counradi II imperatoris Gesta vol. XI.

A Pannonhalmi szent-Benedek Rend története (ed. L. Erdélyi; 12 vols.; Budapest, 1902-07), I, 589ff.

Mattheus Parisiensis *Chronica Maiora* (ed. H.R. Luard; 7 vols.; Rolls series; London, 1872-83).

A. Potthast (ed.), *Regesta pontificum Romanorum* (2 vols.; Berlin, 1875).

C. Péterffy (ed.), *Sacra concilia ecclesiae Romanae Catholicae in regno Hungariae celebrata* (2 vols.; Vienna, 1742), vol. I.

J.G. Schwandtner (ed.), *Scriptores rerum Hungaricarum* (3 vols.; Vienna, 1746-48)

    Gesta Hungarorum Simonis de Keza vol. I

    De insignibus vulgo clenodis regni Hungariae vol. II

    Thuróczy's Chronicon Hungaricum vol. I.

E. Szentpétery (ed.), *Regesta regum stirpis Arpadianae critico-diplomatica* (2 vols.; Budapest, 1923-61).

    , *Scriptores rerum Hungaricarum* (2 vols.; Budapest, 1937-38)

    Annonymi–P. magistri–Gesta Ungarorum

    Annales Posonienses

    Simonis de Keza Gesta Ungarorum

    Chronici Hungarici compositio saeculi XIV

    Legenda minor s. Stephani regis

    Legenda maior s. Stephani regis

    Legenda Hartvici de sancto Stephano rege

    Legenda s. Emerici ducis

    Legenda maior s. Gerardi episcopis Csanadiensis

    Legenda ss. Zoerardi et Benedicti

    Passio s. Gerardi episcopi

    Libellus de institutione morum.

L. Závodszky (ed.), *A szent István, szent László és Kálmán korabeli törvények és zsinati határozatok forrásai* (Budapest, 1904).

    Leges s. Stephani regis

    Leges I–III s. Ladislai regis.

B.   SECONDARY WORKS

A. Alföldy, *Magyarország népei és a római birodalom* (The peoples of Hungary and the Roman empire) (Budapest, 1934).
I. Andrássy, *The Development of Hungarian Constitutional Liberty* (translated by A. and I. Ginever; London, 1908).
H. Aubin, "Der Aufbau des Abendlandes im Mittelalter," *Historische Zeitschrift,* 187 (1959), 497ff.
Gy. Balanyi, "Magyar szentek, szentéletű magyarok (Hungarian saints, saintly Hungarians)," *Katolikus Szemle,* 15 (Rome, 1963), 100ff.
        , "Vallásos élet—iskolák (Religious life and early educational standards in Hungary)," in Domanovszky, *Művelődéstörténet,* I, 373ff.
L. Balics, *A római katholikus Egyház története Magyarországon* (A history of the Roman Catholic Church in Hungary) (2 vols in 3; Budapest, 1885-88), vol. I.
J. Balogh, "A magyar királyság megalapitásánk világpolitikai háttere (The political backgound of the beginnings of the Hungarian kingdom)," *Századok,* 66 (1932), 152ff.
        , "Szent Istvan Intelmeinek forrásai (The sources of King Stephen's Admonitions)," *SIE,* II, 237ff.
        , "Szent Istvan kapcsolatai Cseh,—Német,—Franciaországgal s Belgiummal (King Stephen's foreign relations with Bohemia, Germany, France, and Belgium)," *SIE,* I, 449ff.
        , "The Political Testament of Saint Stephen, King of Hungary," *Hungarian Quarterly,* 4 (1938), 389ff.
M. Oberschall Bárány, *Konstantinos Monomachos császár* (The Crown of Emperor Constantine Monomachos) (Budapest, 1937)
G. Bárczi, "Hozzászólas a történeti forráskutatások kérdéséhez (Some remarks on the present status of historical research)," *Magyar Nyelv,* 57 (1961), 413ff.
F. Barlow, "Edward the Confessor's Early Life and Character," *English Historical Review,* 80 (1965), 225ff.
        , *The English Church, 1000-1066: A Constitutional History* (Hamden, Conn., 1963).
H. Barré, "L'oeuvre mariale de saint Gerard de Csanád," *Marianum,* 25 (1963), 262ff.

A. Bartha, "Hungarian Society in the Tenth Century," *Acta historica*, 9 (1963), 333ff.

E. Bartoniek, *Magyar történeti forráskiadványok* (Published sources of Hungarian history) (Budapest, 1942).

R. Békefi, "Árpádkori közoktatásügy (Education in Hungary in the Árpádian age)," *Századok*, 30 (1896), 207ff.; 310ff.; 413ff.

, *A káptalani iskolák története Magyarországon 1540-ig* (History of the cathedral schools in Hungary prior to 1540) (Budapest, 1910).

E. Békesi, "Középkori magyar írók: szent Gellért (Medieval Hungarian authors: Gerard of Csanád)," *Katholikus Szemle*, Budapest, 1896, 369ff.

F. v. Bezold, "Die Lehre von der Volkssouverinität während des Mittelalters," *Historische Zeitschrift*, 36 (1876), 313ff.

K. Bihlmeyer-F.X. Funk, *Kirchengeschichte* (2 vols.; 8th rev. ed.; Paderborn, 1930).

B. Bischoff, "Das griechische Element in der abendländischen Bildung des Mittelalters," *Byzantinische Zeitschrift*, 44 (1951), 27ff.

A. Bodor, "Szent Gellért Deliberatiojának főforrásai (The main sources of Gerard's Deliberatio)," *Századok*, 77 (1943), 173ff.

J.F. Böhmer *et al* (ed.), *Regesta imperii: Salisches Haus* (Graz, 1951).

, vol. II (Hildesheim, 1967).

, *Regesta imperii: Papstregisten, 911-1024* (rev. repr. Vienna-Cologne-Graz, 1969).

Th. v. Bogyay, *Lechfeld, 955* (Munich, 1955).

, Review of *The Holy Crown of Hungary* by P.J. Kelleher, *Byzantinische Zeitschrift*, 45 (1952), 419ff.

, "Ujabb szent István kutatások (Latest research on King Stephen)," *Katolikus Szemle*, 23 (Rome, 1971), 289ff.

, "Über den Stuhlweissenburger Sarkophag des hl. Stephen," *Ungarn Jahrbuch*, 4 (1972), 9ff.

A. Boeckler, "Die Stefanskrone," *Herrschaftsziechen und Staatssymbolik* (ed. P.E. Schramm); vol. 13, pt. 3 of the *Schriften der Monumenta Germaniae historica* (Stuttgart, 1956).

J. Bóna, "Cunpald fecit: a petőházi kehely és a frank térítés kezdetei a Dunántúlon (Cunpald fecit: the beginnings of Frankish missionary activity in Transdanubia)," *Soproni Szemle*, 18 (1964), 127ff.; 218ff.

Gy. Bónis, "Die Entwicklung der geistlichen Gerichtsbarkeit in Ungarn vor 1526," *Zeitschrift der Savigny Stiftung für Rechtsgeschichte*, Kan. Abt., 80 (1963), 174ff.

A. Brackmann, *Gesammelte Aufsätze* (2nd rev. ed.; Cologne-Graz, 1967), including the following:

"Die Anfänge der abendländischen Kulturbewegung in Osteuropa und deren Träger," 1938

"Kaiser Otto III und die staatliche Umgestaltung Polens und Ungarns," 1939

"Die Ostpolitik Ottos des Grossen," 1926

"Die politische Wirkung der kluniazenischen Bewegung," 1929

"Die Ursachen der geistigen und politischen Wandlung Europas im 11 und 12 Jahrhundert," 1934

"Zur Entstehung des ungarischen Staates," 1940.

A. v. Brandt, *Werkzeug des Historikers* (2nd ed.; Stuttgart, 1960).

H. Breszlau, "Zu den Urkunden König Stephanus von Ungarn," *Archiv für Urkundenforschung*, 6 (1916), 65ff.

M. Büdinger, *Ein Buch ungarischer Geschichte 1058-1100* (Leipzig, 1866).

Ch. Brooke, "Gregorian Reform in Action: Clerical Marriage in England, 1050-1200," in his *Medieval Church and Society* (New York, 1972), 69ff.

R. Buchner, "Geschichtsbild und Reichsbergriff Hermanns von Reichenau," *Archiv für Kulturgeschichte*, 42 (1960), 37ff.

        , "Kulturelle und politische Zusammengehörigkeitsgefühle im Europäischen Frühmittelalter," *Historische Zeitschrift*, 207 (1968), 562ff.

J.B. Bury, "The Treatise: de administrando imperio," *Byzantinische Zeitschrift*, 15 (1906), 517ff.

E.M. Buytaert, "Saint John Damascene, Peter Lombard, and Gerhoch of Reichersberg," *Franciscan Studies*, 10 (1950), 323ff.

E. Caspar, "Gregor VII in seinen Briefem," *Historische Zeitschrift*, 130 (1924), 1ff.

Cs. Csapodi, *A legrégibb magyar könyvtár benső rendje* (Organization of the oldest known Hungarian library) (Budapest, 1957).

K. Csiky, *Magyar alkotmánytan* (Handbook of the Hungarian constitution) (Budapest, 1879).

L.J. Csóka, "Hol született szent Márton (Where Martin of Tours was born)," *Vigilia*, 34 (1969), 379ff.

———, "A magyarok és a kereszténység Géza fejedelem korában (The Hungarians and Christianity during the reign of Géza)," *SIE*, I, 269ff.

———, *A latin nyelvű történeti irodalom kialakulása Magyarországon a XI-XIV században* (The development of Latin historical literature in Hungary during the 11th-14th centuries) (Budapest, 1967).

———, "Szent István Intelmeinek és törvényeinek szerzősége (Authorship of the Admonitions and laws of King Stephen)," *Vigilia*, 29 (1964), 453ff.

———, "Wolfgangus monachus ad ungaros missus est," *ibid.*, 37 (1972), 701ff.

E.R. Curtius, *European Literature and the Latin Middle Ages* (tr. W.R. Trask; New York, 1953).

A.F. Czajkowski, "The Congress of Gniezno in the Year 1000," *Speculum*, 24 (1949), 339ff.

A.S. Czermann, *Die Staatsidee des heiligen Stephan* (Klagenfurt, 1953).

B. Czobor (ed.), *Die historischen Denkmäler Ungarns* (2 vols.; Budapest-Vienna, 1896).

Ch. Dawson, "The Hungarian Middle Ages," *Hungarian Quarterly*, 5 (1939), 585ff.

J. Deér, "Aachen und die Herrschersitze der Árpáden," *Mitteilungen des Institutes für österreichische Geschichtsforschung*, 79 (1971), 1ff.

———, *Die hl. Krone Ungarns* (Vienna, 1966).

———, *A magyar királyság megalakulása (Formation of the Hungarian Kingdom) (Budapest, 1938).*

———, *Pogány magyarság, keresztény magyarság* (Heathen and Christian elements in early Hungarian society) (Budapest, 1942).

———, "A szentistváni Intelmek kérdéséhez (Essay on King Stephen's Admonitions)," *Századok*, 76 (1942), 435ff.

———, "Szent István politikai és egyházi orientációja (The political and ecclesiastical orientation of King Stephen)," *Katolikus Szemle*, 1 (Rome, 1949), 27ff.

———, "Der Weg zum Goldenen Bulle Andreas II von 1222," *Schweizer Beiträge zur allgemeinen Geschichte*, 10 (1952), 104ff.

D. Dercsényi, "Az újabb régészeti kutatások és a pannóniai kontinuitás kérdése (Continued 'Pannonian' history in the light of latest archaeology)," *Századok*, 81 (1947), 11ff.

S. Domanovszky, "Anonymus és a II Géza korabeli Gesta (Anonymus and the Hungarian *gesta* of the reign of Géza II)," *Századok,* 67 (1933), 38ff.; 163ff.

, (ed.), *Magyar művelődéstörténet* (Hungarian cultural history), vol. I: *Ősműveltség és középkori kultúra* (Early and medieval Hungarian culture) (Budapest, n.d.).

F. Dölger, Review of P.J. Kelleher, *The Holy Crown of Hungary* in *Historisches Jahrbuch,* 73 (1954), 262ff.

F. Dölger, *Byzanz und die europäische Staatenwelt* (rev. ed.; Darmstadt, 1964): "Europas Gestaltung im Spiegel der frankisch-byzantenischen Auseinandersetzung des 9 Jahrhunderts" "Die mittelalterliche Kultur auf dem Balkan als byzantenisches Erbe" "Rom in der Gedankenwelt der Byzantiner."

F. Dvornik, *The Making of Central and Eastern Europe* (London, 1949).

F. Eckhart, "The Holy Crown of Hungary, *Hungarian Quarterly,* 6 (1940), 633ff.

, "Staatsrecht und Privatrecht in Ungarn im Mittelalter," *Ungarische Jahrbücher,* (1929), 426ff.

S. Eckhardt, "I Endre francia zarándokai (French pilgrims visiting at the court of Andrew I)," *Magyar Nyelv,* 32 (1936), 38ff.

L. Elekes *et al, Magyarország története 1526-ig* (Hungarian history until 1526) (vol. I of a set of six volumes; Budapest, 1961).

Gy. Ember, Review of D. Kosáry, *Bevezetés Magyarország történetének forrásaiba és irodalmába* in *Századok,* 107 (1973), 458ff.

L. Erdélyi, *Árpádkor* (Age of the Árpáds) (Budapest, 1931).

, *Magyar történelem: művelődés és államtörténet* (Constitutional and cultural history of Hungary) (2 vols.; Budapest, 1936-38).

, (ed.), *A pannonhalmi Szent Benedek-Rend története* (A history of the Benedictines of Pannonhalma) (12 vols.; Budapest, 1902-07), vol. I.

J.A. Endres, "Studien zur Geschichte der Frühscholastik: Gerhard von Csanád," *Philosophisches Jahrbuch,* 26 (1913), 349ff.

C. Erdmann, "Die Anfänge der staatlichen Propoganda im Investiturstreit," *Historische Zeitschrift,* 154 (1936), 491ff.

, *Forschungen zur politischen Ideenwelt des Frühmittelalters* (ed. F. Baethgen; Berlin, 1951).

K. Eszláry, "Ansegise apát és Lévita Benedek kapituláréinak és szent István törvényeinek hasonlatosságai (Essay on the similarities between the Capitularies of Abbot Ansegise and Benedict Levita, and the laws of King Stephen of Hungary)," *A IX Magyar Találkozó Krónikája* (ed. F. Somogyi: Cleveland, OH, 1970), 28ff.

Z. Falvy, "A Pray kódex zenei paleográfiája (The musical paleography of the Pray codex)," repr. from *Zenetudományi tanulmányok,* Budapest, 1954.

G. Fehér, "A bolgár egyház kisérletei és sikerei hazánkban (Successful attempts at missionarization by the Bulgarian Church in Hungary)," *Századok,* 61-62 (1927), 1ff.

J. Félegyházy, "Történelmi irodalmunk kezdetei (Origins of Hungarian historical literature)," *Vigilia,* 34 (1969), 329ff.

G. Ferdinándy, "Die Thronfolge im Zeitalter der Könige aus dem Árpádienhause," *Ungarische Rundschau,* 2 (1913), 759ff.

A. Fest, "Medieval Contacts Between England and Hungary," *Hungarian Quarterly,* 6 (1940), 252ff.

H. Fichtenau, *Grundzüge der Geschichte des Mittelalters* (2nd ed.; Vienna, 1948).

I. Fodor, "Őstörténetünk korai szakaszainak néhány fő vonása (Certain basic characteristics of early Hungarian history)," *Történelmi Szemle,* 15 (1972), 1ff.

V. Fraknói, *A magyar nemzet műveltségi állásának vázlata és a keresztenység behozatalának története* (An outline of national culture, and the introduction of Christianity to Hungary) (Pest, 1861).

——, *Magyarország egyházi és politika kapcsolatai a római Szentszékkel* (Relations between Hungary and the Holy See) (3 vols.; Budapest, 1901-03), vol. I.

——, "Die Thronfolgerung im Zeitalter der Árpáden," *Ungarische Rundschau,* 2 (1913), 135ff.

B. Gebhardt (ed.), *Handbuch der deutschen Geschichte* (4 vols.; 8th ed.; Stuttgart, 1954-60), vol. I.

F.A. Gombos (ed.), *Catalogus fontium historiae Hungaricae* (4 vols.; Budapest, 1937-41).

——, "Szent István háborúja II Konrád német czászárral (King Stephen's war with Emperor Conrad II)," *SIE,* II, 107ff.

——, "Szent István a külföldi történetírásban (King Stephen by non-Hungarian authors)," *SIE,* III, 279ff.

H. Gotefend, *Zeitrechnung des deutschen Mittelalters und der Neuzeit* (2 vols.; Hannover, 1891-92).

H. Grundmann, "Freiheit als religiöses, politisches und persönliches Postulat im Mittelalter," *Historische Zeitschrift,* 183 (1957), 23ff.

P. Gulyás, *A könyvnyomtatás Magyarországon a XV és XVI században* (Hungarian bookprinting in the 15th-16th centuries) (Budapest, 1931; 3 vol. repr. rev., 1961)

Gy. Györffy, "A Magyar nemzetségtűl a vármegyéig, a törzstűl az országig (From the 'Magyar' clan to the country; from the tribe to the state)," *Századok,* 92 (1958).

, "Anonymus Gesta Hungarorumának kora es hitelessége (Age and trustworthiness of Anonymus' Gesta Hungarorum)," *Irodalomtörténeti Közlemények,* 74 (1970), 1ff.

, *Az Árpád-kori Magyarország történeti földrajza* (Geographia historica Hungariae tempore stirpis Arpadianae) (Budapest, 1963).

, "A besnyűk európai honfoglalalásának történetéhez(Essay on the European conquest of the Petchenegs)," *Történelmi Szemle,* 14 (1971), 281ff.

, "A honfoglalásról újabb történeti kutatások tükrében (About the Hungarian conquest in the light of recent research)," *Valóság,* 1973, no. 7-8.

, "Honfoglalás előtti népek és események Anonymus Gesta Hungarorumában (Anonymus' report about peoples and events prior to the Hungarian conquest)," *Ethnographia,* 76 (1965), 411ff.

, *Krónikáink és a magyar őstörténet* (Les chroniques hongroises et l'histoire primitive des Hongrois) (Budapest, 1948).

, "Zu den Anfängen der ungarischen Kirchenwesens auf Grund neuerer geschichts-kritischen Ergebnisse," *Archivum historiae politicae,* 7 (1969), 79ff.

A.M. Haas, "Mittelalterliches Mönchtum," *Neue Zürcher Zeitung,* Aug. 14, 1965, 11.

Gy. Granasztói, "Gentilizmus: a barbár etnikai tudat kérdése (Some questions concerning the barbarian ethnic conscienciousness)," *Századok,* 107 (1973), 114ff.

I. Haller, *Das Papsttum: Idee und Wirklichkeit* (2n ed.; 5 vols.; Stuttgart, 1953-59).

B. Hamilton, "The Monastic Revival in Tenth Century Rome," *Studia monastica,* 4 (1962), 35ff.

K. Hampe, *Deutsche Kaisergeschichte* (16th ed., ed. F. Baethgen; Heidelberg, 1963).

, *Das Hochmittelalter* (5th ed.; Graz, 1963).

K. Hampe, "Kaiser Otto III und Rom," *Historische Zeitschrift,* 140 (1929), 513ff.

T. Hajdú, "Szent Gellért Deliberatio c. művének méltatása (Essay on Gerard of Csanád's Deliberatio)," in Erdélyi, *Rendtörténet,* I, 381ff.

A. Hauck, *Kirchengeschichte Deutschlands* (9th ed.; 5 vols. in 6; Berlin, 1958), vol. III.

A. Häussling, Review of O. Nussbaum, *Klöster, Privatmönch, und Privatmesse* in *Zeitschrift für katholische Theologie,* 85 (1963), 75ff.

A. Hatto, "Walter von der Vogelweide's Ottonian Poems," *Speculum,* 24 (1949), 542ff.

F. Heer, *Aufgang Europas* (Vienna, 1949).

, *Europäische Geistesgeschichte* (2nd ed.; Stuttgart, 1965).

C.J.v. Hefele, *Conciliengeschichte* (6 vols.; 2nd rev. ed.; Freiburg i. Br., 1873-90), vols. V-VI.

Hg. "Anfang Europas," *Neue Zürcher Zeitung,* July 10,1965 , 22.

A. Hof, "Plenitudo potestas und Imitatio Imperii zur Zeit Innozenz' III," *Zeitschrift für Kirchengeschichte,* 66 (1954), 39ff.

H. Hoffmann, "Von Cluny zum Investiturstreit," *Archiv für Kulturgeschichte,* 45 (1963), 165ff.

, "Ivo von Chartres und die Lösung des Investiturproblems," *Deutsches Archiv für Erforschung des Mittelalters,* 15 (1959), 393ff.

K. Hoffmann, "Der Dictatus papae Gregors VII als Index einer Kanonensammlung," *Studi Gregoriani,* 1 (1947), 531ff.

P. Hilsch, "Der Bischof von Prag und das Reich in sächsischer Zeit," *Deutsches Archiv,* 28 (1972), 1ff.

R. Holtzmann, *Geschichte der sächsischen Kaiserzeit* (Munich, 1941), repr. 1967).

B. Hóman, *Geschichte des ungarischen Mittelalters* (2 vols.; Berlin, 1940-43), vol. I.

, *Magyar középkor* (The Hungarian Middle Ages) (Budapest, 1938).

, *Történetírás és forráskritika* (Hungarian historiography) (Budapest, 1938).

, –Gyula Szekfű, *Magyar történet* (Hungarian history) (6th ed.; 5 vols.; Budapest, 1939), vol. I.

(ed.), *A magyar történetírás új útjai* (A new approach in Hungarian historiography) (Budapest, 1931).

E. Horváth, "Medieval Hungary," *South Eastern Affairs*, 1 (1931), 1ff.

J. Horváth, *Árpádkori latinnyelvű irodalmunk stílusproblémái* (Some questions raised as to the style of the Latin literature of the Árpádian age) (Budapest, 1954).

, *A magyar irodalmi műveltség kezdetei* (The origins of Hungarian literary culture) (2nd ed.; Budapest, 1944).

J. Horváth, Jr., "A Gellért legendák forrásértéke (The legends of Gerard of Csanád as historical sources)," *M.T.A. nyelv. s irod. oszt. közleményei*, 13 (1958), 21ff.

A. Huber, "Beiträge zur älteren Geschichte Österreiches; Über die älteste ungarische Verfassung," *MIÖG*, 6 (1885), 385ff.

A. Hürten, "Gregor der Grosse und der mittelalterliche Episkopat," *Zeitschrift für Kirchengeschichte*, 73 (1962), 16ff.

F. Ibrányi, "Szent Gellért teológiája (The theology of Gerard of Csanád)," *SIE*, I, 495ff.

E. Iglói, *A régi orosz irodalom története* (A history of old Russian literature) (Budapest, 1962).

A. Ijjas, "A keleti és nyugati egyház dialógusához (On the eastern-western dialogue in the Church)," *Vigilia*, 37 (1972), 392ff.

G. Inczefi, "A földrajzi nevek értelmének néhány kérdéséhez (Meaning and importance of some geographical names)," *Magyar Nyelv*, 60 (1964), 80ff.

G. Istványi, "Die mittelalterliche Philologie in Ungarn," *Deutsches Archiv*, 4 (1964), 80ff.

E. v. Ivánka, "Das 'Corpus areopagiticum' bei Gerhard von Csanád," *Traditio*, 15 (1959), 205ff.

, "Görög szertartás és középkori magyarság Erdélyben (Greek liturgy and the Hungarians in medieval Transylvania)," *Erdélyi Tudósító*, 20 (1941), 100ff.

, "Szent Gellért Deliberatioja (Gerard of Csanád's Deliberatio)," *Századok*, 76 (1942), 497ff.

E. Pap Ivántsi, "A magyar Aranybulla mint alkotmanybiztosíték (The Hungarian Golden Bull as a guarantee of constitutional life)," *Uj magyar út*, Munich, May, 1951.

W.R. Jones, "Saints in Service: the Political and Cultural Implications of Medieval Hagiolatry," *Cithara*, 10 (1970), 33ff.

C. Juhász, "Die Beziehungen der Vita Gerardi maior zur Vita minor," *Studien und Mitteilungen zur Geschichte des Benediktiner-Ordens,* 47 (1929), 129ff.

———, "Gerhard der Heilige, Bischof von Marosburg," *ibid.,* 48 (1930), 1ff.

L. Juhász, "A Képes Krónika szövegkritikájához (Textual criticisms of the Picture Chronicle)," *Filológiai Közlöny,* 12 (1966), 23ff.

E.H. Kantorowicz, "Inalienability," *Speculum,* 29 (1954), 488ff.

J. Karácsonyi, *Szent Gellért csanádi püspök élete és művei* (Life and work of Gerard of Csanád) (Budapest, 1887).

———, "Szent Gellért püspök müncheni kódexe (The Munich codex of Gerard of Csanád's work)," *Magyar Könyvszemle,* n.s. 2 (1894), 10ff.

———, *Szent István király élete* (Life of King Stephen) (Budapest, 1904).

———, *Szent István király oklevelei és a Szilveszter bulla* (Budapest, 1896).

T. Kardos, *Középkori kultúra, középkori költészet: a magyar irodalom keletkezése* (Medieval culture and poetry: the origins of Hungarian literature) (Budapest, 1941).

G. Karsai, "Az Anonymus kódex első levele (The first leaf of the Anonymus codex)," *Magyar Könyvszemle,* 84 (1968), 42ff.

———, "Névtelenség, névrejtés és szerzőnév a középkori krónikákban (Authorship of, anonymity and hidden identity in the medieval chronicles)," *Századok,* 97 (1963), 666ff.

St. Katona, *Historia critica regum Hungariae* (40 vols in 42; Buda, 1778-1801).

———, *Historia pragmatica Hungariae* (3 vols.; Buda, 1782 etc.).

F. Kempf, "Das Problem der Christianitas im 12 und 13 Jahrhundert," *Historisches Jahrbuch,* 79 (1960), 104ff.

F. Kern, "Recht und Verfassung im Mittelalter," *Historische Zeitschrift,* 120 (1919), 1ff.

W. Kienast, "Die französische Stämme bei der Königswahl," *ibid.,* 206 (1968), 1ff.

K. Kniewald, "A Hahóti-kódex jelentősége a magyarországi liturgia szempontjából (The importance of the Hahóti codex-Zagreb MS 126—for the Hungarian liturgy)," repr. from *Magyar Könyvszemle,* 1938.

———, "A Pray-kódex miserendje (The ordinary of the Mass in the Pray codex)," repr. from *Teológia,* 1939.

K. Kniewald, "A Pray-kódex sanctoraleja (The sanctorale of the Pray codex)," repr. from *Magyar Könyvszemle*, 1939.

J. Koch (ed.), *Artes liberales von den antiken Bildung zur Wissenschaft des Mittelalters* (Leiden-Cologne, 1959).

J. Közi-Horváth, "Magyarország és Nyugateurópa (Hungary and western Europe)," *Catholic Hungarians' Sunday*, Youngstown, OH, Jan. 15, 1961, 1.

Gy. Kornis, *Die Entwicklung der ungarischen Kultur* (Berlin, 1933).

D. Kosáry (ed.), *Bevezetés a magyar történelem irodalmába* (An introduction to Hungarian historical literature) (3 vols.; Budapest, 1951-58), vol. III.

——, (ed.), *Bevezetés Magyarország történetének forrássaiba és irodalmába* (An introduction to the sources and literature in Hungarian history) (vol. I of a planned set; Budapest, 1970).

——, *A History of Hungary* (Cleveland-New York, 1941).

Z. J. Kosztolnyik, "The Importance of Gerard of Csanád as the First Author in Hungary," *Traditio*, 25 (1969), 376ff.

——, "The Negative Results of the Enforced Missionary Policy of King Stephen I of Hungary: the Uprising of 1046," *Catholic Historical Review*, 59 (1973), 569ff.

——, "De facultate resistendi: Two Essential Characteristics of the Hungarian Golden Bull of 1222," *Studies in Medieval Culture*, V.

A. Kovács, "IV Béla levele a pápához (A letter of Béla IV of Hungary to the Pope)," *Hungária*, Munich, Dec. 26, 1952, 7.

Gy. Kristó, "Anjou-kori krónikáink (Hungarian chronicles of the Angevin age)," *Századok*, 101 (1967), 457ff.

——, "Anonymus magyarországi írott forrásainak kérdéséhez (Les sources manuscrites du notaire Anonyme, auteur des Gesta Hungarorum)," *Magyar Könyvszemle*, 99 (1972), 166ff.

——, "Kézai Simon és a XIII század végi köznemesi ideológia néhány vonása (The outlook of the Hungarian lesser nobility expressed in the Gesta Hungarorum of Simon de Keza)," *Irodalomtörténeti Közlemények*, 76 (1972), 1ff.

—— and F. Makk, "Krónikáink keletkezéstörténetéhez (Some remarks on the history of origins of Hungarian chronicles)," *Történelmi Szemle*, 15 (1972), 198ff.

J. Kudora, *A magyar katholikus egyházi beszéd irodalmának ezeréves története* (A thousand years of Catholic preaching in Hungary) (Budapest, 1902).

F. Kűhár, "A Pray-kodéx rendeltetése, sorsa, szellemtörténeti ertéke (Purpose, fate, and ideological value of the Pray codex)," *Magyar Könyvszemle,* 63 (1939), 213ff.

———, "Szent Gellért Bakonybélben (Gerard's sojourn at Bél)," *Pannonhalmi Szemle,* 2 (1927), 305ff.

H. Kühner, *Neues Papstlexikon* (Zurich, 1956).

B.L. Kumorowitz, "Die erste Epoche der ungarischen privatrechtlichen Schriftlichkeit im Mittelalter, bzw. im XI und XII Jahrhundert," *Études historiques* (2 vols.; Budapest, 1960), I, 253ff.

G. Labuda, "Bazoar Anonymus Gallus krónikájában (Bazoar in the Chronicle of Gallus Anonymus)," *Századok,* 104 (1970), 173ff.

G. Ladner, "Die mittelalterliche Reform-Idee und ihr Verhältnis zur Idee der Renaissance," *MIÖG,* 60 (1952), 31ff.

J. Leclercq, *L'Amourdes lettres et le désir de Dieu* (Paris, 1957).

G. Leff, *Medieval Thought* (Baltimore, 1958).

A. Leopold, "Magyar emlékek Bécsben (Hungarian memories in Vienna)," *Bécsi Magyar Évkönyv* (Vienna, 1958), 67ff.

M. Linzel, "Die Kaiserpolitik Ottos des Grossen," in his *Ausgewählte Schriften* (2 vols.; Berlin, 1961), II, 201ff.

A. Lhotsky, *Europäisches Mittelalter* (Vienna, 1970).

———, *Quellenkunde zur mittelalterlichen Geschichte* Österreichs (Graz, 1963).

R. Lüttich, *Ungarnzüge in Europa im 10 Jahrhundert* (Berlin, 1910).

C.A. Macartney, *The Medieval Hungarian Historians* (Cambridge, 1953).

———, "Studies on the Earliest Hungarian Historical Sources," *Archivum Europae centro-orientalis* 4 (1938), 456ff.

E. Mályusz, "La chancellerie royale et la rédaction des chroniques dans la Hongrie médiévale," *Le Moyen Age,* 75 (1969), 51ff.; 219ff.

———, "A Thuróczy Krónika XV századi kiadásai (The 15th century editions of the Thuroczy Chronicle)," *Magyar Könyvszemle,* 83 (1967), 1ff.

M. Manitius, *Geschichte der lateinischen Literatur des Mittelalters* (3 vols.; Munich, 1911-31), vol. II.

H. Marczali, "A középkori elmélet a királyságról (The medieval theory on kingship)," *Budapesti Szemle,* 65 (1891), 367ff.

————, Magyarország története az Árpádok korában (Hungary in the age of the Árpáds) (vol. II of the *Magyar nemzet története,* ed. S. Szilágyi; 10 vols.; Budapest, 1896).

————, *Ungarns Geschichtsquellen im Zeitaleter der Arpaden* (Berlin, 1882).

————, *et al* (ed.), *Enchiridion fontium historiae Hungarorum* (Budapest, 1901).

D. Márkus (ed.), *Corpus Iuris Hungarici: Magyar törvénytár, 1000-1895* (20 vols.; Budapest, 1899 etc.).

B. Menczer, *A Commentary on Hungarian Literature* (in the Amerikai Magyar Kiado "Hungarian Scholarship" series; Castrop-Rauxel, 1956).

Th. Meyer, "Papsttum und Kaisertum im hohen Mittelalter," *Historische Zeitschrift,* 187 (1959), 1ff.

————, "Staatauffassung in der Karolingerzeit," *ibid.,* 173 (1952), 46ff.

L. Mezey, "A latin írás magyarországi történetéből (Essay on the history of Latin literature in Hungary)," *Magyar Könyvszemle,* 82 (1966), 1ff.; 205ff.; 285ff.

————, "Litteratura grammatica et musica," *Irodalomtörténeti Közlemények,* 74 (1970), 653ff.

————, "Pannonia quae et Ungria," *Vigilia,* 35 (1970), 795ff.

————, "A Pray kódex keletkezése (Essay on the origins of the Pray codex)," *ITK,* 75 (1971), 109ff.

E. Mikkers, "Eremitical life in western Europe during the eleventh and twelfth centuries," *Citeaux: commentarii Cistercienses,* 14 (1963), 44ff.

W. Mohr, *Kie karolingische Reichsidee: aevum Christianum* (Münster, 1962).

E. Moór, "Az Árpád-monarchia kialakulásának kérdéséhez (Essay on the formation of the Arpad monarchy)," *Századok,* 104 (1970), 350ff.

————, "A Kakázuson túli állítólagos 'szavard magyarok' kérdéséhez fő tekintettel annak a chazar-problémával való kapcsolatára (Some remarks about the so-called 'Savard-Magyars' beyond the Caucasian Mountains and the relationship with the Khazar question)," *Századok,* 105 (1971), 961ff.

Gy. Moravcsik (ed.), Konstantinos Porphyrogennetos: *De administrando imperio* (Budapest, 1949; new edition with English translation by R.J. H. Jenkins, London, 1962).

———, "Die archaisierenden Namen der Ungarn in Byzanz," *Byzantina Studia* (Budapest, 1967), 320ff., a repr. of BZ, 30 (1929-30), 247ff.

———, "Bölcs Leó Taktikája mint magyar történeti forrás (The *Tactica* of Leo VI the Wise as a source of Hungarian history)," *Századok,* 85 (1951), 334ff.

———, *Byzantium and the Magyars* (Amsterdam-Budapest, 1970).

———, "Görögnyelvű monostorok szent István korában (Greek monasteries in Hungary during the reign of Stephen)," *SIE,* I, 299ff.

———, "The Holy Crown of Hungary," *Hungarian Quarterly,* 4 (1938), 656ff.

D.G. Morin, "Un théologien ignoré du XIe siecle: l'eveque-martyr,Gérard de Csanád, O.S.B.," *Revue Bénédictine,* 27 (1910), 516ff.

K.F. Morrison, Review of W. Mohr's *Karolingische Reichsidee* in *Speculum,* 38 (1963), 648ff.

A. Murray, "Pope Gregory VII and his Letters," *Traditio,* 22 (1966), 149ff.

S. Nagy, "Amiben szent István is tévedett (King Stephen, too, made mistakes)," *Magyarság,* Pittsburgh, Pa., Sept. 2, 1960, 7.

W. Neuss, *Das Problems des Mittelalters* (Kolmar im Elsass, n.d.).

Gy. Német, "A magyar kereszténység kezdetei (The origins of Hungarian Christianity)," *Budapesti Szemle,* 256 (1940), 14ff.

W. Ohnsorge, "Die Legation des Kaisers Basileos II an Heinrich II, " *Historisches Jahrbuch,* 73 (1954), 61ff.

———, "Otto I und Byzanz, " *Festschrift zur Jahrtausendfeier der Kaiserkrönung Ottos des Grossen* (3 vols.; Graz-Cologne, 1962), I, 107ff.

E. Mátra Ompolyi, *A bölcsészet története Magyarországon a skolasztika korában* (A history of scholastic philosophy in Hungary) (Budapest, 1878)

———, "Gellért az első magyar skolasztikus (Garard of Csanád, the first Hungarian scholastic scholar)," *Figyelő,* 4 (1878), 209ff.

V. Padányi, *Vérbulcsú* (Chieftain Búlcsú) (in *Történelmi tanulmányok* series of the Pázmány Free University, Buenos Aires, 1954)

E. Patzelt, *Die karolingische Reianssance* (2nd ed.; Graz, 1965)

, "Die Mission Cyrills und Methodius in verfassungsrechtlicher Schau," *Studi medievali*, 5 (1964), 241ff.

Gy. Pauler, *A magyar nemzet története az árpádházi királyok alatt* (A history of the Hungarian nation during the reign of the Árpáds) (2 vols.; Budapest, 1893)

, Review of J. Karácsonyi, *Szent Gellért* in *Századok*, 22 (1888), 57ff.

F. Pelsőczy, "Szent István király Intelmeiről (About King Stephen's Admonitions)," *Vigilia*, 75 (1971)

M. Perlbach, "Die Kriege Heinrichs III gegen Böhmen, 1039-41," *Forschungen zur deutschen Geschichte*, 10 (1870), 427ff.

E. Petrovich, "Szent Margit skóciai királynő emléke (The memory of Saint Margaret of Scotland)," *Vigilia*, 37 (1972), 128ff.

, "Szent Mór pécsi péspök (St. Maurus, bishop of Pecs)," *ibid.*, 36 (1971), 85ff.

G. Pilati, *Chiesa e stato nei primi quindeci secoli* (Rome-New York, 1961)

J. Pintér, *Magyar irodalomtörténet* (History of Hungarian literature) (8 vols; Budapest, 1930-41), vol. I

A. Pleidell, "A magyar várostőrténet első fejezete (The beginnings of town developments in Hungary)," *Szazadok*, 38 (1934), 1ff.; 158ff.; 276ff.

G. Post, "Two Notes on Nationalism in the Middle Ages," *Traditio*, 9 (1953), 281ff.

A. Potthast, *Bibliotheca historica medii aevi* (2 vols.; 2nd rev. ed.; Berlin, 1896)

G. Pray, *Annales regum Hungariae* (5 vols.; Vienna, 1764 etc.)

M. Prikkel, "A Pray kódex," in Erdélyi, *Rendtörténet*, I, 439ff.

F. Prinz, "Die bischöfliche Stadherrschaft im Frankreich vom 5 bis 7 Jahrhundert," *Historische Zeitschrift*, 217 (1973), 1ff.

, *Frühes Mönchtum in Frankreich* (Munich, 1965)

, "Zur geistigen Kultur des Mönchtums in spätantiken Gallien und im Merowingerreich," *Zeitschrift für bayerische Landesgeschichte*, 26 (1963), 29ff.

J. Quaster, "Oriental Influence in Gallican Liturgy," *Traditio*, 1 (1943), 58ff.

P. Radó, *Beiträge zur Bibliographie der ungarischen Liturgiegeschichte* (Pannonhalma, 1942)

, "Esztergomi könyvtárak liturgikus Kéziratai (The liturgical MSS of the Esztergom libraries)," *Pannonhalmi főapátsági főiskola 1940-41 évkönyve,* (Pannonhalma, 1941), 86ff.

, "Le plus ancien livre liturgique de la Hongrie: l'évangéliaire de l'archéveque Szelepcsényi, " repr. from *Magyar Könyvszemle,* 1939

, *Index codicum manu scriptorum liturgicorum regni Hungariae* (Budapest, 1941)

, *Libri liturgici manu scripti bibliothecarum Hungariae* (Budapest, 1947)

, "A magyar liturgia eredete a XIszázadban(The origins of Hungarian liturgy in the eleventh century)," *Vigilia,* 22 (1957), 391ff.

P. Ratkos, "A Pray kódex keletkezése és funkciója (The origins and purpose of the Pray codex)," *Századok,* 102 (1968), 941ff.

K. Redl, "Problémák Gellért püspök Deliberatiojában (Some questions concerning Gerard of Csanád's Deliberatio)," *Irodalomtörténeti Közlemények,* 69 (1965), 211ff.

Gy. Rónay, "Szent Gellért," *Vigilia,* Dec. 1946, 47ff.

, "Szent István király legendái (The legends of King Stephen)," *Vigilia,* 36 (1971), 527ff.

H. Rost, *Die Wahrheit über das Mittelalter, nach protestantischen Urteilen* (Leipzig, 1924)

E. Sackur, *Richard, Abt von St. Vannes* (Breslau, 1886)

J. v. Sawicki, "Zur Textkritik und Entsethungsgeschichte der Gesetze König Stefan des Heiligen," *Ungarische Jahrbücher,* 9 (1929), 395ff.

D. Schäfer, "Die Ungarnschalcht von 955." *Historische Zeitschrift,* 97 (1906), 538ff.

F. Schiller, "Das erste ungarische Gesetzbuch und das deutsche Recht," *Festschrift für Heinrich Brunner* (Weimar, 1910), 379ff.

H.F. Schmid, "Otto I und der Osten," *Festschrift zur Jahrtausenfeier,* as cited above, 70ff.

Ph. Schmitz, *Geschichte des Benediktinerordens* (2 vols.; Zurich, 1947-48)

G. Schnürer, *Kirche und Kultur im Mittelalter* (3 vols.; 2nd ed.; Paderborn, 1927-28)

P.E. Schramm, "Die Anerkennung Karl des Grossen als Kaiser," *Historische Zeitschrift,* 172 (1951), 449ff.

, *Kaiser, Rom und Renovatio* (2 vols.; 2nd ed.; Darmstadt, 1957)

E. Schwartz, "750 Jahre Stift St. Gotthard in Ungarn," *Cisterzienser Chronik,* 45 (1933), 97ff.

W. Schwarz, "Der Investiturstreit in Frankreich," *Zeitschrift für Kirchengeschichte,* 43 (1924), 92ff.

K. Schünemann, "Ostpolitik und Kriegsführung im deutschen Mittelater," *Ungarische Jahrbücher,* 17 (1937), 31ff.

G. Sebestyén, *Az Árpádok története* (A history of the Árpáds) (Budapest, 1929)

J. Semmler, "Die Beschlüsse des Aachener Konzils im Jahre 816," *Zeitschrift* für Kirchengeschichte, 74 (1963), 15ff.

F.X. Seppelt, *Geschichte der Päpste* (5 vols.; Munich, 1949-57)

J. Card. Serédi (ed), *Emlékkönyv szent István király halálának kilencszázadik évfordulóján* (Memorial volume to the 900th anniversary of the death of King Stephen) (3 vols.; Budapest, 1938), cited *SIE*

J.T. Smith, *Parallels Between the Constitutional History of England and Hungary* (London, 1849)

G. Silagi, *Untersuchungen zur Deliberatio des Gerhard von Csanád* (Munich, 1967).

F. Somogyi, "A magyar szentkorona és annak története (The Hungarian Crown and its history)," *Catholic Hungarians' Sunday,* Cleveland, OH, Aug. 15, 1952, 6

P. Sörös, "Collatio," in Erdélyi, *Rendtörtünet,* I, 597ff.

J. Sőtér, *Francia-magyar kapcsolatok* (French-Hungarian contacts) (Budapest, 1941)

R. Sprandel, "Struktur und Geschichte des merowingischen Adels," *Historische Zeitschrift,* 193 (1961), 33ff.

G. Stadmüller, "Geschichte der ungarischen Grossmacht des Mittelalters," *Historisches Jahrbuch,* 70 (1951), 151ff.

W.v. den Steinen, *Der Kosmos des Mittelalters* (2nd rev. ed.; Bern-Munich, 1967)

R.J. Strayer, "The Laicization of French and English Society," *Speculum,* 15 (1940), 76ff.

V. Strommer (ed), *Szent Benedek Emlékkönyv, 529-1929* (A memorial volume to St. Benedict of Nursia) (Pannonhalma, 1929)

J. Szalay, "Gérard, Saint, de Csanád," *Catholicisme* (ed. G. Jacquemet; 6 vols to date; Paris, 1951 etc.), IV, col. 1868f.

J. Szekfű, *Der Staat Ungarn: eine Geschichtsstudie* (Stuttgart, 1918)

R. Szentiványi (ed), *Catalogus concinnus librorum manuscriptorum Bibliothaecae Batthyanyianae* (Szeged, 1958)

J. Szentmihályi, Review of D. Kosáry, *Bevezetés Magyarország történetenek forrásaiba és irodalmába* in *Magyar Könyvszemle,* 87 (1971), 255ff.

E. Szentpétery, "Beiträge zur Geschichte des ungarischen Urkundenwesens," *Archiv für Urkundenforschung,* 16 (1939), 157ff.

——, "Szent István oklevelei (The diplomas of King Stephen)," *SIE,*

J. Szinnyei (ed), *Magyar írók élete és munkái* (Lives and works of Hungarian authors) (14 vols.; Budapest, 1891-1914)

J. Szűcs, "Gentilizmus: a barbár etnikai tudat kérdéséhez (Some remarks on primitive ethnic consciousness)," *Történelmi Szemle*, 14 (1971), 188ff.

———, "Nationalität und Nationalbewusstsein im Mittelalter," *Acta historica*, 18 (1972), 1ff.; 245ff.

A. Nagy Tasnády, "A Thousand Years of Hungarian Constitution," *Hungarian Quarterly*, 5 (1939), 9ff.

P. Teleki, *The Evolution of Hungary and Her Place in European History* (New York, 1923)

G. Tellenbach, *Libertas: Kirche und Weltordnung im Zeitalter des Investiturstreites* (Stuttgart, 1936)

F. Teller, *Magyarország középkori hangjegyezett kódexei* (The medieval Hungarian musical MSS) (Budapest, 1944)

I. Timkó, *Keleti kereszténység, keleti egyházak* (Eastern Christianity, eastern Churches) (Budapest, 1972)

———, "A latin és görög szertartású kereszténység együttélése Szent István uralmának idejében (The coexistence of Latin and Greek Christians in Hungary during the reign of King Stephen)," *Vigilia*, 35 (1970), 727ff.

F. Toldy, *A magyar szentek legendái a carthausi névtelentől* (The legends of Hungarian saints by the anonymous Carthusian) (Pest, 1859)

———, *Geschichte der ungarischen Literatur im Mittelalter* (Pest, 1865)

———, *A magyar nemzeti irodalom története* (A history of Hungarian national literature) (Budapest, 1878)

Z. Tóth, *A Hartvik legenda kritikájához* (Some remarks on the Hartvic Life of King Stephen) (Budapest, 1942)

———, "Tuhutum és Gelou: hagyomány s történelmi hitelesság Anonymus müvében (Tuhutum and Gelou; tradition and accuracy in the writing of the Hungarian Anonymus)," *Századok*, 79-80 (1945-46), 21ff.

J. Udvardy, "Szent Gellárt lelki arca (The spiritual features of Garard of Csanád)," *Vigilia*, 35 (1970), 577ff.

M. Uhlirz, "Kaiser Otto III und das Papsttum," *Historische Zeitschrift,* 162 (1940), 258ff.

W. Ullmann, *Medieval Papalism* (London, 1949)

P. Váczy, "Deutschlands Anteil in der Begründung des ungarischen Königtums," *Ungarn,* 1 (1941), 12ff.

, *Die erste Epoche des ungarischen Königtums* (Pecs, 1935)

, "A korai magyar történet néhány kérdéséhez (Some questions concerning early Hungarian history)," *Századok,* 92 (1958), 265ff.

, *A középkor története* (Medieval history) (Vol. II of *Egyetemes történet,* ed. B. Hóman; 4 vols.; Budapest, 1935-37.

, "A központi királyság kialakulása szent István korában (Centralization of royal power in Hungary during the reign of King Stephen)," *SIE,* II, 33ff.

D. Vargha, "Szent István a magyar kódexirodalomban (King Stephen in Hungarian codex literature)," *SIE,* III, 357ff.

(ed), *Szent Mór Emlékkönyv* (Memorial volume to St. Maurus, second bishop of Pecs) (Pécs, 1936)

E. Varjú, *A gyulafehérvári Batthyány Könyvtár* (The Batthyány Libraray at Alba-Julia) (Budapest, 1899)

J. Vas, "Szent István miséje (The Mass of King Stephen)," *Vigilia,* 37 (1972), 517ff.

A. Vízkelety, "Eine deutsche Fassung der Stephanslegende aus dem Jahre 1471," *Magyar Könyvszemle,* 84 (1968), 129ff.

Gy. Volf, "Első keresztény térítőink (The first Christian missionaries in Hungary)," *Budapesti Szemle,* 85 (1896), 17ff.

L. Wallach, "Charlemage and Alcuin," *Traditio,* 9 (1953), 127ff.

J.M. Wallace-Hadrill, "The *via regia* of the Carolingian Age," in *Trends in Medieval Thought* (ed. B. Smalley; New York, 1965), 22ff.

W. Wattenbach, *Deutschlands, Geschichtsquellen im Mittelalter* (2 vols.; Berlin, 1893-43; 6th rev. ed.)

P. Wirth, "Das bislang erste literarische Zeugnis für die Stefanskrone aus der Zeit zwischen dem X und XIII Jahrhundert," *Byzantinische Zeitschrift,* 53 (1960), 79ff.

W. Wühr, *Studien zu Gregor VII* (Munich, 1930)

F. Zagiba, "Die altbayerische Kirchenprovinz Salzburg, und die hl. Slawenlehrer Cyrill und Method," a repr. of the Proceedings of the 1963 Salzburg Slavic Congress

M. Zalán, "Árpádkori magyar vonatkozású kéziratok az osztrák könyvtárak kézirattáraiban (MSS related to the Arpadian age of Hungarian history now in Austrian libraries)," *Pannonhalmi Szemle,* 1 (1926), 46ff.

O. Zarek, *Die Geschichte Ungarns* (Zurich, 1938)

L. Závodszky *(ed), A szent István, szent László és Kálmán korabeli törvények és zsinati hatarozatok forrásai* (Sources of the legal enactments and acts of synods held during the reigns of St. Stephen, St. Ladislas and Coloman the Learned) (Budapest, 1904)

I. Zoltvány, "A magyarországi bencés irodalom a tatárjárás előtt (Benedictine literature in Hungary prior to the Mongol invasion of 1241-42)," in Erdélyi, *Rendtörténet,* I, 337.

* * *

Only recently was I able to gain access to the following:

A. Bartha, *A IX - X századi magyar társadalom* (Hungarian social structure in the ninth-tenth centuries) (Budapest, 1968)

J. Szűcs, "Társadalomelmélet, politikai teória és történetszemlélet Kezai Simon Gesta Hungarorumában (Social outlook, political theory, and historial views in the
Századok, 107 (1973), 569ff., and 823ff.

E. Tóth, "Szent Márton pannonhalmi széletéshely-legendájának kialakulása (Formation of the lengend concerning the birthplace of St. Martin of Tours as that at Pannonhalma, Hungary)," *Vigilia,* 39 (1974), 306ff.

INDEX

Aba, Samuel, 1041-44, elected king, 12; had support of churchmen but lacked social prestige, 12; is impatient with his opposition, 58-59, 60, 63, 64; is murdered in 1044, 12, 58.

Ajtony, lord of the southern region, 5-6; *legenda,* 5, 5-6; received no aid from the Byzantine court, 31, and is defeated by Duke Csanád, 6, 7; his seat of government, Marosvár, will be known as Csanád, 15; is also known as Kean, 5.

Almos, x; first elected Magyar ruler, 2.

Andrew I, 1046-60, determined to continue King Stephen's policies, 12, 73-74; issues Ecclesiastical Constitution in 1047, 71, 73-74; submissive to the German court at first, 54; crowned king, 65; his reign, 72-76; had plans to influence German politics through the papal curia, 77-78; his downfall and death, 76-77.

Anonymus, *P. dictus magister,* Hungarian chronicler, late twelfth -early thirteenth cent., x, 201, 207, 210.

Árpád, the Conqueror, son of Almos, ob. 907, 1.

Astric of Pécsvárad, monk, sent by Stephen to Rome to negotiate papal recognition of Hungary as a Christian kingdom, 8; was a boyhood friend of Pope Sylvester II, 9; represented the Hungarian hierarchy at the Synod of Frankfurt, 1007, 22.

Atelcosu [Etelköz], xi, 1, 2.

Augsburg, battle of, August, 955, 2.

Béla I, 1060, 78-80, younger brother and successor of Andrew I, 72, 74, 78; his relations with Poland, 76; shattered the plans of Henry III to incorporate Hungary into the German empire, 67, 77; accepted his crown from the hands of the bishops and the army, but not from the nobles, 78; from his brother, he accepted the princely-one-third of the realm's territory for his maintenance, 74; circumstances surrounding his death are not clear, 39, 80-81; was a born leader, 80.

Beneta, bishop and friend of Gerard of Csanád, escaped the bloodbath in 1046 and informed Andrew I about conditions in the realm, 70-71.

Boleslaw of Poland, 15.

Chronicon pictum, mid-fourteenth century Hungarian chronicle, vii, ix-x, x-xi, 201.

Conrad II, German emperor, attacked Hungary in 1030, and suffered defeat, 10, 15; attack was not well planned, 30, and there was no cooperation between him and the Byzantine court, 15, 29-30.

Constantine VII Porphyrogenitus, Byzantine emperor and chronicler, xi, 1.

Council, known at first as a national assembly, 3, or council of elders, 7, 9; approved of Stephen as ruler,

EAST EUROPEAN MONOGRAPHS

The *East European Monographs* comprise scholarly books on the history and civilization of Eastern Europe. They are published by the *East European Quarterly* in the belief that these studies contribute substantially to the knowledge of the area and serve to stimulate scholarship and research.

Political Ideas and the Enlightenment in the Romanian Principalities, 1750-1831. By Vlad Georgescu. 1971.

America, Italy and the Birth of Yugoslavia, 1917-1919. By Dragan R. Zivjinovic. 1972.

Jewish Nobles and Geniuses in Modern Hungary. By William O. McCagg,Jr. 1972.

Mixail Soloxov in Yugoslavia: Reception and Literary Impact. By Robert F. Price. 1973.

The Historical and National Thought of Nicolae Iorga. By William O. Oldson. 1973.

Guide to Polish Libraries and Archives. By Richard C. Lewanski. 1974.

Vienna Broadcasts to Slovakia, 1938-1939: A Case Study in Subversion. By Henry Delfiner. 1974.

The 1917 Revolution in Latvia. By Andrew Ezergailis. 1974.

The Ukraine in the United Nations Organization: A Study in Soviet Foreign Policy. 1944-1950. By Konstantin Sawczuk. 1975.

The Bosnian Church: A New Interpretation. By John V. A. Fine, Jr., 1975.

Intellectual and Social Developments in the Habsburg Empire from Maria Theresa to World War I. Edited by Stanley B. Winters and Joseph Held. 1975.

Ljudevit Gaj and the Illyrian Movement. By Elinor Murray Despalatovic. 1975.

Tolerance and Movements of Religious Dissent in Eastern Europe. Edited by Bela K. Kiraly. 1975.

The Parish Republic: Hlinka's Slovak People's Party, 1939-1945. By Yeshayahu Jelinek. 1976.

The Russian Annexation of Bessarabia, 1774-1828. By George F. Jewsbury. 1976.

Modern Hungarian Historiography. By Steven Bela Vardy. 1976.

Values and Community in Multi-National Yugoslavia. By Gary K. Bertsch. 1976.

The Greek Socialist Movement and the First World War: The Road to Unity. By George B. Leon. 1976.

The Radical Left in the Hungarian Revolution of 1848. By Laszlo Deme. 1976.

Hungary between Wilson and Lenin: The Hungarian Revolution of 1918-1919 and the Big Three. By Peter Pastor. 1976.

The Crises of France's East-Central European Diplomacy, 1933-1938. By Anthony J. Komjathy. 1976.

Polish Politics and National Reform, 1775-1788. By Daniel Stone. 1976.

The Habsburg Empire in World War I. Robert A. Kann, Bela K. Kiraly, and Paula S. Fichtner, eds. 1977.

The Slovenes and Yugoslavism, 1890-1914. By Carole Rogel. 1977.

German-Hungarian Relations and the Swabian Problem. By Thomas Spira. 1977.

The Metamorphosis of a Social Class in Hungary During the Reign of Young Franz Joseph. By Peter I. Hidas. 1977.

Tax Reform in Eighteenth Century Lombardy. By Daniel M. Klang. 1977.

Tradition versus Revolution: Russia and the Balkans in 1917. By Robert H. Johnston. 1977.

Winter into Spring: The Czechoslovak Press and the Reform Movement 1963-1968. By Frank L. Kaplan. 1977.

The Catholic Church and the Soviet Government, 1939-1949. By Dennis J. Dunn. 1977.

The Hungarian Labor Service System, 1939-1945. By Randolph L Braham. 1977.

Consciousness and History: Nationalist Critics of Greek Society 1897-1914. By Gerasimos Augustinos. 1977.

Emigration in Polish Social and Political Thought, 1870-1914. By Benjamin P. Murdzek. 1977.

Serbian Poetry and Milutin Bojic. By Mihailo Dordevic. 1977.

The Baranya Dispute: Diplomacy in the Vortex of Ideologies, 1918-1921. By Leslie C. Tihany. 1978.

The United States in Prague, 1945-1948. By Walter Ullmann. 1978.

Rush to the Alps: The Evolution of Vacationing in Switzerland. By Paul P. Bernard. 1978.

Transportation in Eastern Europe: Empirical Findings. By Bogdan Mieczkowski. 1978.

The Polish Underground State: A Guide to the Underground, 1939-1945. By Stefan Korbonski. 1978.

The Hungarian Revolution of 1956 in Retrospect. Edited by Bela K. Kiraly and Paul Jonas. 1978.

Boleslaw Limanowski (1835-1935): A Study in Socialism and Nationalism. By Kazimiera Janina Cottam. 1978.

The Lingering Shadow of Nazism: The Austrian Independent Party Movement Since 1945. By Max E. Riedlsperger. 1978.

The Catholic Church, Dissent and Nationality in Soviet Lithuania. By V. Stanley Vardys. 1978.

The Development of Parliamentary Government in Serbia. By Alex N. Dragnich. 1978.

Divide and Conquer: German Efforts to Conclude a Separate Peace, 1914-1918. By L. L. Farrar, Jr. 1978.

The Prague Slav Congress of 1848. By Lawrence D. Orton. 1978.

The Nobility and the Making of the Hussite Revolution. By John M. Klassen. 1978.

The Cultural Limits of Revolutionary Politics: Change and Continuity in Socialist Czechoslovakia. By David W. Paul. 1979.

On the Border of War and Peace: Polish Intelligence and Diplomacy in 1937-1939 and the Origins of the Ultra Secret. By Richard A. Woytak. 1979.

Bear and Foxes: The International Relations of the East European States 1965-1969. By Ronald Haly Linden. 1979.

Czechoslovakia: The Heritage of Ages Past. Edited by Ivan Volgyes and Hans Brisch. 1979.

Prima Minister Gyula Andrassy's Influence on Habsburg Foreign Policy. By Janos Decsy. 1979.

Citizens for the Fatherland: Education, Educators, and Pedagogical Ideals in Eighteenth Century Russia. By J. L. Black. 1979.

A History of the "Proletariat": The Emergence of Marxism in the Kingdom of Poland, 1870-1887. By Norman M. Naimark. 1979.

The Slovak Autonomy Movement, 1935-1939: A Study in Unrelenting Nationalism. By Dorothea H. El Mallakh. 1979.

Diplomat in Exile: Francis Pulszky's Political Activities in England, 1849-1860. By Thomas Kabdebo. 1979.

The German Struggle Against the Yugoslav Guerrillas in World War II: German Counter-Insurgency in Yugoslavia, 1941-1943. By Paul N. Hehn. 1979.

The Emergence of the Romanian National State. By Gerald J. Bobango. 1979.

Stewards of the Land: The American Farm School and Modern Greece. By Brenda L. Marder. 1979.

Roman Dmowski: Party, Tactics, Ideology, 1895-1907. By Alvin M. Fountain, II. 1980.

International and Domestic Politics in Greece During the Crimean War. By Jon V. Kofas. 1980.

Fires on the Mountain: The Macedonian Revolutionary Movement and the Kidnapping of Ellen Stone. By Laura Beth Sherman. 1980.

The Modernization of Agriculture: Rural Transformation in Hungary, 1848-1975. Edited by Joseph Held. 1980.

Britain and the War for Yugoslavia, 1940-1943. By Mark C. Wheeler. 1980.

The Turn to the Right: The Ideological Origins and Development of Ukrainian Nationalism, 1919-1929. By Alexander J. Motyl. 1980.

The Maple Leaf and the White Eagle: Canadian-Polish Relations, 1918-1978. By Aloysius Balawyder. 1980.

Antecedents of Revolution: Alexander I and the Polish Congress Kingdom, 1815-1825. By Frank W. Thackeray. 1980.

Blood Libel at Tiszaeszlar. By Andrew Handler. 1980.

Democratic Centralism in Romania: A Study of Local Communist Politics. By Daniel N. Nelson. 1980.

The Challenge of Communist Education: A Look at the German Democratic Republic. By Margrete Siebert Klein. 1980.

The Fortifications and Defense of Constantinople. By Byron C.P. Tsangadas. 1980.

Balkan Cultural Studies. By Stavro Skendi. 1980.

Studies in Ethnicity: The East European Experience in America. Edited by Charles A. Ward, Philip Shahshko, and Donald E. Pienkos. 1980.

The Logic of "Normalization:" The Soviet Intervention in Czechoslovakia and the Czechoslovak Response. By Fred Eidlin. 1980.

Red Cross. Black Eagle: A Biography of Albania's American Schol. By Joan Fultz Kontos. 1981.

Nationalism in Contemporary Europe. By Franjo Tudjman. 1981.

Great Power Rivalry at the Turkish Straits: The Montreux Conference and Convention of 1936. By Anthony R. DeLuca. 1981.

Islam Under the Double Eagle: The Muslims of Bosnia and Hercegovina, 1878-1914. By Robert J. Donia. 1981.

Five Eleventh Century Hungarian Kings: Their Policies and Their Relations with Rome. By Z.J. Kosztolnyik. 1981.